Ex Libris

Betty Holtzman

FRANZ BOAS

THE MIND OF

PRIMITIVE

MAN

Revised Edition

With a new Foreword by
Melville J. Herskovits

THE FREE PRESS, *New York*
COLLIER-MACMILLAN LIMITED, *London*

For information, address:

THE FREE PRESS
A DIVISION OF THE MACMILLAN COMPANY
60 Fifth Avenue, New York, N.Y. 10011

Collier-Macmillan Canada, Ltd., Toronto, Ontario

Library of Congress Catalog Card Number: 63-9984

First edition copyrighted 1911 by The Macmillan Company

Copyright renewed 1939 by Franz Boas

FIRST FREE PRESS PAPERBACK EDITION 1965

Foreword

THE QUESTION OF RACE as a factor in human affairs has only been raised in relatively recent times. The differences in physical type which mark off the major groupings of mankind, in earlier days figured but little in evaluating intellectual and cultural worth. Such aspects of the human form as pigmentation, eye color, hair form and color and facial contours did, of course, not go unnoticed. But they were not assigned social, economic and political significance until about the late seventeenth century, with the era of European expansion over the world.

Theories of racial superiority and inferiority were given systematic expression only at about the middle of the nineteenth century, and ran in two main currents. Earliest came the attempt to justify, on scientific grounds, the institution of Negro slavery. Here the writings of Americans such as J. C. Nott and C. R. Gliddon led the way, stimulating the thinking of such an English proponent of the anti-abolitionist movement as James Hunt, among others. Then, on the continent of Europe, came the works of the Comte de Gobineau in France and Houston Stewart Chamberlain in Germany. The writings of these men centered on establishing the thesis of the intellectual and cultural superiority of the Aryan race—the tall, blond, blue-eyed north European type, which later came to be called by the term Nordic.

The works of the early American and British race theorists were lost sight of after the overthrow of slavery in the United States. The point of view of the Europeans, however, flourished, especially in Germany, where it became one of the prime elements in Nazi ideology, and thus became a principal cause of the holocaust of the second World War. It was at this time that the word "racism" was coined to denote the utilization of the concept of race for political ends.

It must not be thought that racism went unchallenged. But the anthropologists who refused to accept a racial interpretation of history were scattered, their attempts to rectify the

5

distortions of their science diffuse, while their researches, for the most part, ignored the political and social implications of the doctrine they rejected. It was, therefore, not until the publication of *The Mind of Primitive Man* that the anti-racists could refer to a single work which, in the best scientific tradition derived its conclusions from measured, objective analysis, and presented its data in terms of their wider implications, marshalling the known facts to bring them to bear on disputed questions.

From the moment of its appearance, this book became a prime target for those who supported the thesis of racial superiority. It is not chance that the version of it that was published in Germany in 1914, called *Kultur und Rasse*, was one of the volumes marked for the Nazi book-burning of May 10, 1933. Its vitality is attested by the attacks still directed against it and its author, two decades after his death and five after publication of the original edition, by neo-racists reacting against the drive toward racial integration in the United States and the downfall of the colonial system in the broader world.

Franz Boas was born on July 9, 1858, at Minden, Germany. He studied at Heidelberg and Bonn Universities before going to Kiel where, at the age of 23, he was awarded the degree of Doctor of Philosophy. His thesis, *Contribution toward the Understanding of the Color of Water*, was in his major subject, physics. But it was his minor, geography, that most influenced his later career, though his mathematical training as a physicist was put to telling use in his researches into questions of racial differences and of human heredity. His geographical interests lay in the field of human, or cultural geography. They led him logically, and as it turned out, irrevocably to the new discipline of anthropology. As a result of his field trip to the Arctic, he became fascinated with Eskimo culture—so different from anything he had known, yet so well adapted to the harsh environment in which these people lived and so satisfying to them. The scientific challenge of accounting for the similarities and differences in the ways of peoples of varied physical type, living in different natural habitats, absorbed him, and the questions thus posed framed problems to the study of which he devoted the rest of his life.

Boas first visited the United States in 1884, on his return from his research among the Eskimo. He had accepted a position with the Berlin Ethnological Museum, and also became involved in university life, attaining the rank of Docent. It was at this time, also, that he initiated his long-term researches into the life of the Indians of the North Pacific Coast of North America. The freedom of the American intellectual world, contrasted to the rigidity of the German hierarchical system, appealed to him, and in 1887 he joined the journal *Science*, married, and established his residence in New York City. In 1889 he received his first American academic appointment, at Clark University, remaining there until 1892, when he left to go to Chicago to become a member of the staff of the World Columbian Exposition and later of the Field Museum.

He returned to New York in 1896, accepting a position at the American Museum of Natural History. From 1899 to 1905 he held his museum post conjointly with a professorship of anthropology at Columbia University. After 1905, he functioned exclusively at Columbia, from which institution he sent forth the students who, with him, were to play such an important role in shaping anthropological science. He retired in 1937, five years before his dramatic death in 1942, at a luncheon given by him at the Columbia Faculty Club for his friend Professor Paul Rivet of Paris, then a refugee from the Nazi oppression whose racial perversions Boas had consistently fought.

An indefatigable worker, his productiveness has rarely been matched. A steady stream of monographs, articles in scientific journals, and reviews came from his pen. He founded one scholarly publication and edited another for eighteen years, in addition to initiating and editing a monograph series. Uncompromising in his feeling that no concession to his readers should obscure the stark scientific quality of his data and his concepts, he wrote as he felt the requirements of a given problem dictated. His most important contributions, such as his analysis of the significance of family and fraternal variability in the formation of physical types; or the approach to the study of language in terms of the structure of the language studied instead of the categories of Indo-European tongues;

or the importance of the psychological component in behavior for an understanding of culture, now anthopological
commonplaces, appeared in professional journals and monographs of restricted circulation. Of the more than six hundred
items in his personal bibliography, only a few are for the
general reader. Of books, besides the present one, there can
be cited only his *Primitive Art*, the collaborative text-book he
edited, *General Anthropology*, and his *Anthropology and
Modern Life*. A few years before he died he was induced to
bring together a collection of his scientific papers, which
appeared under the title *Race, Language and Culture*.

The history of the present book is not without interest. The
ideas which make up its core were first expressed in a paper
dated 1894, entitled "Human Faculty as Determined by
Race." This was an address delivered by Boas as Vice-
President of the American Association for the Advancement
of Science and Chairman of its Section of Anthropology, at
its Brooklyn meeting. The title first appeared in Boas' presi-
dential address to the American Folklore Society, in 1901.
The ideas which in the initial versions make up the germ of
the conceptions found in this book in its present form, were
worked into a series of lectures delivered in 1910 before the
Lowell Institute, Boston, and later, in Spanish, at the National
University of Mexico.

The first edition of the book appeared in 1911, and went
through several printings before Boas revised it, as he said, to
take account of the findings of researches carried on since the
book was initially written. Later results confirmed his earlier
conclusions, regarding which he had felt "ever-increasing certainty." These conclusions are succinctly given: "There is no
fundamental difference in the ways of thinking of primitive
and civilized man. A close connection between race and personality has never been established. The concept of racial type
as commonly used even in scientific literature is misleading
and requires a logical as well as biological definition."

It is important, however, that this book not be thought of
as only a treatise on the subject of race and race differences.
Even in its earlier form, it lay bare the anatomy of the whole
science of man, demonstrating that human capacity as manifested in forms of thought and behavior is essentially a con-

tinuing contrapuntal play between what is physically inherited and what has been learned—that is, between physical endowment and culture. It has been observed, and correctly, that the German title of this book, *Culture and Race,* more aptly describes its content than does its English designation.

The 1911 edition reflected a preoccupation with hereditary processes that was to continue and be the more strongly emphasized in its rewriting. In this, it foreshadowed a trend that was to change almost completely the sub-science of physical anthropology from one concerned primarily with the classification of human types into a specialized science of human biology. Even when the 1938 edition appeared, the genetic study of man was in its infancy. In the work entitled *Changes in the Bodily Form of Descendants of Immigrants,* which presents the results of a study Boas carried out for the Dillingham Commission on Immigration of the United States Congress, he examined the role of the environment in influencing physically inherited human traits. Demonstrating, as it did, the plasticity of the human organism, it was one of the first to bring the resources of biometrics to bear on the study of man, a mathematical approach of which Boas was a creative master.

In considering the cultural side of the human experience, Boas ranged widely. The case for holding race, language and culture as independent variables is cogently put and extensively documented. Most of the points he made to show the cultural achievements of "primitive" man, especially the examples he gives, have become axiomatic in anthropology. Scattered throughout the latter chapters we find valuable precepts setting forth principles of scientific method for the study of culture, such as this one (p. 201):

In scientific inquiries we should always be clear in our own minds that we always embody a number of hypotheses and theories in our explanations, and that we do not carry the analysis of any given phenomenon to completion. If we were to do so, progress would hardly be possible, because every phenomenon would require an endless amount of time for thorough treatment. We are only too apt, however, to forget entirely the general, and for most of us purely traditional, theoretical basis which is the foundation of our reasoning, and to assume that the result of our reasoning is absolute truth.

Considering the pace of anthropological developments since Boas rewrote this book, it is striking how valid his basic approach and his fundamental theses remain. Certain of his concepts are no longer current, and some of the terms he used have understandably fallen into disuse. Thus the word "primitive," which he is at such pains to define, and which, even in his discussion of it is seen to be functionally difficult as a valid classificatory device, is being less and less heard. Not only because of its diffuse meaning, but also because of the invidious connotations it has come to carry, it is giving way to more precise, descriptive and non-evaluative terms, such as the word "nonliterate." Similarly, the concept of progress, which bulks large in Boas' thinking, has come under heavy attack because of its hidden, culture-bound implications.

Or, to take another instance, the very idea of race, so important in this book, has come to be realized as having scientific no less than social disutility. Following the lead of Boas, with the stress he laid on the need to study dynamic hereditary processes of human physical form, rather than to remain content to classify the end-results of these processes as manifest in populations of adults, the very concept of race is found to represent a scientific dead-end. In the final chapter, we find that events have overtaken the discussion of the "race problem," though even here one comes on scientific generalizations of continuing value.

The essential contribution of this book, as seen more than two decades after its appearance, is never actually made formally explicit in its pages. This is its demonstration of how, in human culture, the plurality of forms represents an overlay of the unities which exist in the endowments, needs and aspirations of all men. It thus adumbrates what we have come to call *cultural relativism*, which, arising out of the unities in cultural diversity, builds on a realization of the devotion all peoples have for their particular way of life. More than this; in the chapter on the role of emotional association in shaping judgements, Boas lays the psychological groundwork for what, since his death, has become a new field, the comparative study of values. This is a field whose importance derives not only from its study of a neglected aspect of the scientific reality of culture, but also from the fact that it provides the basis for a cogent philosophy in a world where contacts between peoples having different ways of life are constantly increasing in incidence and intensity.

This, Boas' most "popular" work, thus merits the closest reading. In reading it, we would do well to keep in mind two summary comments on the work of its author. The first, by an early student of Boas, A. L. Kroeber, who became one of our most distinguished cultural anthropologists, was made a year after Boas' death:

Boas' scientific contribution . . . consisted of, first, the recognition and originating of a vast number of new problems; second, answers which so far as they went were sound to an amazing degree; and third, the fact that his answers were, as they should be, restricted: he saw through the fallacies of others and refrained from committing his own. With all his boundless energy for pushing on, he knew where to stop, and rigorously respected the borders of proof.

Sixteen years later, J. M. Tanner, a British physical anthropologist who knew Boas only through his writings, in a *Memoir* of the American Anthropological Association commemorating the centenary of Boas' birth wrote of his studies of human growth:

Some of Boas' findings, of course, have not been verified by later events. Some of his interpretations need amendment. Sometimes he too failed to see all that lay implicit in his data. The astonishing thing is how seldom a questionable finding, a dubious interpretation, or a missed opportunity found its way into Boas' work. He was a remarkable innovator, who nevertheless made few mistakes —and no major ones. He was a man of enormous width of interest, yet his writings in this small sector show no trace of dispersion of talent. On the contrary, most of his work

makes the other writers of his time look like dilettantes; it
is he who penetrates beneath the surface.

MELVILLE J. HERSKOVITS

Northwestern University
June 25, 1962

Note: For those interested in the biography of the author of
this book, there are several items that are readily available.
The first was published as a memorial to Franz Boas shortly
after his death. The reference is as follows: *Franz Boas,
1858–1942* by A. L. Kroeber and others, *Memoir 61*, Ameri-
can Anthropological Association, July-September, 1943.
In this Memoir will be found the definitive bibliography of
Boas' published works. There is also an intellectual biography:
M. J. Herskovits, *Franz Boas, The Science of Man in the
Making,* Charles Scribner and Sons, New York, 1953.
Finally, the hundredth anniversary of the birth of Boas was
marked by the anthropologists of the United States with the
following Memoir: *The Anthropology of Franz Boas* (W.
Goldschmidt, ed.), *Memoir 89*, American Anthropological
Association, October, 1959 (also published by Howard
Chandler, Publishers, San Francisco).

M. J. H.

Contents

Preface   17

1   Introduction   19
Double meaning of primitiveness, 19.—The
White race having achieved the highest civilization said to represent the highest physical type,
20.—Does cultural achievement depend upon
hereditary aptitude alone? 21.—Many races contributed to the origin of civilization, 22.—Early
civilization in America, 23.—Interpretation of
rapidity of development, 23.—Decline of primitive cultures, 25.—Spread of civilization, 27.—
Summary, 29.—The problem, 31.

2   Historical Review   32
Boulainvilliers and Gobineau, 32.—Klemm, 33.
—Carus, 34.—Morton, 34.—Nott and Gliddon,
35.—Houston Stewart Chamberlain, 36.—Madison Grant, 37.—Palaeontologist, 37.—Stoddard,
38.—von Eickstedt, 38.—Influence of contact of
races and of modern biology, 40.—Ethnologists, 43.

3   The Composition of Human Races   45
The meaning of types, 45.—The meaning of
variability, 47.—The analysis of populations as
composed of different elements, 50.—Determination of differences between traits, 51.—
Regular distribution of many variable phenomena, 51.—Measurements of degree of variability, 53.—Description of differences between
types, 55.

4   The Hereditary Characteristics of Human Races   60
Racial heredity, 60.—Forms common to several
racial types, 61.—Genetic differences of forms
apparently identical, 61.—Laws of heredity, 62.

13

—Inbreeding, 63.—Variability of family lines and of fraternities, 66.—Race a complex of distinct genetic lines, 69.—Relations between family line and fraternal variabilities, 70.— Differences between human races and races of domesticated animals, 74.—Impossibility of constructing original "pure types," 75.—Rate at which individual and social characters develop, 77.

5 The Instability of Human Types   78
Morphological development of man, 79.—Domestication, 80.—Influence of environment upon organisms, 87.—Human races living under different conditions, 88.—Modification of form due to environment, 89.—Growth, 90.—Identical twins, 96.—Influence of selection, 97.

6 The Morphological Position of Races   99
Parallel development, 99.—Distribution of "higher" and "lower" traits among races, 101.— Significance of such traits, 102.—Size and structure of brain in various races, 103.—The principal races of man, 104.—Europeans, Australians, Pygmy types, 107.—Relations between Mongolid and European, 108.—Areas of specialization of races, 110.

7 Physiological and Psychological Functions of Races 113
Variability of functions, 113.—Variability of tempo of development, 114.—Tempo of development of different races in the same environment and of the same race in different types of environment, 116.—Mental tests, 117.—Motor habits, 119.—Frequency of crime, 121.—Mental diseases, 121.—Pronunciation, 122.—Studies of personality, 122.—Behavior of identical twins, 123.—Ethnological observations regarding personality, 123.—Inhibition, 125.—Improvidence, 127.—Lack of concentration, 127.—Prelogical thought, 128.—Lack of originality, 129.—Rela-

tion of genetic and cultural conditioning of behavior, 130.—Effect of continued civilization,
132.—Lack of proof of change in faculties, 132.
—Relapse of individuals into primitive life,
134.—Influence of early life, 135.—Distribution
of mental traits in different races, 135.

8   Race, Language and Culture   137
    Relations between type, language and culture,
    137.—Classification from the three points of
    view irreconcilable, 137.—Permanence of type
    and change of language, 138.—Permanence of
    language and change of type, 139.—Permanence
    of type and language and change of culture,
    141.—Hypothesis of original correlation be-
    tween type, language and culture, 143.—Lack of
    time relation between the three features, 145.—
    The evaluation of languages and cultures, 146.

9   Early Cultural Traits   149
    Definition of culture, 149.—Animal habits com-
    pared with human culture, 150.—Culture in
    palaeolithic times, 153.—Traits common to all
    cultures, 154.—Isolated parallelisms, 154.—
    Similarities due to historical causes, 157.—Old
    World and New World, 158.—Simple and com-
    plex cultures, 159.—Advance of rational ex-
    planations, 161.

10 The Interpretations of Culture   162
    Explanations by analogy, 162.—Evolutionary
    theory, 164.—Examples, 164.—Development of
    agriculture and of domestication of animals,
    166.—Development of the family, 168.—Cus-
    toms do not always develop in the same way,
    168.—Different customs developing from a
    single source, 169.—Convergent evolution, 170.
    —Lack of comparability of data, 171.—Influ-
    ence of geographical environment, 173.—Eco-
    nomic determinism, 176.—Bastian's elementary
    ideas, 177.—Culture as determined by race, 178.

11 The Mind of Primitive Man and the Progress of
    Culture   180
    Definition of primitiveness, 180.—Progress of
    technique, 181.—Progress in intellectual work,
    184.—Participation in cultural achievements,
    185.—Social organization, 187.—Characteristics
    of languages of primitive tribes, 188.—Funda-
    mental characteristics of primitive thought and
    language, 189.—The categories of language,
    190.—Attributes, 192.—Grammatical forms,
    193.—Abstract terms, 195.—Numerals, 197.—
    The influence of language upon thought, 198.—
    Importance of tradition, 199.—Gradual enlarge-
    ment of the social unit, 202.

12 The Emotional Associations of Primitives   204
    Interrelations between various aspects of primi-
    tive life, 204.—Subconscious character of auto-
    matic actions and their emotional tone, 205.—
    Taboo, 207.—The incest group, 208.—The
    effect of propaganda, 210.—Examples of auto-
    matic reactions, 211.—Effects of education, 213.
    —Customs based on irrational processes, 213.—
    Secondary explanations, 214.—Association of
    ideas through similar emotional values, 215.—
    Ritual, 216.—Nature myths, 216.—Art, 217.—
    Varying associations of widely distributed traits,
    219.—Substitution of causal explanations for
    emotional associations, 222.

13 The Race Problem in Modern Society   226
    Modern race theories, 226.—Critique of the
    concept of race, 227.—Intermingling of Euro-
    pean types, 228.—Attempts to describe culture
    as determined by race, 231.—Population of the
    United States, 232.—Eugenics, 237.—The Negro
    problem in the United States, 238.

    Bibliography   243

Preface

SINCE 1911, when the first edition of *The Mind of Primitive Man* was published much work has been done in all the branches of science that have to be considered in the problem with which the book deals. The study of heredity has made important strides and has helped to clear up the concept of race. The influence of environment upon bodily form and behavior has been the subject of many investigations and the mental attitudes of "primitive" man have been studied from new points of view. For this reason a large part of the book had to be rewritten and rearranged.

The first statement of some of the conclusions reached in the book were made in an address delivered by the author as vice-president of the Section of Anthropology of the American Association for the Advancement of Science, in 1895. Ever since that time the subject has remained one of his chief interests. The result of his studies has been an ever-increasing certainty of his conclusions. There is no fundamental difference in the ways of thinking of primitive and civilized man. A close connection between race and personality has never been established. The concept of racial type as commonly used even in scientific literature is misleading and requires a logical as well as a biological redefinition. While it would seem that a great number of American students of biology, psychology and anthropology concur with these views, popular prejudice, based on earlier scientific and popular tradition, has certainly not diminished, for race prejudice is still an important factor in our life. Still worse is the subjection of science to ignorant prejudice in countries controlled by dictators. Such control has extended particularly to books dealing with the subject matter of race and culture. Since nothing is permitted to be printed that runs counter to the ignorant whims and prejudices of the governing clique, there can be no trustworthy science. When a publisher whose pride used to be the number and value of his scientific books announces in his calendar a book trying to show that race mixture is not harmful, withdraws the same book after a dictator comes into power, when great cyclopedias are rewritten according to prescribed tenets, when scientists either do not dare or are not allowed to publish results contradicting the prescribed doctrines, when others, in order to advance their own material interests or blinded by uncontrolled emotion follow blindly the prescribed road no confidence can be placed in their statements. The suppression of intellectual freedom rings the death knell of science.

FRANZ BOAS

NEW YORK
COLUMBIA UNIVERSITY
January, 1938

Chapter 1

Introduction

A SURVEY OF OUR GLOBE shows the continents inhabited by a
great diversity of peoples different in appearance, different in
language and in cultural life. The Europeans and their
descendants on other continents are united by similarity of
bodily build, and their civilization sets them off sharply
against all the people of different appearance. The Chinese,
the native New Zealander, the African Negro, the American
Indian present not only distinctive bodily features, but each
possesses also his own peculiar mode of life. Each human type
seems to have its own inventions, its own customs and beliefs,
and it is very generally assumed that race and culture must be
intimately associated, that racial descent determines cultural
life.

Owing to this impression the term "primitive" has a double
meaning. It applies to both bodily form and culture. We are
accustomed to speak both of primitive races and primitive
cultures as though the two were necessarily related. We
believe not only in a close association between race and
culture; we are also ready to claim superiority of our own
race over all others. The sources of this attitude spring from
our every-day experiences. Bodily form has an aesthetic
value. The dark color, the flat and wide nose, the thick lips
and prominent mouth of the Negro; the slanting eye and
prominent cheekbones of the East Asiatic do not conform to
those ideals of human beauty to which we of West European
traditions are accustomed. The racial isolation of Europe and
the social segregation of races in America have favored the
rise of the so-called "instinctive" aversion to foreign types,
founded to a great extent on the feeling of a fundamental
distinctiveness of form of our own race. It is the same feeling
that creates an "instinctive" aversion to abnormal or ugly
types in our own midst, or to habits that do not conform to
our sense of propriety. Furthermore such strange types as are

19

members of our society occupy, very generally, inferior positions and do not mingle to any great extent with members of our own race. In their native land their cultural life is not as rich in intellectual achievement as our own. Hence the inference that strangeness of type and low intelligence go hand in hand. In this way our attitude becomes intelligible, but we also recognize that it is not based on scientific insight but on simple emotional reactions and social conditions. Our aversions and judgments are not, by any means, primarily rational in character.

Nevertheless, we like to support our emotional attitude toward the so-called inferior races by reasoning. The superiority of our inventions, the extent of our scientific knowledge, the complexity of our social institutions, our attempts to promote the welfare of all members of the social body, create the impression that we, the civilized people, have advanced far beyond the stages on which other groups linger, and the assumption has arisen of an innate superiority of the European nations and of their descendants. The basis of our reasoning is obvious: the higher a civilization, the higher must be the aptitude for civilization; and as aptitude presumably depends upon the perfection of the mechanism of body and mind, we infer that the White race represents the highest type. The tacit assumption is made that achievement depends solely, or at least primarily, upon innate racial ability. Since the intellectual development of the White race is the highest, it is assumed that its intellectuality is supreme and that its mind has the most subtle organization.

The conviction that European nations possess the highest aptitude supports our impressions regarding the significance of differences in type between the European race and those of other continents, or even of differences between various European types. Unwittingly we pursue a line of thought like this: since the aptitude of the European is the highest, his physical and mental type is also highest, and every deviation from the White type necessarily represents a lower feature.

This unproved assumption underlies our judgments of races, for other conditions being equal, a race is commonly described as the lower, the more fundamentally it differs from our own. We interpret as proof of a lower mentality anatomical peculiarities found in primitive man which resemble traits occurring in lower forms of the zoological series; and we are troubled by the observation that some of the "lower" traits do not occur in primitive man, but are rather found in the European race.

The subject and form of all such discussions show that the idea is rooted in the minds of investigators that we should expect to find in the White race the highest type of man.

Social conditions are often treated from the same point of view. We value our individual freedom, our code of ethics, our free art so highly that they seem to mark an advancement to which no other race can lay claim.

The judgment of the mental status of a people is generally guided by the difference between its social status and our own, and the greater the difference between their intellectual, emotional and moral processes and those which are found in our civilization, the harsher our judgment. It is only when a Tacitus deploring the degeneration of his time finds the virtues of his ancestors among foreign tribes that their example is held up to the gaze of his fellow-citizens; but the people of imperial Rome probably had only a pitying smile for the dreamer who clung to the antiquated ideals of the past.

In order to understand clearly the relations between race and civilization, the two unproved assumptions to which I have referred must be subjected to a searching analysis. We must investigate how far we are justified in assuming achievement to be primarily due to exceptional aptitude, and how far we are justified in assuming the European type—or, taking the notion in its extreme form, the Northwest European type —to represent the highest development of mankind. It will be advantageous to consider these popular beliefs before making the attempt to clear up the relations between culture and race and to describe the form and growth of culture.

It might be said, that, although achievement is not necessarily a measure of aptitude, it seems admissible to judge the one by the other. Have not most races had the same chances for development? Why, then, did the White race alone develop a civilization which is sweeping the whole world, and compared with which all other civilizations appear as feeble beginnings cut short in early childhood, or arrested and petrified at an early stage of development? Is it not, to say the least, probable that the race which attained the highest stage of civilization was the most gifted one, and that those races which have remained at the bottom of the scale were not capable of rising to higher levels?

A brief consideration of the general outlines of the history of civilization will give us an answer to these questions. Let our minds go back a few thousand years, until we reach the time when the civilizations of eastern and western Asia were in their infancy. The first great advances appear. The art of writing is invented. As time passes, the bloom of civilization bursts forth now here, now there. A people that at one time represented the highest type of culture sinks back into obscurity, while others take its place. At the dawn of history we see civilization cling to certain districts, taken up now by one people, now by another. Often, in the numerous conflicts of these times the more civilized people are vanquished. The conqueror learns the arts of life from the conquered and carries on their work. Thus the centers of civilization are shifting to and fro over a limited area, and progress is slow and halting. At this period the ancestors of the races that are today among the most highly civilized were in no way superior to primitive man as we find him now in regions that have not come into contact with modern civilization.

Was the civilization attained by these ancient people of such a character as to allow us to claim for them a genius superior to that of any other race?

First of all, we must bear in mind that none of these civilizations was the product of the genius of a single people. Ideas and inventions were carried from one to the other; and, although intercommunication was slow, each people which participated in the ancient development contributed its share to the general progress. Proofs without number have been forthcoming which show that ideas have been disseminated as long as people have come into contact with one another. Neither race nor language limit their diffusion. Hostility and timid exclusiveness against neighbors are unable to hinder their flow from tribe to tribe and they filter through distances that are measured by thousands of miles. Since many races have worked together in the development of the ancient civilizations, we must bow to the genius of all, whatever group of mankind they may represent, North African, West Asiatic, European, East Indian or East Asiatic.

We may now ask, did no other races develop a culture of equal value? It would seem that the civilizations of ancient Peru and of Central America may well be compared with the ancient civilizations of the Old World. In both we find a high stage of political organization, division of labor and an elaborate ecclesiastical hierarchy. Great architectural works were undertaken, requiring the co-operation of many individuals. Plants were cultivated and animals domesticated; the art of writing had been invented. The inventions and knowledge of the peoples of the Old World seem to have been somewhat more numerous and extended than those of the races of the New World, but there can be no doubt that the general status of their civilization measured by their inventions and knowledge was nearly equally high.[1] This will suffice for our consideration.

What, then, is the difference between the civilization of the Old World and that of the New World? It is essentially a difference in time. The one reached a certain stage three thousand or four thousand years sooner than the other.

Although much stress has been laid upon the greater rapidity of development of the races of the Old World, it is not by any means conclusive proof of exceptional ability. It may be adequately conceived as due to the laws of chance. When two bodies run through the same course with variable rapidity, sometimes quickly, sometimes slowly, their relative position will be the more likely to show accidental differences, the longer the course they run. If their speed is constantly accelerating, as has been the case in the rapidity of cultural development, the distance between these bodies, due to chance only, will be still wider than it would be if the rate were uniform. Thus two groups of infants a few months old will be much alike in their physiological and psychical development; youths of equal age will differ much more; and among old men of equal age, one group will be in full possession of their

[1] A general presentation of these data will be found in Buschan and MacCurdy.

powers, the other on the decline; due mainly to the acceleration or retardation of their development, which is, to a great extent determined by causes that are not inherent in their bodily structure, but largely due to their modes of life. The difference in period of development does not always signify that the hereditary structure of the retarded individuals is inferior to that of the others.

Applying the same reasoning to the history of mankind we may say that the difference of a few thousand years is insignificant as compared to the age of the human race. The time required to develop the existing races is a matter of conjecture, but we may be sure that it is long. We also know that man existed in the Eastern Hemisphere at a time that can be measured by geological standards only, and that he reached America not later than the beginning of the present geological period, perhaps a little earlier. The age of the human race must be measured by a span of time exceeding considerably one hundred thousand years (Penck). As the initial point of cultural development we must assume the remotest times in which we find traces of man. What does it mean, then, if one group of mankind reached a certain stage of cultural development at the age of one hundred thousand years and another at the age of one hundred and four thousand years? Would not the life history of the people, and the vicissitudes of their history, be fully sufficient to explain a delay of this character, without necessitating the assumption of a difference in their aptitude to social development? Such retardation would be significant only if it could be shown that it occurs regularly and at all times in one race, while in other races greater rapidity of development is the rule.

If the achievements of a people were a measure of their aptitude, this method of estimating innate ability would hold good not only for our time but would be applicable under all conditions. The Egyptians of 2000 or 3000 B.C. might have applied the argument in their judgment of the people of northwestern Europe who lived in the Stone Age, had no architecture and a very primitive agriculture. They were "backward people" like many so-called primitive people of our time. These were our ancestors, and the judgment of the ancient Egyptians would now have to be reversed. Precisely in the same way must the customary estimate of the Japanese of one hundred years ago be reversed on account of their adoption of the economic, industrial and scientific methods of the western world. The claim that achievement and aptitude go hand in hand is not convincing. It must be subjected to an exhaustive analysis.

At present practically all the members of the White race participate to a greater or lesser degree in their advancement, while in none of the other races has such civilization as has been attained at one time or another been able to reach all the constituent tribes or peoples. This does not necessarily mean that all the members of the White race had the power of developing with equal rapidity the germs of civilization. Civilization, originated by a few members of the race, gave a stimulus to the neighboring tribes who, without this help, would have required a much longer time to reach the high level which they now occupy. We do observe a remarkable power of assimilation, which has not manifested itself to an equal degree in any other race.

Thus the problem presents itself of discovering the reason why the tribes of ancient Europe readily assimilated the civilization that was offered to them, while at present we see primitive people dwindle and become degraded before its onslaught instead of being elevated by it. Is not this a proof of a higher organization of the inhabitants of Europe?

I believe the reasons for the present rapid decline of primitive culture are not far to seek, and do not necessarily lie in a greater ability of the races of Europe and Asia. First of all, in appearance, these people were more alike to civilized man of their times than the races of Africa, Australia and America to the European invaders of later periods. When an individual had been assimilated in culture, he merged readily in the mass of the population and his descendants soon forgot their foreign ancestry. Not so in our times. A member of a foreign race always remains an outsider on account of his personal appearance. The Negro, no matter how completely he may have adopted what is best in our civilization is too often looked down upon as a member of an inferior race. The physical contrast in bodily appearance is a fundamental difficulty for the rise of primitive people. In early times in Europe, it was possible for colonial society to grow by accretion from among the more primitive natives. Similar conditions are still prevalent in many parts of Latin America.

Furthermore, the diseases which nowadays ravage the inhabitants of territories newly opened to the Whites were not so devastating. On account of the permanent contiguity of the people of the Old World who were always in contact with one another, they were subject to the same kinds of contagion. The invasion of America and Polynesia, on the other hand, was accompanied by the introduction of new diseases among the natives of these countries. The suffering and devastation wrought by epidemics which followed the discovery are too well known to be described in full. In all cases in which a material reduction in numbers occurs in a thinly settled area, the economic life as well as the social structure is almost completely destroyed, and with these the mental vigor and power of resistance decays.

At the time when Mediterranean civilization had made important strides forward, the tribes of northern Europe had profited to a considerable extent by their achievements. Although still sparsely settled, the tribal units were large as compared to the small bands encountered in many parts of America, in Australia or on the small islands of Polynesia. We may observe that populous communities of extensive areas have withstood the inroads of European colonization. The outstanding examples are Mexico and the Andean highlands where the Indian population has recovered from the impact of European immigration. The small North American tribes and those of eastern South America have succumbed. The Negro race also seems capable of surviving the shock.

Furthermore, the economic stresses brought about by the conflict between modern inventions and native industries are far more fundamental than those produced by contact between the industries of the ancients and those of less advanced people. Our methods of manufacture have reached such perfection that the industries of the primitive people of our times are being exterminated by the cheapness and plentiful supply of the products imported by the White trader; for the primitive tradesman is entirely unable to compete with the power of production of our machines, while in olden times there was only rivalry between the hand-products of the native and of the foreigner. When a day's work suffices for obtaining efficient tools or fabrics from the trader, while the manufacture of the corresponding implements or materials by the native himself would have required weeks, it is but natural that the slower and more laborious process should be given up speedily. In some regions, and particularly in America and in parts of Siberia, the primitive tribes are swamped by the numbers of the immigrating race, which is crowding them so rapidly out of their own haunts that no time for gradual assimilation is given. In olden times there was certainly no such vast inequality in numbers as we observe in many areas at the present time.

We conclude from these considerations that in ancient Europe the assimilation of the more primitive tribes to those of advanced economic, industrial and intellectual achievement was comparatively easy; while primitive tribes of our times have to contend against almost insurmountable difficulties inherent in the vast contrast between their own condition of life and our civilization. It does not necessarily follow from these observations that the ancient Europeans were more gifted than other races which have not been exposed to the influences of civilizations until more recent times (Gerland; Ratzel).

This conclusion may be corroborated by other facts. In the Middle Ages the civilization of the Arabs and Arabized Berbers had reached a stage which was undoubtedly superior to that of many European nations of that period. Both civilizations had sprung largely from the same sources, and must be considered branches of one tree. The people who were the carriers of Arab civilization in the Sudan were by no means of the same descent as the Europeans, but nobody will dispute the high merits of their culture. It is of interest to see in what manner they influenced the Negro races of Africa. At an early time, principally between the second half of the eighth and the eleventh centuries of our era, northwestern Africa was invaded by Hamitic tribes, and Mohammedanism spread rapidly through the Sahara and the western Sudan. We see that since that time large empires were formed, and disappeared again in struggles with neighboring States, and that a relatively high degree of culture was attained. The invaders intermarried with the natives; and the mixed races, some of which are almost purely Negro, have risen high above the level of other African Negroes. The history of Bornu is perhaps one of the best examples of this kind. Barth and Nachtigal (1) have made us acquainted with the past of this State, which has played a most important part in the eventful history of North Africa.

Why, then, have the Mohammedans been able to exert a deep influence upon these tribes, and to raise them to nearly the same standard which they had attained, while in most parts of Africa the Whites have not been capable of assimilating Negro culture to an equal degree? Evidently on account of the different method of introduction of culture. While the relations between the Mohammedans and the natives were similar to those of the ancients and the tribes of Europe, the Whites send only the products of their manufactures and a few of their representatives into the Negro country. A real amalgamation between the more highly educated Whites and the Negroes has never taken place. The amalgamation of the Negroes by the Mohammedans is facilitated particularly by the institution of polygamy, the conquerors taking native wives, and raising their children as members of their own family.

The spread of Chinese civilization in eastern Asia may be likened to that of the ancient civilization in Europe. Colonization and amalgamation of kindred tribes and in some cases extermination of rebellious subjects, with subsequent colonization have led to a remarkable uniformity of culture over a large area.

When, finally, we consider the inferior position held by the Negro race of the United States, where the Negro lives in the closest contact with modern civilization, we must not forget that the antagonism between the races is as strong as ever and that the inferiority of the Negro race is dogmatically assumed (Ovington). This is a formidable obstacle to the Negro's advance and progress, even though schools and universities are open to him. We might rather wonder how much, against heavy odds, has been accomplished in a short period. It is hardly possible to predict what would be the achievements of the Negro if he were able to live with the Whites on absolutely equal terms.

Our conclusion drawn from the foregoing considerations is the following: Several races have developed a civilization of a type similar to the one from which our own has sprung, and a number of favorable conditions have facilitated its rapid spread in Europe. Among these, similar physical appearance, contiguity of habitat and moderate difference in modes of manufacture were the most potent. When, later on, Europeans began to spread over other continents, the races with which they came into contact were not equally favorably situated. Striking differences of racial types, the preceding isolation which caused devastating epidemics in the newly discovered countries, and the greater advance in technical processes made assimilation much more difficult. The rapid dissemination of Europeans over the whole world destroyed all promising beginnings which had arisen in various regions. Thus no race except that of eastern Asia was given a chance to develop independently. The spread of the European race cut short the growth of the existing germs without regard to the mental aptitude of the people among whom it was developing.

On the other hand, we have seen that no great weight can be attributed to the earlier rise of civilization in the Old World, which is satisfactorily explained as due to chance. In short, historical events appear to have been much more potent in leading races to civilization than their innate faculty, and it follows that achievements of races do not without further proof warrant the assumption that one race is more highly gifted than another.

After having thus found an answer to our first problem, we turn to the second one: In how far are we justified in considering those anatomical traits in regard to which foreign races differ from the White race as marks of inferiority? In one respect the answer to this question is easier than that to the former. We have recognized that achievement alone is no satisfactory proof of an unusual mental ability of the White race. It follows from this, that anatomical differences between the White race and others can be interpreted as meaning superiority of the former, inferiority of the latter, only if a relation between anatomical form and mentality can be proved to exist.

Too many investigations relating to mental characteristics of races are based on the logical fallacy of first assuming that the European represents the highest racial type and then interpreting every deviation from the European type as a sign of lower mentality. When the formation of the jaws of the Negroes is thus interpreted without proof of a biological connection between the forms of the jaw and the functioning of the nervous system an error is committed that might be paralleled by a Chinaman who would describe Europeans as hairy monsters whose hirsute body is a proof of a lower status. This is emotional, not scientific reasoning.

The question that must be answered is: In how far do anatomical traits determine mental activities? By analogy we associate lower mental traits with theromorphic, brutelike features. In our naive, every-day parlance, brutish features and brutality are closely connected. We must distinguish here, however, between the anatomical characteristics of which we have been speaking and the muscular development of the face, trunk and limbs due to habits of life. The hand, which is never employed in activities requiring those refined adjustments which are characteristic of psychologically complex actions, will lack the modeling brought about by the development of each muscle. The face, the muscles of which have not responded to the innervations accompanying deep thought and refined sentiment will lack in individuality and expressiveness. The neck that has supported heavy loads, and has not responded to the varied requirements of delicate changes of position of head and body, will appear massive and clumsy. These physiognomic differences must not mislead us in our interpretations. We are also inclined to draw inferences in regard to mentality from a receding forehead, a heavy jaw, large and heavy teeth, perhaps even from an inordinate length of arms or an unusual development of hairiness. A careful consideration of the relation of such traits to mental activities will be required, before we can assume as proven their significance.

It appears that neither cultural achievement nor outer

appearance is a safe basis on which to judge the mental aptitude of races. Added to this is the one-sided evaluation of our own racial type and of our modern civilization without any close inquiry into the mental processes of primitive races and cultures which may easily lead to erroneous conclusions.

The object of our inquiry is therefore an attempt to clear up the racial and cultural problems involved in these questions. Our globe is inhabited by many races, and a great diversity of cultural forms exists. The term "primitive" should not be applied indiscriminately to bodily build and to culture as though both belonged together by necessity. It is rather one of the fundamental questions to be investigated whether the cultural character of a race is determined by its physical characteristics. The term race itself should be clearly understood before this question can be answered. If a close relation between race and culture should be shown to exist it would be necessary to study for each racial group separately the interaction between bodily build and mental and social life. If it should be proved not to exist, it will be permissible to treat mankind as a whole and to study cultural types regardless of race.

We shall thus have to investigate primitiveness from two angles. First of all we shall have to inquire whether certain bodily characteristics of races exist that doom them to a permanent mental and social inferiority. After we have cleared up this point we shall have to discuss the traits of the mental and social life of those people whom we call primitive from a cultural point of view, and see in how far they coincide with racial groups and describe those features that distinguish their lives from those of civilized nations.

Chapter 2

Historical Review

THE PROBLEM of the relations between race and culture has engaged the attention of many investigators. Only few have attacked it impartially and critically. Judgment has been influenced too often by racial, national and class prejudice.

The theory that racial descent determines the character or ability of a people or of a social class has been held for a long time. Linné, in his description of racial types, ascribes to each mental characteristics. The whole theory of a privileged aristocracy is based on the assumption of a close correlation between individual excellence and descent from a noble line. Until the end of the eighteenth century the organization of European society favored the assumption of a close correlation between descent and culture. When Boulainvilliers in 1727 studied the political history of France he concluded that the old aristocracy was descended from the Franks and the bulk of the population from the Celtic population, and inferred that the Franks must have had a superior mental endowment. Among more recent writers John Beddoe refers to the mental characteristics of the various types of Scotland and England, and A. Ploetz ascribes mental characteristics to the various races.

Gobineau developed these ideas with stronger emphasis upon the permanence of physical form and mental functions of all races. His essential viewpoints appear in the following statements: "1. Wild tribes of the present have always been in this condition, no matter with what higher cultural forms they may have come into contact, and will always remain in this condition; 2. the wild tribes can continue to exist in a civilized mode of life only if the people who created this mode of life are a nobler branch of the same race; 3. the same conditions are necessary when two civilizations influence each other strongly, borrow from each other, and create a new civilization composed of the elements of their own; two

32

civilizations can never be mixed; 4. civilizations originating in races entirely foreign to each other can form only superficial contacts, they can never penetrate each other and will always be mutually exclusive." On the basis of the identification of historical and racial data, Gobineau develops his idea of the paramount excellence of the Northwest European. His work may be considered the first systematic development of this thought. It has exerted a remarkably strong influence.

Klemm's (1843) division of mankind into an active or "male" and a passive or "female" half is based on cultural considerations. He decribes the activities of the European as those of the active half and says[1] that their mental characteristics are strong will power, desire for mastery, independence, freedom; activity, restlessness, longing for expansion and travel; progress in every direction; an instinctive inclination for investigation and testing, stubborn resistance and doubt. Persians, Arabs, Greeks, Romans, the Germanic peoples, and also Turks, Tartars, Tcherkess, the Inca of Peru and Polynesians[2] belong to this group. His description of the body form of the passive half of mankind is based very largely on general impressions derived from the appearance of the Mongolids.[3] He acknowledges that there are differences between Mongols, Negroes, Papuans, Malays and American Indians, but he emphasizes as unifying characters, the dark pigmentation, the form of the skull, and most important of all "the passivity of the mind." According to his theory the passive half of mankind had spread at an early time over the whole globe and is represented by the conservative part of the populations of Europe. The active race developed in the Himalayas, gradually spread over the whole world and became the dominant race wherever they went. He assumes that many of the most important inventions were made by the passive race, but that they did not progress beyond a certain point. He sees as the moving power in the life of man the struggle for a union between the active and passive races that will represent mankind completely, and the aim of which is civilization. Klemm's opinions were accepted by Wuttke.

[1] Vol. I, p. 197.
[2] Vol. IV, p. 451.
[3] Vol. I, p. 198.

Carl Gustav Carus (1849) recognizes that Klemm's division is essentially a cultural one. His own views which he first expressed in his *System of Physiology* (1838) are based on speculation. He believes that the conditions of our planet must be reflected in all living forms. The planet has day and night, dawn and dusk, and so there are some animals active, and plants blooming in daylight, others at night, still others at dawn or dusk. So it must be with man, and for this reason there can be only four races, a day race, a night race, a dawn race and a dusk race. These are, respectively, Europeans and West Asiatics, Negroes, Mongols, American Indians. After having found these groups he claims, following Morton, that the size of the brain of the day race is great, of the night race small, and those of the dawn and dusk races intermediate. He also interprets the facial form of the Negro as being similar to that of animals. The remaining argument is derived from what at his time seemed to be the cultural conditions of the human races. Among the different races he gives prominence to the Hindu, the creator of truth, the Egyptian, the creator of beauty, and the Jew, the creator of human love. The duty of mankind is to develop in each race to the fullest extent its own inborn characters.

Among early American writers Samuel G. Morton based his conclusions upon a careful investigation of racial types. His general views were largely influenced by the interest in the question of polygenism or monogenism, which dominated the minds at that period. He reached the conclusion that there must have been a multiple origin of human races, and claimed that the distinguishing characteristics of races were intimately associated with their physical build. He says: "[The Caucasian race] is distinguished by the facility with which it attains the highest intellectual development. . . . In their intellectual characteristics the Mongols are ingenious, imitative and highly susceptible to cultivation. . . . The Malay is active and ingenious and possesses all the habits of a migratory, predacious and maritime people. . . . In their mental characteristics the Americans are averse to cultivation, slow, cruel, boisterous, revengeful and fond of war, and entirely destitute of maritime adventure. . . . In disposition the Negro is joyful, flexible and indolent, while the many groups that constitute this race possess a singular diversity of character of which the far extreme is the lowest strain of humanity."

Referring to particular groups he says, "The mental faculties of the Eskimo from infancy to old age, present a continued childhood; they reach a certain limit and expand no further"; and of the Australians; "It is not probable that this people as a body are capable of any other than their slight degree of civilization." His point of view appears clearly in the footnote added to this remark: "This moving picture is derived from the great majority of observers of Australian life. The reader may consult Dawson's 'Australia' for some different views, which, however, appear to be biased by a genuine and active spirit of benevolence." In the appendix to Morton's work, George Combe, the phrenologist, discusses the relation between the form of the head and character, and dwells particularly on the fact that the brain of the European is the largest and that of the Negro the smallest, inferring from this a corresponding intellectual status. There is no discussion of the contradiction between this statement and the data given in Morton's work, according to which the advanced people of America have smaller heads than the so-called barbarous tribes.

Morton was followed by a number of writers whose views were colored by their endeavor to defend slavery as an institution. To them the problem of polygeny and monogeny was important particularly because the distinct origin and the permanence of type of the Negro seemed to justify his enslavement. The most important writings of this group are those of J. C. Nott and George R. Gliddon. Nott in his introduction to *Types of Mankind* says: "The grand problem, more particularly interesting to all readers, is that which involves the *common origin* of races; for upon the latter deduction hang not only certain religious dogmas, but the more practical question of the equality and perfectibility of races— we say 'more practical question,' because, while Almighty Power, on the one hand, is not responsible to Man for the distinct origin of human races, these, on the other, are accountable to Him for the manner in which their delegated power is used towards each other.

"Whether an original diversity of races be admitted or not,

the *permanence* of existing physical types will not be questioned by any Archaeologist or Naturalist of the present day. Nor, by such competent arbitrators, can the consequent permanence of moral and intellectual peculiarities of types be denied. The intellectual man is inseparable from the physical man; and the nature of the one cannot be altered without a corresponding change in the other." In another place he says, "To one who has lived among American Indians, it is in vain to talk of civilizing them. You might as well attempt to change the nature of the buffalo."

A line of argument similar to that of Gobineau was taken up by Houston Stewart Chamberlain. His influence seems also more due to the fact that he presented in an attractive form current views, than to his scientific accuracy and penetrating thought. He says (2): "Why should we enter into lengthy scientific inquiries to determine whether there are different races and whether racial descent is of value, how this is possible, etc.? We turn the tables and say: it is evident that there are racial differences; it is a fact of immediate experience that the genealogy of a race is of decisive importance; all you have to do is to investigate how these differences came about and why they are there. You must not deny the facts to protect your ignorance. . . . Whoever travels the short distance from Calais to Dover feels as though he had reached a new planet—such is the difference between the French and English notwithstanding the many ties that unite them. At the same time the observer may see by this example the value of the purer inbreeding. By its insular position England is practically isolated, and there has been reared the race which at the moment is undeniably the strongest in Europe." He formulates his principles as follows: "It is a fundamental law that the development of a great civilization requires first of all excellent stock; next inbreeding with proper selection and finally an old mixture of different but closely related lines of great excellence, which, however, must be followed by a period of isolation." He derived these statements from the experience of husbandry, transferring its rules to human societies. He tries to support this procedure by historical examples that, to his mind seem to sustain his views. He ascribes degeneration particularly to continued mingling of heterogeneous elements.

Chamberlain's (1) lack of scientific method is made clear by his statement in a letter to Cosima Wagner in which he acknowledges tô have used a diplomatic trick (einen diplomatischen Schachzug) to prove his point (22nd of May, 1899).

The influence of Gobineau and Chamberlain and of the current race prejudices are also reflected in the writings of Madison Grant.

His book is a dithyrambic praise of the blond, blue-eyed long-headed White and his achievements and he prophesies all the ills that will befall mankind because of the presence of Negroes and dark-eyed races. The entire argument is based on the dogmatic assumption that wherever a people exhibits eminent cultural characteristics these must be due to a leaven of Nordic blood. As an example may be quoted the following: "To what extent the Nordic race entered into the blood and civilization of Rome it is not difficult to say. The traditions of the Eternal City, its organization of law, its military efficiency as well as Roman ideals of family life, loyalty and truth, point clearly to a Nordic rather than to a Mediterranean origin." In this passage, as throughout his writings, the main thesis is assumed as proven, and is then applied to "explain" cultural phenomena, and biological facts are juggled to suit the fancies of the author. In some places he stresses headform as fundamental, in others as irrelevant. Stature is sometimes given great importance as a dominant hereditary feature; later it is claimed to be the first trait likely to vanish in cases of mixture. Notwithstanding the slight importance assigned to environmental influences, he claims that the native American population by the middle of the nineteenth century was rapidly becoming a distinct type, and was on the point of developing physical peculiarities of its own.

Unfortunately biologists, who in their own sciences enjoy a well-earned reputation, permit themselves to follow the lead of uncritical race enthusiasts. An eminent palaeontologist states his own position in the New York Times, April 8, 1924.

"The Northern races as is well known to anthropologists,

include all those peoples which originally occupied the western plateau of Asia and traversed northern Europe, certainly as early as 12,000 B.C. In the country which they occupied the conditions of life were hard, the struggle for existence severe, and this gave rise to their principal virtues, as well as to their faults, to their fighting qualities and to their love of strong drink. Increasing beyond the power of their own country to support them, they invaded the countries to the south, not only as conquerors but as contributors of strong moral and intellectual elements to more or less decadent civilizations. Through the Nordic tide which flowed into Italy came the ancestors of Raphael, Leonardo da Vinci, Galileo, Titian. . . . Columbus from his portraits and from busts, *authentic or not,* was clearly of Nordic ancestry."

Lothrop Stoddard writes: "Every race is the result of ages of development which involve specialized capacities which make the race what it is and make it capable of creative achievement. These specialized capacities (which are particularly marked in the superior races, being relatively recent developments) are highly unstable. They are what the biologists call 'recessive' characteristics. Hence, when a highly specialized stock interbreeds with a different stock the new, less stable specialized characteristics are bred out, the variation, no matter how great its potential value to human progress, being irretrievably lost. This occurs even in the mating of two superior stocks if these stocks are widely dissimilar in character; the valuable specializations of both breeds cancel out and the mixed offspring tends strongly to revert to generalized mediocrity." Further on the author says that "civilization is the body and race the soul," and that civilization is "the result of the creative urge of the superior germ plasm." This is playing with biological and cultural terms, not science.

E. von Eickstedt has made an attempt to establish the foundations of a race psychology. Notwithstanding his claims to a strictly logical argumentation his reasoning seems to be based on the same fallacy as all the others. He is influenced by the modern Gestalt-psychology and considers that "we see the evident fact of a race-psychological element" that consequently it must have a structure and that bodily build and mental behavior of races must be considered a unit. From an aesthetic, pictorial point of view this is true enough, as in a landscape topographic form, plant life, animal life and human culture belong to the picture, although a structural unity in the sense of causal relations cannot be given. Soil and climate favor certain forms of life, but they do not determine what plants, animals and forms of culture exist. A scientific study of the totality of phenomena should never lead to an omission of the study of causality. The presence of a number of traits in a picture is not necessarily due to their causal relation. Correlations may be fortuitous, not causal. The proof of causal relation is indispensable. Differences in mental traits of races must be proved, not assumed, to be biologically determined and external influences must be proved, not assumed, to exist. Only if the exact proof can be given that individual behavior depends upon bodily build, and that what may be true of the individual is also true of the racial group, or if the relative importance of heredity and environment in individual and racial behavior is determined is it possible to look at them as a totality, except from an aesthetic and emotional point of view. Von Eickstedt is aware of the "extraordinary plasticity of the dispositions given by heredity," but they do not find a place in his discussion.

I shall not attempt to follow in detail the historical development of modern theories which claim that racial descent determines the mental and cultural qualities of the individual. It is however, worth while to consider the conditions that favored their growth. At present the belief that race determines mental behavior and culture rests on strong emotional values. Race is considered as a unifying link between individuals and a call for race allegiance. A new group concept is replacing that of nationality, or is being added to it, just as in earlier times the concept of nationality replaced that of group allegiance to the feudal lord, and the religious bond holding together all Christianity—a tie still potent in Islam. Its sentimental effect is analogous to the class consciousness of the modern communist, or that of the nobleman who still believes in the physical and mental superiority of the nobility. Groupings of this kind are ever present. The only problem is why the biological grouping has come to be of such importance at the present time, and whether it has any justification.[4]

It seems likely that the development of modern trade and travel brought the existence of foreign races to the notice of wide circles that in earlier times had no personal knowledge of distinct types of man. The superior power that the European owes to his inventions and that enables him to subject and exploit foreign peoples, even peoples of high culture, gives emphasis to the feeling of European superiority. It is worth noting that before the officially fomented drive against Jews in Germany and the traditional anti-Jewish feeling in Poland and Russia the feeling used to be nowhere more intense than among the English who first came into close contact with foreign races, and that it developed at an early time in America where the presence of a large Negro population kept alive a constant awareness of racial differences. However, other causes must have contributed to such popular feeling because the same attitude is not developed as strongly among the Spaniards, Portuguese and French although it is not entirely absent. The modern French pose of equality of all races is presumably dictated more by political reasons, such as the need of soldiers, than by an actual absence of all feeling of race differences. The attitude of the Parisian is fundamentally different from that of the colonial administration.

The permeation of our whole thinking by biological viewpoints is probably a much more important element in the development of the opinion that culture is determined by descent.

The development of physiological psychology which neces-

[4] A historical presentation of race theories has been given by Theophile Simar: *Etude Critique sur la Fondation de la Doctrine des Races*, Brussels, 1922. The presentation, however, misses much of its force because a Catholic and anti-German point of view dominate the whole book. The author misinterprets the views of all those authors who dwell upon the difference in the "genius of cultures," as defending the theory of hereditary determination. This appears particularly in his discussion of Herder and of the whole Romantic school. See also Jacques Barzun, *Race, A Study of Modern Superstition*, New York, 1937.

sarily treats of organic determinants of mental functions, has left its impress upon modern psychology, and has led to a comparative neglect of the influence of the experience of an individual upon his behavior. In recent years the behavioristic and Freudian schools have turned away from this one-sided attitude, and a more critical view is also held by many psychologists of other schools. Nevertheless, in many quarters the popular view still prevails that all psychological tests reveal an organically determined mentality. It is believed therefore that innate intelligence, emotional character and volition may be determined by psychological tests. This is essentially a biologically oriented psychology.

The current methods of biology give added strength to these views. At present no subject attracts wider attention of both scientists and general public, than the phenomena of heredity. A vast amount of material has been accumulated that proves how thoroughly the bodily form of the individual is determined by his ancestry. The successes of breeders of plants and animals who raise varieties that fulfill certain demands made upon them suggest that by similar methods national physique and mentality might be improved, that inferior strains might be eliminated and superior ones increased in number. The importance of heredity has been expressed in the formula, "Nature not nurture," meaning that whatever man is or does depends upon his heredity, not upon his bringing up. Through the influence of Francis Galton (2, 3) and his followers the attention of the scientist and the public has been called to these questions. To this has been added the study of the hereditary character of pathological conditions and of the general constitution of the body.

The combined influence of physiological psychology and of biology seems to have strengthened the view that the mental and cultural functions of individuals are determined by heredity and that environmental conditions are negligible.

A constitutional determination of mentality is assumed which brings it about that a person of a certain type will behave in a way corresponding to his habitus and that, therefore, the composition of a population will determine its mental behavior. Added to this is the assumption that the hereditary character of mental traits has been proved, or that it must exist because all heredity is controlled by Mendelian[5] laws. Since these involve the permanence of existing traits in the population, we must expect that the same mental traits will reappear constantly. Only on this basis can Eugen Fischer (1) say that he considers it proved by many observations that the human races and their crosses are distinct in their hereditary mental characteristics. "It is, however, only a question of the fuller or a more restricted development, of a quantitative increase or decrease in intensity of mental qualities common to all human groups (and distinct from those of animals), the combination of which results in varied forms. A clear understanding of the origin of these forms is made still more difficult by the influence of the history of the people (i.e., by environmental conditions) which as in the individual, may develop the innate qualities in the most varied ways." And in another place,[6] "To a great extent the form of mental life as we meet it in various social groups, is determined by environment. Historical events and conditions of nature further or impede the development of innate characteristics. Nevertheless, we may certainly claim that there are racially hereditary differences. Certain traits of the mind of the Mongol, the Negro, the Melanesian and of other races are different from our own and differ among themselves."

The most serious studies made in this direction refer to the interrelation between individual constitution and mental life rather than to the hereditary characteristics of mental traits of races.

The differences in cultural life have also been approached from an entirely different point of view. We shall not dwell on the ideas of the rationalists of the eighteenth century, who, with Rousseau, believed that there existed a happy, simple, natural life. We are rather concerned with the views of those who saw and felt clearly the individuality of each type of cultural life, but who interpreted it not as an expression of innate mental qualities but as a result of varied external conditions acting upon general human characteristics. The

[5] See p. 62.
[6] Fischer 2: p. 512.

understanding of the character of foreign cultures is much more definite among all members of this group. Herder who had a marvelous aptitude for entering into the spirit of foreign forms of thought and who saw clearly the value of the manifold ways of thinking and feeling among the different peoples of the world, believed that natural environment was the cause of the existing biological and cultural differentiation. The geographical point of view was stressed by Karl Ritter who studied the influence of environment upon the life of man. He believed that even continental areas could impose their geographical character upon their inhabitants.

The fundamental point of view of this group has been expressed by Theodor Waitz. He says: "We assert, moreover, in opposition to the usual theory, that the degree of civilization of a people, or of an individual, is exclusively the product of his mental capacity; that his capacities, which designate merely the magnitude of his performances, depend on the degree of cultivation which he has reached."

Since that time ethnologists in their studies of culture have concentrated their attention upon the differences in cultural status and have disregarded racial elements completely. The similarity of fundamental customs and beliefs the world over, without regard to race and environment, is so general that race appeared to them as irrelevant. The works of Herbert Spencer, E. B. Tylor, Adolf Bastian, Lewis Morgan, Sir James George Frazer, and among the more recent ones, those of Durkheim, Lévy-Bruhl, to mention only a few, notwithstanding material differences in point of view, reflect this attitude. We do not find in their writings any mention of racial differences. On the contrary, it is only the difference between culturally primitive man and civilized man that is relevant. The psychological basis of cultural traits is identical among all races, and similar forms develop among all of them. The customs of the South African Negro or of the Australian are analogous and comparable to those of the American Indian, and the customs of our European predecessors find their parallels among the most diverse peoples. The whole problem of the development of culture is therefore reduced to the study of psychological and social conditions which are common to mankind as a whole, and to the effects of historical happenings and of natural and cultural environment. This disregard of races appears also in Wundt's general *Folk Psychology*, and Sumner's *Science of Society*, and in most of the modern sociological discussions. To those who seek to establish an evolution of culture, parallel to organic evolution, the varying forms fall into an orderly array no matter what the bodily form of the carriers of the culture. The sociologist who tries to establish valid laws of cultural development assumes that their manifestations are the same the world over. The psychologist finds the same form of thinking and feeling in all races that are on similar levels of culture.

It may be granted that the ethnologist is not sufficiently interested in the problem of the relation between bodily build and cultural form, because his attention is directed to the similarities of culture the world over which justify the assumption of a fundamental sameness of the human mind regardless of race; but this does not signify that finer differences may not exist that go by unnoticed on account of general similarities.

The problem remains whether there is a more or less intimate relation between the bodily structure of racial groups and their cultural life.

Chapter 3

The Composition of Human Races

BEFORE ATTEMPTING an analysis of the relation between race and culture we must obtain a clear conception of what we mean by the terms race and culture.

The anatomist who studies the form of the human body is interested, first of all, in those characteristics which are common to mankind as a whole, and general anatomical descriptions deal with the organs of the body primarily as though no individual differences existed. At the same time we know that this is merely a convenient generalization, that in reality no two individuals have an identical form.

More penetrating study shows also that certain groups of mankind are somewhat alike among themselves and differ more or less strikingly from other groups. These differences are sometimes quite considerable and appear even in external characteristics. The European has wavy or straight hair, is slightly pigmented, has a narrow face, thin lips and a narrow, high nose. The Negro has frizzly hair, dark skin, dark brown eyes, thick lips and a wide, flat nose. The differences between the two groups stand out so clearly that, when comparing the two races, we disregard those peculiarities that distinguish various groups of Europeans and of Negroes. The European who visits Central Africa sees at once the distinguishing traits of the Negro.

Similar impressions are created even when the differences are not quite so striking. When Caesar's legions encountered the German followers of Ariovistus they were impressed by their blue eyes and blond hair and by other pronounced features that were rare among Romans, although not entirely unknown to them. This contrast between the two groups must have created an impression of racial distinction.

In the same way a Swede from the interior provinces who at home has comparatively speaking few opportunities of seeing people with dark eyes and black hair will be impressed by this feature, while the Scotchman, who is thoroughly familiar with black hair and dark eyes may not consider it a particularly distinguishing characteristic. Furthermore, to the Swede who is accustomed to see blue eyes, blond hair, tall bodies and long heads, the people of northern Germany will appear partly similar to the Swedish type, partly distinct; while to the North German it will rather seem that in the northern country the distribution of individual forms is different from that prevailing at home. In Sweden the light, tall, blond individuals with whose appearance the German is quite familiar, are more numerous than in his home country, the darker ones are rarer.

According to our familiarity with the bodily forms found in various localities, we are apt to establish these as definite concepts according to which we classify the great variety of human types. We pursue the same process in the classification of our general experiences, which always depends upon the character of our previous impressions, and only to a lesser extent upon objective characteristics. The naive classification of human types does not represent a grouping according to biological principles, but is based on subjective attitudes.

Nevertheless there is a tendency to give biological reality to classifications arrived at quite irrationally and dependent upon previous individual experiences. Thus it happens that we claim mixed descent for a population that contains a number of types which have been conceptualized. This is the case, for instance, in southeastern Norway where an unusually large number of brunettes live. By the same procedure it has been claimed that the Pueblo Indian population consists of Pueblo, Navaho and Ute types. In these cases a composite descent is possible, but it cannot be proved satisfactorily by the identification of individuals with types abstracted from previous observations in other localities.

We must bear in mind that groups impressing us as a conglomerate of different conceptualized types may actually be of common descent, and that others appearing to us as representatives of one type may include groups of distinct origin.

A race must not be identified with a subjectively established type but must be conceived as a biological unit, as a population derived from a common ancestry and by virtue of its descent endowed with definite biological characteristics. To a certain extent these may be unstable because subject to a multitude of outer influences, for the biological character of the genealogical group finds expression in the way in which the body is shaped under varying conditions of life.

The difficulties that we find in defining races is due to the variability of local forms. The similarities of forms inhabiting contiguous areas make it necessary to define clearly what we mean when we speak of racial characteristics and of differences between races.

This problem confronts us in the study of man just in the same way as we encounter it in the study of animals and plants. It is easy to describe what distinguishes a lion from a mouse. It is almost as easy to give a satisfactory description that enables us to distinguish the type of the Swede from the type of the Central African Negro. It is, however, difficult to give a satisfactory description that will set off a Swede against a North German, or a lion of North Africa against a lion from Rhodesia. The reason is clear. Not all Swedes are alike, and some cannot be distinguished from North Germans, and the same is true of lions of different localities. The variability of each group is considerable, and if we want to know what a Swede is we must know all the different forms that may be found among the descendants of a group of "pure" Swedes.

Among the Swedes of our present period some are tall, some short; the hair is blond or dark, straight or wavy; the eyes vary from brown to blue; the complexion is light or dark; the face more or less delicate. So it is with the Negroes: The degree of darkness of skin; the amount of projection of the teeth; the flatness of the nose; the frizzliness of the hair—all these traits show a considerable degree of variability. When we compare these two distinct types they appear to us fundamentally different notwithstanding their variability. Certain human types are thus sharply set off from others, as the Negro by his frizzly hair from the straight-haired Mongol; the Armenian by his narrow nose from the flat-nosed Negro; the Australian by his pigmentation from the rosy-hued Scandinavian. On the other hand, when we compare contiguous groups, like the Swedes and North Germans, or the Negroes of the Cameroons with those of the Upper Congo, we find essentially the same range of individual forms, but each occurring with a different frequency in each area. Those forms which are frequent in one district may be more or less rare in the other.

It is a characteristic feature of all living beings that individuals descended from the same ancestors are not identical, but differ among themselves more or less, not only in outer form but also in details of structure and in chemical characteristics. Brothers and sisters are not alike in bodily form; the chemical composition of the blood may be quite different.

W. Johannsen studied the descendants of self-fertilized beans. Since all had an identical ancestry we might be inclined to suppose that they all would be alike. All the beans he measured were descendants of a single bean raised in 1900 and belonged to the third generation which was raised in 1903. The length of these beans varied from 10 to 17 mm.[1] The distribution of sizes in per cent of their frequency is interesting.

Length in mm.	10–11	11–12	12–13	13–14	14–15	15–16	16–17
	0.4	1.4	4.7	21.3	45.2	25.2	1.8

The reason for these variations is easily understood. There are so many uncontrollable conditions that influence the development of the organism that even with identical ancestry the same form and size cannot always be expected. If we could control all the conditions beginning with the formation of the sex cells and following through fertilization and growth, and if we could make all of these uniform, then we should, of course, expect the same result in every case.

We are dealing here with the fundamental difference between a constant and a variable phenomenon which must be clearly held in mind if we want to understand the meaning of the term "race."

Wherever we are in a position to control a phenomenon completely we can also give a complete definition. To give an example: A cubic centimeter of pure water at its greatest density may be considered as completely defined. Its size,

[1] Johannsen, p. 174

composition and density are known and we suppose that there is nothing to prevent our preparing a cubic centimeter of pure water at greatest density whenever we might wish to do so, and since it is completely defined, since nothing remains uncertain in regard to its character, we expect the same results when we study its characteristics. The weight of this quantity of pure water at greatest density is expected to be the same every single time it is weighed at the same place, and in case it should not be the same we should suppose that an error had been made, in regard to the size, purity or density. If we are less accurate in our definition and ask simply for the characteristics of one cubic centimeter of water, there will be uncontrolled conditions of temperature and purity that bring it about that the water will not behave always in just the same way; and the more numerous the uncontrolled conditions the more variable may be the behavior of the samples. However, the water will not behave like mercury or oil, and therefore within certain limits we may still define its characteristics that are determined because we are dealing with more or less pure water. We may say that the sample that we are studying is a representative of a class of objects that have certain characteristics in common but which differ among themselves in minor respects. These differences will be the greater the more uncontrolled conditions are present.

Exactly the same conditions prevail in every incompletely defined phenomenon. The samples are not always the same. A study of the frequency of occurrences of each particular form belonging to the class shows that they are distributed in a regular way characteristic of the class. A different distribution indicates that we are dealing with another set of circumstances, with another class. An accurate description of any variable phenomenon must therefore consist in an enumeration of the frequency distribution of the characteristics of the individuals that compose the class.

To give only one example: The temperature of a given date at noon in New York is never the same in successive years. Still if we note the temperature of that particular day year after year we find that the same temperatures occur with definite frequency, and the distribution of these frequencies characterizes the temperature of the day selected.

It is just the same with animal forms. It does not matter whether we believe the cause of variation to be due to varying combinations of genetic elements or to accidental conditions of other kinds, it is certain that a very large number of uncontrolled and uncontrollable elements influence development and that the general class characteristics will appear modified in one way or another in each individual. The description of the class requires an enumeration of the frequency of each form and we cannot expect sameness of form in all the individuals composing the group.

Let us suppose now that we are familiar with two distinct individual human forms that have impressed themselves forcibly upon our minds, perhaps one tall and long-headed, the other short and round-headed. We now become familiar with a variable type in which individuals of both types occur. Then we shall be inclined to claim that we find a type composed of two races. We forget that we are perhaps dealing with a type that may vary so much that both forms which stand out as distinct in our minds occur here. Before concluding that we are actually dealing with two distinct types we ought to prove that the ancestral forms do not vary in such a way that both forms might have developed from the same single uniform ancestry. In other words, in a cautious study of racial characteristics we must begin with a description of local forms as they appear to us. We must describe the frequency of the various forms that occur in each local or social unit. After this has been done we may ask ourselves whether the variations are due to varying internal organic conditions or whether we are dealing with a mixed population in which genetically distinct types occur. In some cases a careful analysis of the interrelations of measurements makes it possible to answer this question (Boas 4).

The preliminary work, namely the description of types, must therefore be an enumeration of the frequencies of individuals of distinctive forms.

In a study of racial distributions it will be necessary first of all to determine whether the groups investigated are identical or not. Our previous consideration shows that sameness of two racial groups can be claimed only if the frequency distribution of forms is identical. If the relative frequency of the same form is not the same in the two series, then there must be certain unknown causes which differentiate the two groups that we are comparing. If we find that among 6687 young Italians born in Sardinia 3.9% and among 5328 born in Udine 8.2% have a stature of 167 cm. we must conclude that the two populations are not identical. Conversely we may say that if two populations agree in the frequency distribution of numerous forms, that they are probably identical. This conclusion is not quite as binding as the one from which we conclude diversity, because two populations *may* have the same distribution without being identical, and because other traits, not examined, may show differences in distribution.

It would be very difficult to describe accurately populations in the manner here indicated if the frequency distributions in each group followed different laws. It has, however, been shown that in a great many cases the type of frequency distribution is very much alike. Even a cursory examination of forms shows that extreme aberrant types are rare and that the mass of the population is fairly uniform. Extremely tall and extremely short persons are not common, while an average stature occurs frequently. Thus among the Scotch statures around 172 cm. are numerous; 20% of all Scotchmen have statures between 171 and 173 cm. Only 1% are shorter than 159 cm. and only 1% are taller than 187 cm. Among Sicilians 28% measured between 164 and 168 cm. and only 1.2% were shorter than 152 cm. and 5% taller than 180 cm.[2] The massing around the middle in each group is one of the causes that gives us a strong impression of a type in those cases in which we are dealing with measurements. When we isolate a striking form such as a Roman nose or an upturned nose, or striking hair-colors such as blond or black, or blue and brown eye-colors, these forms may not prevail, but nevertheless we find ourselves inclined to classify the frequent intermediate forms and colors with the extremes that have been conceptualized in our minds.

[2] Boas 6: p. 356; pp. 274–276.

The empirical study of frequency distributions has shown that we can predict with reasonable accuracy the frequency of any form, provided we know certain easily determined values.

The general type of distribution is shown in Fig. 1, in which points on the horizontal line represent the numerical

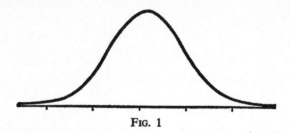

FIG. 1

values of an observation—stature, weight or any other metrical value—while the vertical distances between the horizontal line and the curve represent the frequency of that observation to which the vertical distance belongs.

The curve representing the distribution of variables will be the more contracted laterally and the higher in the middle the more uniform the series, and conversely, the more expanded laterally and the flatter in the middle, the more variable the series. In Fig. 2 two such curves are represented

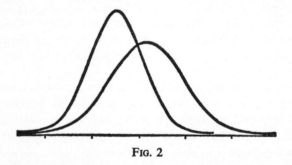

FIG. 2

which show two overlapping phenomena. It will be noticed that those observations that are in the area common to both curves may belong to either group.

A series is the more variable the more frequently strongly deviating types occur. If we determine therefore, the average type and the range of varying forms, we have a measure of the most frequent type and of the degree of its variability. An example will illustrate what is meant.

The frequencies of statures on the next page were observed among 3975 boys 6½ years old and 2518 boys 14½ years old.

This table shows that in a given population boys 14½ years of age are more variable than boys 6½ years of age, and we may express this by figures. We determine the average for each group by adding all the statures and dividing by the number of observations. These give

> Statures of boys 6½ years old, average: 111.78
> Statures of boys 14½ years old, average: 152.14

Then we arrange all the individuals in order and mark the limits of those representing the middle half of our series. This is done easily by counting off one fourth of the number of individuals from each end. The limits for the 6½ year old boys are 108.2 and 115.0 cm., so that the middle half is contained in a span of 6.8 cm. For the 14½ year old boys the corresponding limits are 146.2 and 158.0 cm., so that the middle half is contained in a span of 11.8 cm.

Experience has shown that the distribution of frequencies is in most cases fairly symmetrical around the average, so that one half of the distance in which the middle half of the whole series is contained represents the range of deviations around the average that constitute the middle half of the series. We might thus describe the 6½ year old boys as having a statue of 111.8 ± 3.4 cm., those 14½ years old as having a stature of 152.1 ± 5.9 cm.

It follows from these remarks that an adequate description of a racial type may be given in many cases as the average form of all the individuals observed and the measure of their variability, as just defined. There are some cases in which this description is not adequate, but in a great many cases it is practicable.

When we want to compare two racial types we must compare both their averages and variabilities and, unless both values are the same for the two groups, they cannot be considered as representatives of the same type.

STATURES OF BOYS

BOYS 6½ YEARS		BOYS 14½ YEARS	
Stature in Centimeters	Frequency	Stature in Centimeters	Frequency
	(Per Cent)		(Per Cent)
95– 96.9	0.1	121–122.9	0.1
97– 98.9	0.4	123–124.9	0.1
99–100.9	0.7	125–126.9	0.1
		127–128.9	0.2
		129–130.9	0.2
101–102.9	2.2	131–132.9	0.4
103–104.9	4.9	133–134.9	0.8
105–106.9	9.0	135–136.9	1.2
107–108.9	12.2	137–138.9	2.5
109–110.9	15.5	139–140.9	3.6
111–112.9	15.8	141–142.9	5.2
113–114.9	13.5	143–144.9	5.6
115–116.9	10.9	145–146.9	8.0
117–118.9	6.9	147–148.9	9.1
119–120.9	4.1	149–150.9	10.0
121–122.9	2.2	151–152.9	8.2
123–124.9	0.9	153–154.9	8.8
125–126.9	0.3	155–156.9	8.3
127–128.9	0.3	157–158.8	6.2
129–130.9	0.1	159–160.9	5.7
		161–162.9	4.7
		163–164.9	3.7
		165–166.9	2.4
		167–168.9	1.5
		169–170.9	1.4
		171–172.9	0.9
		173–174.9	0.5
		175–176.9	0.2
		177–178.9	0.2
		179–180.9	0.1

We recognize now that the current method by which a people is described as tall, blond, with elongated heads is not adequate, but that besides describing the prevalent type its variability must be given.

The degree of variability in regard to various physical traits and in different populations is far from uniform. Most of the European types, for instance, are remarkable for their high variability. The same is true of the Polynesians and of some Negro tribes. On the other hand, people like the European Hebrews, and even more so, the single tribes of North American Indians, are, comparatively speaking, characterized by much greater uniformity. The amount of variability differs considerably with regard to different physical features. It is, for instance, obvious that the hair-color and hair-form of North Europeans is much more variable than the hair-color and hair-form of the Chinese. In Europe the colors vary from flaxen to black, with a considerable number of individuals with red hair, and the form varies from straight to high degrees of waviness. Among the Chinese, on the other hand, we do not find equal variations in the darkness of color, since blondes and curly-haired individuals are absent. Similar observations may be made in regard to stature, head-form or any other feature of the body that can be expressed by measurements.

The concept of a type develops in our minds from general impressions. If the majority of a people are tall, long-headed, of light complexion, with narrow faces and straight noses we construct this combination of features as a type. We may perhaps consider as typical that half of the population whose traits are the most frequent and that lie near the most frequent value. Supposing that the features under consideration are mutually independent, one half of the population will have one of the typical traits; one half of these, that is one quarter, will have two combined traits; one half of these, that is one eighth, will have three of the typical traits combined, so that when ten such traits are counted only one in 1024 individuals will combine all the typical traits. The type is not an individual but an abstraction.

So far we have dealt merely with the description of a single racial type. Let us next examine how we are to proceed when we wish to compare different local types.

We have seen that it happens often that among distinct racial types the same individual forms may occur, that, for instance, a German selected at random may be apparently identical with a native of Sweden. This condition prevails in all extended land areas, in Europe as well as in Africa, Asia and America. If the differences were like those between Central Africans and Swedes, so that not a single form were common to the two groups, our problem would be simple; the difference would be obvious and could be expressed with precision. It might be measured and expressed by the difference between the most frequent forms. For instance, if the general average of the skin color of Swedes and that of Negroes were expressed quantitatively, the difference would be so great that the minor differences that occur in Sweden and in Africa might be disregarded and we should be in a position to measure the actual differences between the two groups. However, as soon as the two variables have a certain number of forms in common, difficulties arise. How are we to express the difference between these two series? If each individual of one series could be matched with a corresponding individual of the other one, the two series would be identical.

The larger the number of individuals that can be matched, the greater will be the similarity between the two series. A glance at Fig. 2 shows that the individuals in the area common to both curves are common to both populations. The lower their number the more unlike will be the two populations.

These considerations show that a grouping of human types according only to the difference between their average values is not admissible. Nevertheless most of the classifications of European types that have been attempted are based on this method. Certain subjectively striking forms have been selected and have been called racial types, or a nomenclature has been introduced to distinguish by brief designations various groups in the wide span of variable forms. In the course of time these names have been treated as though they were significant biological types. Particularly the head-form has been so used. The ratio of the greatest breadth of the head expressed in per cents of the length of the head, (i.e., the distance from a point just over the nose to the most prominent point on the back of the head) is called the cephalic index, or length-breadth index. Individuals having an index of less than 75 are called

long-headed or dolichocephalic, those with an index from
75 to 80, mesocephalic, those with an index over 80, short-
headed, round-headed or brachycephalic. Sometimes the limits
are drawn somewhat differently. It is clear that when we speak
of a dolichocephalic *race*, we divide the local grouping on an
arbitrary basis. We may, perhaps, with due caution, say that
a group is dolichocephalic if we mean that the average type
falls in the dolichocephalic division, but we must remember
that many members of the group will belong to the other
divisions, because the type itself is variable. It would also not
be admissible to claim that two groups are racially different
because one happens to fall inside of the limits of what we
call dolichocephalic, the others outside. Most classifications
are based on the segregation of local groups according to
average form. Head-form, stature, pigmentation, hair-form
and other characteristics, such as the form of the face and
nose, are being so used. No attempt has been made to show
that these traits are morphologically of importance, and the
limits of the various groups are arbitrarily chosen. The classifications have a descriptive value, but without further proof
no biological significance.

Roland B. Dixon (3) classifies the individuals composing
each local group according to divisions based on the numerical values of head-form, face-form and nasal form, and he
assumes that the combinations of the various divisions of
these three elements represent fundamental types. Here also
any shift in the arbitrarily chosen limits will give us a
different kind of fundamental racial grouping. The artifi-
ciality of this method is apparent. No proof has been given or
can be given that the selected groupings correspond to reali-
ties, that, for instance, a long-headed, long-faced, narrow-
nosed group represents in any sense a pure racial stock.

The same error is committed when the long-headed, blond
individuals in Europe are arbitrarily set off as a separate
racial group as is so often done at the present time.

The attempts to classify man according to constitutional
types are subject to the same criticism. This classification has
been developed essentially by medical men. Their experience
has led them to recognize a more or less intimate interdependence between bodily form and pathological conditions

so that in many cases body form may be of diagnostic value. Since these judgments are based on impressions, they are conceptualizations of constitutional forms of the same kind as conceptualizations of local types. The basis of this classification is the partial dependence of pathological conditions upon bodily form. When expressed in exact metrical terms, constitutional types are found to be variables similar to those previously discussed (Kretschmer).

The difficulties with which we are confronted are evidently based largely upon the vagueness of the concept of difference between variables. We have seen that the difference of averages does not express the difference between two series; that our judgment of difference will rather depend upon the number of individuals that are common to the two distinct series, upon the degree of overlapping of the curves representing the frequencies of forms in the series that are being compared.

The whole problem becomes clearer, if instead of the term difference, we use the term dissimilarity. The degree of similarity or dissimilarity may, perhaps, best be expressed by the number of individuals that are common to the various types that are being compared.

An ideal solution of the statistical problem of race classification would require the establishment of those extreme local forms that do not show any kind of overlapping and that could therefore be differentiated with absolute certainty. The Europeans, Negroes of Africa and Melanesians, Bushmen, Northern Mongolids, the various Malay groups, Australians and Australoid types of southern Asia, and perhaps some groups of American Indians would be such racial types. It would then be necessary to establish the position of intervening groups by a study of their similarities to the extreme types. For instance, the people of North Africa would have to be compared with the European and Negro types, the people of India with the European, Southern Mongolid, Northern Mongolid and Australian types, and so forth. It would however be an error to assume offhand on the basis of this statistical classification that the extreme types that we have isolated are the oldest and purest types from which all the others have been derived by intermixture, because they may just as well be new varieties that have developed owing to long continued isolation and to the hereditary establishment of chance variations.

A purely statistical treatment cannot solve the problem of the biological relation of races, but it is necessary to bear the statistical considerations in mind when we attempt a biological study.

Chapter 4

The Hereditary Characteristics of Human Races

WE SHALL NOW REEXAMINE from a biological point of view the characteristics of individuals composing a race.

The character of a race is determined primarily by heredity. In loose, every-day parlance we mean by heredity that the offspring repeats the form of the progenitors without material change, that the characteristics of a series of generations will always remain the same. Obviously this is not quite exact, because the descendants of the same couple will not be identical in form, neither when compared with their parents nor among themselves. When we consider a racial group as a whole we assume that, unless conditions change, heredity will bring it about that in successive generations the same frequency distribution of forms is found, or to use the terms which we discussed before, that the class, its variability and its average will remain constant. This thought is clearly in our minds when we discuss the distribution of racial types. We assume these to be constant and to continue in the same way generation after generation unless disturbances of population or perhaps changes in external conditions bring about changes in bodily form.

We might speak in this sense of "racial heredity" when the racial traits are so pronounced that they characterize all members of the race. To use the same example that we used before: blondness, fair complexion, blue or light eyes may be said to be hereditary characteristics of the Swedish race, and black, frizzly hair, dark skin and dark eyes of the African. The child of a Swedish couple will never be an African. When, however, the Swedes are compared with North Germans, or even with Italians, more or less numerous cases are found in which the racial traits overlap, so that a clear distinction cannot be made. The child of a Swedish couple may look like some North German, or even like some Italian. The term "racial heredity" is no longer applicable so far as it signifies a determination of the bodily form of every individual of the race.

There are many traits in regard to which remote races are so similar that such overlapping occurs. The size of the brain, stature, weight and size and form of various internal organs are of this character, so that in regard to none of these can we speak of racial heredity as determining these traits so that the individual by them may be recognized as a member of the race.

It is all important to note that whenever such overlapping exists, a person of a given form who belongs to one population is not biologically, or better genetically, identical with another person who has the same characteristics but who belongs to another population.

To give an example: From a study of the bodily form of a considerable number of families we find that Sicilian couples whose head index lies between 79.5 and 82.5 for both parents, and who have an average index of 80.6 have children whose average index is 79.3, that is 1.3 units under the value of their parents. Bohemian couples whose head index lies within the same limits, and who have an average index of 81.0 have children whose average index is 83.0, or 2 units over that of their parents. This shows that from a genetic point of view the individuals of the same head index in these two groups are not identical.

Similar conditions prevail in regard to other bodily features. In other words, individuals of the same bodily form that belong to two different populations are genetically not identical. Biologists have been led to the same conclusions. Lotry in a careful analysis of the meaning of "species," emphasizes the importance of constitutional identity against apparent gross morphological identity. Constitutional identity can be discovered only by inbreeding and crossing and it is often found that forms apparently alike breed in different ways. It follows from these observations that we must describe each population as a whole, that we must not separate arbitrarily a group of a certain bodily appearance from the rest. The error of identifying individuals of the same bodily appearance but belonging to different populations as members of the same race is made altogether too frequently, even by careful investigators.

During the past twenty-five years numerous studies of heredity, or as it is now generally called, genetics, have been made and their result may be formulated as follows: If the number of offspring of a single pair is infinitely large, then the frequency distribution of forms in the offspring of this pair would be definitely determined by the organic characteristics of the parents, provided there is no disturbance by external conditions. The forms of frequency distribution vary a great deal, but for each pair they are absolutely fixed as long as external conditions influencing bodily form remain the same. This is the most generalized expression of the Mendelian law of inheritance. It is difficult to give exact proof of these conditions in man as well as in those animal species in which the number of offspring is small, but the observations among lower animals and plants and the agreement of the observed conditions in man with those found in lower forms are conclusive. While we cannot say what the specific characteristics of any one individual may be, the group as a whole will always behave in the same way.

It follows from these observations that in a strictly biological study we must study the genetic lines constituting a race before we can gain an insight into the character of the race as a whole.

In higher animals the offspring is always the resultant of the union of two individuals and we do not know a single population of animals or man in which the uniting male and female would represent identical lines of descent. Even in matings of animals of the same litter of brothers and sisters the structure of the sex cells is not the same. The family lines in every population, no matter how uniform its descent, are unequal.

The importance of these considerations will become clearer when we consider the constitution of populations in greater detail.

In a large population which is as little stable in its habitat as that of modern Europe and modern America, the number of ancestors of a single person increases very rapidly, the number of parents being two; of grandparents, four; of great-grandparents, eight; the theoretical number of ancestors twenty generations back would be over a million, or, more accurately, 1,048,576. Twenty generations represent, according to the rate of increase of modern times, about seven hundred years; according to the rate of increase of earlier times, about four hundred years as a minimum. These figures would apply to the series of generations represented by first-born males; for the first-born females the respective numbers would be about five hundred years and three hundred and fifty years. If we consider, however, the actual descent of families, including individuals later born, we might perhaps assume that twenty generations in Europe would represent from eight hundred to nine hundred years, and among primitive peoples perhaps only little less, since in former times the differences between the rapidity of successive generations in Europe and among primitive peoples was not very great. This makes it obvious that it is entirely impossible that as great a number of ancestors as the theory requires can have contributed to the development of the individuals of the present generation. The reason for this is plain. Owing to intermarriages between the same families, large numbers of ancestors will be duplicated in different paternal and maternal lines; and in this way the real ancestry of each individual appears to be much more complex than the purely arithmetical treatment would suggest. The calculation for the ancestor table of the former German Emperor, for instance, is instructive. According to O. Lorenz, the numbers of his ancestors in successive generations were as follows:

GENERATION	THEORETICAL NUMBER	ACTUAL NUMBER
I	2	2
II	4	4
III	8	8
IV	16	14
V	32	24
VI	64	44
VII	128	74
VIII	256	116*
IX	512	177*
X	1024	256*
XI	2048	342*
XII	4096	533*

* These generations are not completely known. The values here given are the maximum values which would be found provided the unknown individuals had had no "loss of ancestors."

A series of forty royal families gives the following averages:

GENERATION	AVERAGE NUMBER
I	2.00
II	4.00
III	7.75
IV	13.88
V	23.70
VI	40.53

When we compare these conditions in the unstable population of the densely populated parts of modern Europe and of America with the conditions among primitive tribes, it becomes at once apparent that the total number of ancestors of each individual in small communities must be much less than the number of ancestors in the modern states just referred to. A characteristic example is presented by the Eskimo of Smith Sound in North Greenland. From all we know, it seems extremely unlikely that this community ever consisted of more than a few hundred individuals. The mode of life of Eskimo communities suggests that originally it consisted of a very few families only. The community has been cut off from the outer world for very long periods; and while there may have been accessions of new individuals from outside a few times every century, on the whole it has remained isolated. It is therefore obvious that the ancestry of this group cannot contain anything like the million of people required by the theory, but that all the individuals must be interrelated through their immediate and remote ancestry.

In a community of this type, the members of which have never numbered more than about two hundred, the ancestors of every single individual from the eighth generation back must have been largely the same, in varying combinations, because the eighth generation would require theoretically two hundred and fifty-six individuals—a greater number than are actually found in the community. Therefore the occurrence of any individual who has not a good many near and remote ancestors in common with the whole rest of the community is highly improbable, if not impossible.

We have tried to determine the loss of ancestors for the South African Bastards, descendants of Hottentots and Boers.

Using the genealogical tables collected by Eugen Fischer (3), the following numbers were found:

| GENERATION | No. of Ancestors of Various Families | | |
	Family I	Family II	Family III
I	2	2	2
II	4	4	4
III	8	8	8
IV	14.1	14.3	16
V	20.1	19.7	32
VI	32.0	—	—

These numbers are similar to those found among the royal houses of Europe.

A somewhat clearer picture is obtained when we determine the number of ascendants, and consider each individual as a member of a fraternity embracing a certain number of children who continue to propagate at the same rate. For a large, mobile population we might furthermore assume that the mates of the succeeding generations are in no way related among themselves or to the members of the family line under consideration. Under these conditions the ancestry of any one individual will be that fraction of the number of ancestors which is obtained by dividing the total number of his ancestors by the number of members of his generation. When, for instance, a couple have two children the average number of parents for each will be 1. When these children marry and have each two children, the total number of individuals in the first generation will be six, because the two children of the original couple have the same parents. The four grandchildren of the original couple will have therefore six grandparents or 1.5 for each. In this way the following ancestral series is obtained for ancestors in direct line of descent.

The apparent contradiction of these values—for instance that four grandchildren have six grandparents—lies in the fact that two of these grandchildren are at the same time direct descendants of another family. The collateral relations are expanding rapidly. A rough approximation of these values

has been given by Jankowsky.[1] It must be remembered that
the actual conditions will depend largely on the mobility of
the population. Whenever the population is sedentary and
relatively small groups are in permanent contact a high degree
of inbreeding with segregation of local groups will result,
while in a freely moving large population the rate at which
inbreeding develops will be much slower.

| GENERATION | NUMBER OF ANCESTORS FOR FAMILIES OF | | | |
	2 Children	3 Children	4 Children	5 Children
I	1	.67	.50	.40
II	1.50	.89	.62	.48
III	2.75	1.63	1.16	.90
IV	5.38	3.21	2.29	1.78
V	10.69	6.40	4.57	3.55
VI	21.34	12.80	9.14	7.11
VII	42.67	25.60	18.29	14.22
VIII	85.34	51.20	36.57	28.44
IX	170.64	102.40	73.14	56.88
X	341.33	204.80	146.28	113.78

Both inbreeding and continued intermixture bring it about
that when the process has been carried on for a long time all
the family lines will be very much alike, while in a population
of mixed descent or without inbreeding the family lines will
be quite distinct. It may, therefore, happen that the bodily
forms in two populations are distributed in the same way, if
only individuals are considered, and still the biological composition of the two series may be quite diifferent. In the one
we may have family lines quite distinct among themselves,
while all the brothers and sisters in each family are much
alike; in the other we may have family lines very much alike,
while brothers and sisters may vary very much among themselves.

The effect of inbreeding has been tested with animals.
Experiments (King) with rats in which brothers and sisters
were mated for 25 successive generations show that the
fraternal variability decreases gradually. It seems likely that

[1] Jankowsky, W., *Die Blutsverwandschaft im Volk und in der Familie*, Stuttgart (1934), pp. 119 ff.

this would indicate both a decrease in variability of family lines and in fraternal variability, but the data do not allow us to distinguish between these two features.

Only a few populations and very few traits have been examined from these points of view. The material so far collected indicates that the differences between the family lines constituting a population are the less, the more stable the population and the longer inbreeding without selection has continued. When the progenitors of these family lines are of distinct bodily form the brothers and sisters in each family are liable to be unlike; if the progenitors are alike in form, then both family lines and fraternities (that is brothers and sisters of each family) will be alike.

The following data relating to the variability of the value of the breadth of head expressed in per cents of the length of the head illustrate the conditions that are found in various local groups.

STANDARD VARIABILITY[2] OF HEAD INDEX

	I TOTAL	II FRATERNAL	III FAMILY LINES	RATIO OF II AND III
Armenians	3.88	3.20	2.20	1.46
Chippewa Indians	3.76	3.32	1.77	1.88
Central Italians	3.62	2.72	2.39	1.14
N. Y. Negro-White	3.51	2.93	1.85	1.58
Bohemians	3.53	2.61	2.37	1.10
Scotch	3.43	2.66	2.17	1.21
Missisauga	3.43	3.10	1.47	2.11
East European Jews	3.40	2.52	2.29	1.10
Worcester, Mass.	3.34	2.36	2.36	1.00
Dutch	3.05	2.33	1.95	1.20
Bastards, South Africa	2.82	2.52	1.26	2.00
Blue Ridge Mountain Whites	2.80	2.09	1.85	1.13

[2] Variability is a measure indicating the degree of scattering of forms as illustrated on p. 53 of this chapter. On account of technical reasons which do not need to be described here it is determined as the value obtained by squaring all the deviations from the average, taking the average of their sum and determining the square root of this average. Inside the limits of the average plus and minus this deviation about 68% of the whole series are

This means that among the Armenians whose head index is on the average 85.6, 68% of the families have an index between 83.4 and 87.8, while the remaining 32% have index values outside of these limits. It also means that 68% of the brothers and sisters have a head index varying between 3.20 units below and 3.20 units above the family mean, while the remainder are outside of these limits. And so with the other values.

The figures for the Bastards are interesting. The Bastards are a people of Hottentot and Dutch descent who have largely intermarried among themselves for the last century. Notwithstanding their mixed descent the family lines are much alike, while brothers and sisters show considerable variations. The conditions among the Chippewa Indians of Canada and particularly among the Missisauga, a local branch of the Chippewa, are quite similar. They are an old inbred mixed population of Indian, French and Irish descent. Among the American Negroes we find also greater uniformity of family lines because they also represent an old mixture of White and Negro.

The meaning of these figures may be more fully illustrated by the following consideration. In the Missisauga population 16% of the families have an index of more than 1.47 units under the average and another 16% of more than 1.47 units over the average.

Since the fraternal variability is ±3.10, or more than twice the variability of the family lines there will be a considerable overlapping among these two groups. (Fig. 3). According to statistical constants about 32% of the lower group will have values over, and the same percentage of the upper group will have values under the general average, so that about 32% of each of the 16%, or about 10% of the extremes of the population will have the same forms. In Worcester on the other hand only 16% of the two extremes will overlap so that only 5% of the two extremes will overlap.

This is still clearer when the extremes selected are farther

---

found. Inside the limits of twice this value about 95% of the whole series are found. This mean square variation is called the standard variation. The probable variation described on p. 33 is about equal to 0.67 of the standard deviation.

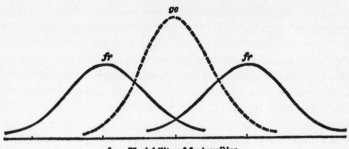

fr = Variability of fraternities
ge = Variability of family lines

FIG. 3

removed from the average. We might consider the group of Missisauga that are more than 2.2 units removed from the average. There are 6.7% of the whole series below and 6.7% above these points. Then, according to statistical constants about 24% of each of these groups or 3.2% of the whole population will overlap. For the Worcester population only 6.7% of each of the extreme groups will overlap so that less than 1% will be common to the two series.[3]

It is well to bear this in mind, for authors like Fritz Lenz minimize the significance of genetic differences within the race.

It should be remembered that this discussion refers to a single trait only. If the traits studied are more numerous the heterogeneity of the families must become still more apparent.

We conclude from this that in most populations family lines differ so much that distinctive lines will always be found. By contrast with this it is impossible to find analogous radical distinctions between whole populations of contiguous areas.

While, therefore, an exact biological definition of a race cannot be given, we can define family lines with much greater precision, and therefore the race must be defined as a complex of family lines. The origin and character of the family lines determine the character of the race.

The results of our consideration are quite in accord with recent views of what constitutes a species of animals or of

[3] As a matter of fact these numbers are too high, because those farther removed from the average will have much less overlapping.

plants. Johannsen's dissolution of the species, or as he calls it, the phenotype, into a series of genotypes is comparable to our analysis of a race. Johannsen was dealing primarily with self-fertilized beans. In this case the phenomenon is naturally much clearer than it can be in cases in which self-fertilization is impossible and where crossing of lines constantly occurs. The view here expressed agrees also with that of O. F. Cook who recognized only the individual and its descendants in the species. He also considers the species a complex of distinct lines.

The more gradual the transition between local types, the more necessary it is to bear this point clearly in mind.

We may call a population heterogeneous in which the family lines are very different because a single family line will not be representative of the whole population. The less the variability of family lines, the more will any one family be a good representative of the whole population. In this sense populations with a low variability of family lines may be called homogeneous. It may well be that in such a case the ancestry is quite diverse, as among the South African Bastards, the descendants of Dutch and Hottentot, and still the families may be so much alike that each represents fairly and adequately the general type of the whole population.

The laws of heredity bring it about that absolute homogeneity will never be found, no matter how much inbreeding has occurred. Until more extended investigations of this question have been carried out we cannot tell what the limit of homogeneity in a population may be.

Even without detailed information it is easy to see that the degree of heterogeneity must vary greatly. The inhabitants of a small stable European village in which the land has been held for centuries by the same families must have a high degree of homogeneity. The same must be the case in small isolated tribes.

Large cities represent the reverse conditions. Owing to the conflux of people of distinct ancestry the family lines will be quite varied. The character of the fraternities and the variability of family lines will undergo constant changes as the integration of the population proceeds until finally a new stable condition is established, provided that no new accession of foreign lines occurs, a condition that in city life is never realized.

The composition of a race may also be looked at from another angle. When we compare two quite distinct types, all the individuals of each type appear to us alike and different from the other type. On the other hand, when two types overlap the individual differences will become more striking and the degree of mutual similarity among the members of each type will not seem so great. When we compare one Negro family with one White family, the minor differences between the brothers and sisters in each of these families seem irrelevant. When we compare, on the other hand, two families that are very much alike, the individual differences will seem much more important, and correspondingly the family resemblances between brothers and sisters will appear slight. In a single family, not compared with any other family, brothers and sisters are simply different. They have only individually different degrees of similarity. Also, when we have a number of identical families, all the individuals will be different and there will be no family resemblances. This does not interfere with the fact that the fraternal variability in the families may be great or small.

This simple consideration shows that fraternal similarity depends entirely upon the composition of the population. In a very heterogeneous population fraternal resemblances will be great. In a homogeneous population they will be small. The same may be said of the similarity between parents and children. It will appear to us the greater, the greater the heterogeneity of the population, while in a comparatively homogeneous population it will practically disappear, because in every family the same type will be represented. When Francis Galton (3) studied this phenomenon he laid great stress upon the degree of similarity between brothers and sisters and parents and children, which he expressed by the so-called coefficient of regression. He determined this in the following way: When fathers or mothers in a given population differ by a certain amount from the general average of the population, then the children will differ from the general population by a certain fraction of this amount; and if one individual differs by a certain amount from the average of the population his or her brothers or sisters will differ on the average from the average of the population by a certain fraction of this amount.

For the populations referred to on page 67 and for the average deviations of the head index of brothers and sisters the following values of these fractions have been found:

Worcester, Mass.	0.50
Bohemians	0.45
East European Jews	0.45
Blue Ridge Whites	0.44
Central Italians	0.44
Dutch	0.41
Scotch	0.40
Armenians	0.30
N. Y. Negro-White	0.28
Chippewa Indians	0.21
Bastards, South Africa	0.20
Missisauga	0.18

For instance, if in Worcester, Massachusetts, an individual has a head index 4 units above the average, then his brothers and sisters would have on the average an index of 4×0.5 or 2 units above the average; while among the Missisauga the brothers and sisters would have on the average a head index of only 4×0.18 or 0.72 above the average.

The differences in these values are due to the varying degrees of heterogeneity of the population. The most homogeneous series have the lowest correlations. The arrangement according to variability of family lines (I) and the ratio between family line and fraternal variability (II) is as follows:

I		II	
Bastards	±1.26	Missisauga	2.11
Missisauga	±1.47	Bastards	2.00
Chippewa	±1.77	Chippewa	1.88
N. Y. Negro-White	±1.85	N. Y. Negro-White	1.58
Blue Ridge Whites	±1.85	Armenians	1.46
Dutch	±1.95	Scotch	1.21
Scotch	±2.17	Dutch	1.20
Armenians	±2.20	Blue Ridge Whites	1.13
East European Jews	±2.29	Central Italians	1.14
Worcester, Mass.	±2.36	East European Jews	1.10
Bohemians	±2.37	Bohemians	1.10
Central Italians	±2.39	Worcester, Mass.	1.00

The agreement between these columns shows that in the selected series the ratio of variability of fraternities measured by the variability of family lines is the greater the more uniform the family lines.

We must recur once more to the discussion of family lines. We assumed in the previous considerations that all the families in a population will have the same fraternal variability. Since the descent of the family lines is not uniform this is not likely and the values given before must be considered approximations to the actual conditions.

It can be shown that within the same population the variability of fraternities increases with the difference between the parents. An investigation of a considerable number of families shows that the variability of the head index within a population increases with the difference of head index between parents (Boas 5).

DIFFERENCE OF HEAD INDEX BETWEEN PARENTS	FRATERNAL VARIABILITY, NEW YORK	CASES	FRATERNAL VARIABILITY, HOLLAND	CASES
0–2.9 units	6.8	1102	5.3	627
3–5.9	6.7	736	5.9	473
6–8.9	8.3	317	5.4	182
9 and more	13.0	108	8.5	66

Felix von Luschan (1) has found a similar phenomenon in the mixed population of southern Asia Minor where a round-headed people of central Asia Minor has intermingled for thousands of years with the long-headed people of the coast of Syria. Here also we find a considerable increase in the variability of the mixed population as compared with the degree of variability found in more homogeneous populations.

The distribution of head-forms in Italy also illustrates this point. In central Italy where the short-headed North Italians and the long-headed South Italians have intermarried, the variability of head-form is high.

These phenomena are expressions of the various forms of Mendelian inheritance to which we referred before (p. 62), to the tendency of individuals of mixed descent to revert in definite numerical ratios in regard to various bodily features to the types from which they are descended.

Human races are often compared with modern races of domesticated animals. There is, however, a fundamental difference. Breeds of domesticated animals are raised by careful selection, and the Mendelian splitting up of families is eliminated by breeding only those individuals that breed true. The variation in a breed of domesticated animals is, therefore, very slight, the more so the more carefully all mixed types are eliminated. In this manner strikingly differentiated races have been developed. Nothing of the kind has happened in man. On the contrary, even where the attempt has been made to prevent intermarriage between different stocks it has never been successful. Social barriers break down and gradually the two types of the population intermingle. This is true even in such rigid caste systems as those of India. It was true of patricians and plebeians in Rome and notwithstanding the recrudescence of forcible prevention of intermarriage in Germany the history of mankind will not be reversed.

More or less specialized local types develop only when small groups are isolated and the small number of ancestors show peculiarities. The smaller the ancestral group, the greater will be the probability that the local group will appear more or less distinct from the type of the general population from which they sprang. When we find, for instance, that in North America a very marked type belongs to the Arctic coast of the continent, and that another type is found in the Mackenzie Basin, still others in well-defined localities on the Pacific Coast, the Mississippi Basin, the Southeast, along the Rio Grande and in Mexico, it seems possible to ascribe their origin to the increase of small isolated groups. Some other instances of the occurrence of peculiar forms in local communities may be explained in this manner. Examples are the unusual frequency of the *os Incae* (the division of the occipital bone by a transversal suture) in Peru and the Pueblos (Matthews 1), the great frequency of the *torus palatinus* (a ridge along the middle line of the palate) among the Lapps and along the eastern shores of the Baltic (Lissauer).

Another phenomenon may be pointed out here which is still little investigated, but which deserves careful attention.

We have seen that in stable communities in sparsely settled countries the relationship between members of a group will be quite close, and that this relationship will necessarily affect the type and its variability. In course of time two areas whose populations have thus developed may be thrown into contact, and numerous intermarriages may occur. It will be seen at once that although the differences between the two types may be apparently only slight, a complete disturbance in the forms of heredity will result, because a great number of individuals of distinct ancestry are thrown together. To give an example —the South Italians and the Spaniards represent two types not very distinct in physical features, but separated for centuries. The small village communities of Italy, as well as those of Spain, have all the characteristics of communities in which endogamic marriages have been continued for a long period. In the Argentine Republic these two types come into contact and intermarry frequently. We have no observations on the result of this mixture upon physical characteristics, but it has been noted that the distribution of male and female births is quite different from that prevailing in families in which both parents are either Spanish or Italian (Pearl 3). It is also conceivable that this may be one of the elements bringing about the change of type of urban populations when compared to rural populations in Europe, and that it may have been active in the change of type observed among the descendants of European immigrants in America.

All attempts to reconstruct the component elements of a population of mixed ancestry are destined to fail. Supposing, for instance, that we did not know a White race and a Negro race, but only Mulattoes. Could we reconstruct a White race and a Negro race? If we knew the laws of inheritance of each individual trait, their interrelations and the changes that may occur owing to mixture; if furthermore we knew what the influences of environment and selection had been, this might seem possible; but these intricate mechanisms are very imperfectly known, and the task would be like that of a person who is to solve a single equation with many unknown quantities and with hardly any guide in the selection of quantities that would fulfill the conditions of the original equation.

This is even more true in types that are akin like those of

Europe and the Near East, whose bodily features are so little divergent that individuals cannot be assigned with certainty to one group or another. All we know is that each group consists of many divergent family lines. The reconstruction of original "pure" family lines from which the modern population is derived cannot be made. Statistical solutions without number can be given, but their biological interpretation would require an exhaustive knowledge of the conditions controlling the effects of mixtures of distinct family lines.

We are not able to predict, even statistically, much less individually, what the result of the intermingling of two races will be. Much less are we able to reverse the process and determine the types from which a population may have sprung.

We have so far discussed racial types as shown in the adult. We have to consider the way in which hereditary characteristics find expression in the development of the individual. Specific racial characteristics—that is, traits the individual variation of which is small as compared to the racial differences—are generally established very early in life. A. Schultz has shown that the characteristic features of the Negro and White are noticeable in fetal life. The more pronounced the difference between two types, the earlier it is established. During this time the differentiation of racial types is more marked than individual differentiation. In the course of growth both racial and individual character become more and more emphasized and this process continues throughout life. For this reason the characteristics of local types are often most distinct in adult males who have a longer and more intense period of development than females. They are least marked in children. The most generalized racial types will be found among children, the most specialized types among adult males. This may be illustrated by an analysis of the form of the nose of Indian, Chinese and White children, which is much more alike than it is in adults. The bridge of the nose is low, its elevation over the face slight, the upper eyelid often has an inner fold which gives an apparent slanting position to the eye. This is found particularly in Mongolids and Indians but also quite frequently in White children. It disappears with the increased elevation of the nose over the plane of the face.

The proportions of limbs and body of young children of these three races are not very different.

Accompanying the differentiation of types we find also a differentiation of individual characteristics. After a certain age has been reached the rate of individual differentiation exceeds that of racial differentiation. Racial characteristics that have not become established before this time do not develop in later life. The age at which marked progress in individualization occurs is not the same for all traits. Pigmentation is established shortly after birth. Head-form is established at the age of one or two years. The most typical development of the nose occurs during adolescence.

We may express this in another way. The most generalized types are found in the youngest individuals. The process of specialization occurs during childhood and the greatest degree of specialization is found among adult men. The affinities between distantly related racial groups may therefore be discovered most easily by a comparison of fetal forms and of young children. It is hardly possible at the present time to make definite statements in regard to this matter because too little is known about the anatomical forms of the young in Australians, Bushmen, Negritos or American Indians, and these belong to the most important groups whose position is to be determined.

It seems likely that the various groups have each a characteristic rate of development for various bodily traits. It is uncertain whether in such cases environmental conditions play an important role or whether we are dealing with hereditary traits. A comparison of Jewish and non-Jewish children attending different schools shows that young Jewish children grow first more rapidly than non-Jewish children, while later on the rate of growth of the latter is greater than that of the Jewish children. Under equal social conditions no such difference appeared. The order of eruption of permanent teeth among South African Negroes and American Whites is not the same. The observed differences between these groups are much smaller than those found in family lines in which there are clear evidences of hereditary tendencies in regard to size as well as to tempo of development.

Chapter 5

The Instability of Human Types

THE DEVELOPMENT of the races of man cannot be fully understood as long as we consider the bodily form as absolutely stable. We must investigate the genesis of the various types.

While it is not our object to discuss and describe in detail the probable development of the human races, a few general considerations cannot be omitted.

The mammalian fauna of the late tertiary differs fundamentally from that of modern times. Very few forms of that period, for instance beaver and marmot, survive. In most genera important changes of form have taken place in the span of time that has since elapsed. The modifications which have occurred in all the higher forms of mammals make it very improbable that man should have existed at this time, and up to the present no remains have been found that would suggest his presence. On the contrary, the few oldest specimens from the early quaternary like the Javanese skeleton of *Pithecanthropus erectus*, the Pekin skeletons, and the quaternary jaw found at Heidelberg, are decidedly distinct from the present forms of man. Towards the latter part of the quaternary true human types appear, particularly the Neanderthal man—so called from the Neander Valley in Germany where the first skeleton of this type was found. It is still decidedly different from living races of man. We may discover a single Neanderthaloid feature in a single individual here and there—more frequently in some races than in others—but no races of the Neanderthal type survive.

It seems that even at this early period mankind was not uniform, for forms found at Piltdown in England[1] and in the Grimaldi caves near Mentone represent distinct types.

Forms closely associated with modern man appear in the period immediately following the disappearance of Neander-

---

[1] A theory which has since been discredited—Ed.

thal man. The palaeontological data, fragmentary as they are, show a change of forms beginning with the oldest known prehuman and human remains. We cannot show by palaeontological evidence how the modern types developed, but we are able to prove that the most ancient types differed from those of our time, and ceased to exist.

A gradual change in human types is also indicated in the morphological forms of living man. To quote the words of Wiedersheim:

"In the course of his phylogenetic development the body of Man has undergone a series of modifications which still in part find expression in his ontogeny. There are indications that changes in his organization are still continuing, and that the Man of the future will be different from the Man of to-day." The best illustrations of these changes are found in the forms of organs which are undergoing reduction. Thus we may observe that in modern man the little toe is often two-jointed, a phenomenon presumably due to lack of functional use. The teeth also show a tendency to gradual reduction, especially in the variable size of the molars and of the upper outer incisors. A similar reduction may be observed at the lower end of the thorax, where the development of ribs and sternum shows great variations.

The significance of these phenomena lies in the fact that in the evolutionary series the abnormal occurrences, which are found in different races in varying frequency, appear as new developments, which, if they should become normal, would increase the differentiation between man and the lower forms. The actual proof of increasing frequency of these features, and of their becoming permanent characteristics, has not been given, but seems plausible.

This inference is strongly supported by the occurrence of rudimentary, functionless organs, and by the temporary appearance of lower features during ontogenetic development.

Besides these progressive variations, there are others that recall forms occurring among the higher mammals and which from this point of view may be called regressive. The specifically human forms have come to be fairly well stabilized, while the older forms occur rarely. Many traits of the skeleton and muscular system belong to this class. They have been observed in all races of mankind, but with unequal frequency. Some of them are determined by physiological causes and should not be considered as fixed hereditary traits, but from a purely morphological point of view they may be interpreted as indications of the line along which the human type has developed.

There is another point of view that must be borne in mind if we want to gain a clear understanding of the significance of racial types. Man is not a wild form, but must be compared to the domesticated animals. He is a self-domesticated being.

It is quite a number of years since Fritsch, in his studies of the anthropology of South Africa, pointed out that a peculiar difference exists in the form of the body of the Bushman and the Hottentot as compared to that of Europeans, in that the former exhibit slenderer forms of the bones, that the bone is very solid in its structure; while in the European the skeleton appears heavier, but of more open structure. Similar differences may be observed in a comparison between the skeletons of wild and those of domesticated animals; and this observation led him to the conclusion that the Bushmen are in their physical habitus to a certain extent like wild animals, while the Europeans resemble in their structure domesticated animals.

This point of view—namely, that the human race in its civilized forms must be compared, not with the forms of wild animals, but rather with those of domesticated ones—seems to me a very important one; and a somewhat detailed study of the conditions in which various races are found suggests that at the present time, and all over the world, even among the most primitive types of man, changes incident to domestication have taken place.

There are three different types of changes due to domestication which must be clearly distinguished. The bodies of domesticated animals undergo considerable transformations, owing to the change in nutrition and use of the body; secondly, selection, and lastly, crossing, have played an important part in the development of races of domesticated animals.

Some changes of the first class are due to a more regular and more ample nutrition; others to a new diet imposed by man; still others to the different manner in which the muscular and the nervous systems are put into use. These changes are not quite the same among carnivorous and among herbivorous animals. The dog and the cat, for instance, are fairly regularly fed when they are found in domestication; but the food given to them differs in character from the food which the wild dog and cat eat. Even among people whose diet consists almost entirely of meat, dogs are generally fed boiled meat, or rather the boiled, less nutritious parts of animals; while among other tribes which utilize to a great extent vegetable food, dogs are often fed mush and other vegetable material. The same is true of our cats, whose diet is not by any means entirely a meat diet. The exertions which wild carnivorous animals undergo to obtain food are incomparably greater than those of the corresponding domesticated forms; and for this reason the muscular system and the central nervous system may have undergone considerable changes.

The muscular exertions of herbivorous animals, as far as they are fed on pastures, are not so materially changed. The grazing habits of cattle and sheep in domestication are about the same as the grazing habits of wild animals of the same class; but the rapid movements and the watchfulness required for protecting the herd against animals of prey have completely disappeared. Stable-fed animals live under highly artificial conditions, and material changes of diet occur in them.

Changes due to these causes may be observed in the oldest types of domesticated animals, such as are found in the neolithic villages of Europe, in which native European species appear in domesticated form (Keller; Studer). They may also be observed in the dogs of the various continents, which differ markedly from the wild species from which they are derived. Even the Eskimo dog, which is a descendant of the gray wolf and still interbreeds with the wolf, differs in bodily form from the wild animal (Beckmann). Modifications may also be observed in slightly domesticated animals, like the Chukchee reindeer, which differs in type from the wild reindeer of the same area.[2] I think it very unlikely, judging

[2] Bogoras, pp. 73 et seq.; compare with Allen.

82 / The Mind of Primitive Man

from our knowledge of the methods of domestication practised by tribes like the Eskimo and Chukchee, that any material amount of artificial selection has contributed to the modifications of form found in these races of primitive domesticated animals. Their uniformity is still fairly well marked, but they have assumed traits different from the wild species, even though they still interbreed with the wild forms. Admixture of blood of wild reindeer is favored by the Chukchee.

A certain kind of selection may occur in early forms of domestication by preventing or encouraging mating and by interference with the bringing up of young animals. Wherever castration is practised, where milk is used, where young animals are slaughtered or taken away from their mothers and given to other animals highly artificial conditions prevail. Although these do not lead to any kind of conscious selection of forms they disturb the natural composition of the herd and may lead to bodily modifications.

A more marked differentiation of domesticated forms does not seem to occur until man begins to select and to isolate, more or less consciously, particular breeds. Opportunity for such isolation has been the greater, the older the domestication of any particular species. We find, therefore, that the number of distinct breeds have come to be greatest in those animals which have been under domestication for the longest periods.

The number of varieties of domesticated species has also been increased by unintentional or intentional crossing of different species, from which are derived many breeds whose ancestry it is often difficult to unravel.

In the development of the races of man, change of mode of life and crossing have been most strongly active. The condition of the tribes of man the world over is such, that there are none whose mode of nutrition is strictly analogous to that of wild animals, and a consideration of early human culture shows that similar conditions have prevailed for a long period. In all those cases in which man practises agriculture, when he is the owner of herds of domesticated animals which are used for food, the food-supply has become regular, and is obtained by an application of the muscular system in highly specialized directions. Examples of this condition are, for instance, the Central African Negroes, who have their gardens near their villages, the cultivation of the gardens being essentially the work of the women, while the men are engaged in various specialized industrial pursuits. Neither is the manner of the use of the body which is applied by wild animals for protection against enemies found among these tribes. In combat muscular strength alone is not decisive, but excellence of weapons and strategy count as much as mere strength and agility. The conditions among the American agricultural Indians of the Mississippi Valley or of those of the South American forests are similar in character.

As an example of a pastoral people among whom considerable regularity in nutrition obtains, we might mention the reindeer-breeders of Siberia or the cattle-breeders of Africa.

We know, of course, that among all these people, periods of starvation occur, due to a failure of the crops or to epidemics in the herds; but the normal condition is one of fairly regular and ample food-supply.

The conditions among fishing tribes are not very different; owing to methods of storing provisions, and to the super-abundance of food-supply obtained in one season and sufficient to last for the rest of the year, the nutrition of these people is also fairly regular. Here also, the kind of muscular exertion required for obtaining food is specialized, and differs from that required from the simple pursuit of game.

Associated with these conditions are also the characteristic selections of food-stuffs by different tribes, such as the exclusive meat diet of some tribes—most pronounced among the Eskimo—and the exclusive vegetable diet of others—well developed, for instance, in southern Asia. Both of these have, in all probability, a far-reaching effect upon the bodily form of these races.

All these differences are of minor importance when compared to the effect of the artificial change of food-stuffs by means of fire. The art of cookery is universal. By its means the character of the food and with it the demands made upon the digestive organs are materially changed. The invention of fire dates back to very early times. Remains of hearths have been found in palaeolithic strata, which according to conservative estimates date back 50,000 years. The use of fire and the application of methods of leeching have enabled man to utilize vegetable products that otherwise would be harmful (Ida Hahn). The potato, the California acorn, the casava, the Australian Cycas and perhaps the wild oats are examples.

We may say with justice that one of the most fundamental conditions of domestication set in when fire was first applied to the preparation of food.

Besides the use of fire, artificial means of protection against climate and enemies are important features in the process of domestication because they modify essentially the conditions of propagation and the course of individual development. Under protecting influences the chances of survival of varying forms and hence the composition of the population may be materially altered. Tools and the use of clothing as protection against the climate are the most important inventions of this kind. The use of tools goes back to very great antiquity. In fact, the earliest presence of man is known only from the occurrence of stone implements and must be assigned to the early part of the glacial period. To the earliest stone tools undoubtedly made by the hand of man may be ascribed an age of at least 150,000 years. Evidence of the use of clothing occurs also in palaeolithic times, at about the same time that evidence of the use of fire is available.

We conclude that the time of domestication of man must have begun with the early quaternary, and that it became intensive with the discovery of the use of fire.

The second group of causes which is most potent in developing distinct races of domesticated animals—namely, conscious selection—has probably never been very active in the races of man. We do not know of a single case in which it can be shown that intermarriage between distinct types of the same descent was prohibited; and whatever selection there may have been in the development of primitive society seems to have been rather that type of natural selection which encourages the mating of like with like, or such intricate selection as is due to the social laws of intermarriage, which prevented or encouraged intermarriages of relatives of certain grades, and often also of members of different generations.

Thus among certain tribes it is customary for children of a man to marry those of his sister, while the children of brothers and the children of sisters are not allowed to intermarry. Similar restrictions are found in great number, and may possibly have had a certain selective effect, although their operation can hardly be assumed to have had very marked results upon the form of the human body. Customs that prescribe the killing of twins or of children showing abnormalities of form or color may also have had a slight selective influence.

In some cases social laws have had the indirect effect of perpetuating distinctions between separate parts of a population, or at least of retarding their complete amalgamation. This is the case where laws of endogamy relate to groups of distinct descent, and may be observed, for instance, among the castes of Bengal, where the low castes are of the characteristic South Indian type, while the highest castes preserve the type of the tribes of northwestern India (Risley and Gait). The numerous intermediate castes show, however, that the laws of endogamy, even where they are as stringent as those of India, cannot prevent blood-mixture. Whether or not in extreme cases endogamy in small groups, as among the ancient Egyptians, has led to the development of well-defined types, is a question that cannot be answered, but it is certain that none of these types, when found in a large population, have survived.

The third element of domestication has been very important in the development of the races of man. Crossings between distinct types are so markedly common in the history of primitive people, and so markedly rare in the history of wild animals, that in this case the analogy between domesticated animals and man becomes very clear. Cases of hybrid forms of higher wild animals are rare almost everywhere; while domesticated animals have been crossed and recrossed without end. Crossings between the most distinct types of man are also of common occurrence. As an instance, we might mention the intermarriages between the Hamitic tribes of the Sahara and the Negro tribes of the Sudan (Nachtigal 2); the mixtures between the Negritos and Malay, which are of such common occurrence in the Malay Peninsula (Martin, pp.

1011–1012) and which are probably to a great extent a cause of the peculiar distribution of types in the whole Malay Archipelago; the mixtures which have taken place in Fiji; that of the Ainu and Japanese in the northern part of Japan; of European and Mongol in eastern Europe; not to speak of the more recent mixtures between European and other races which were incident to the gradual distribution of the Europeans over the whole world.

The distinguishing traits of human races are in many cases analogous to those by which domesticated animals are characterized.[3] Melanism, that is a strong increase of pigment, and leucism, that is marked loss of pigment, belong here. The black bear, the black panther and the mole have black coat color, but on the whole black hair is not common in wild mammals. Individuals with black hair are found in various species. Black mice, rabbits, roes, giraffes, tigers, ermines have been observed.

Even rarer is blond hair and the general scarcity of pigment that finds expression in the light color of the skin and in blue eyes. This loss, however, is found in many domesticated strains, particularly in pigs and horses. The great variation in the size of the face belongs to the same class. The shortening of the face as in certain breeds of sheep, pigs, horses and dogs, and its lengthening in other breeds compare well with the excessive forms found in the Whites on the one hand, and the Negroes on the other. Frizzly hair is not characteristic of wild animals, but similar forms are found in domestication. The hair of the poodle dog is somewhat similar in form to that of the Negro. The excessive length of the hair of the head may also well have developed owing to conditions of

[3] The importance of considering races as domesticated forms has been emphasized by Johannes Ranke. He compared the pigmentation of domesticated animals and of man. Eduard Hahn (1896) recognized the similarities in the conditions of life of man and of domesticated animals. I have called attention to the cultural and anatomical conditions in 1910. B. Klatt (1912) pointed out changes in the form of the skull and Friedenthal studied the conditions of hair and skin. The pigmentation of the eye was investigated by Hauschild in 1909. The forms of the human body as expressions of domestication have been fully discussed by Eugen Fischer.

domestication. Wild animals with such excessive hair length are unknown, but lengthening of the mane is found in the domesticated horse, and of body hair in cats and dogs. Great variation in stature is also characteristic of domesticated animals as against wild forms.

Important functional changes are also common to man and to domesticated animals. The periodicity of sexual functioning has been lost in man and in a number of domesticated animals. The milk secreting glands which in wild animals develop periodically have become permanent in some of our domesticated animals and in man. It seems also that anomalies of sexual behavior such as homosexuality are characteristic of domesticated animals and of all races of man.

The process of human domestication can be studied in its results only. The direct influence of environment may be investigated experimentally and statistically.

An examination of organisms, plants and animals shows that in many cases the form will vary according to environmental influences. This is particularly evident in plants. Plants that grow habitually in the plains when transported to high altitudes assume the form of Alpine plants. Due to the strong insolation and the cool nights their leaves become small and their stems are shortened. Conversely, Alpine plants transplanted to the plains develop larger leaves and their stems are elongated (Haberlandt). The Ranunculus growing in water has much reduced leaves, while those parts growing in the air have a continuous surface. Plants growing in arid soil have thick impermeable outer epidermis walls; they excrete wax and have deeply imbedded stomata. These traits are often lost when they are cultivated in moisture.

O. F. Cook expresses similar observations as follows: "Zoologists speculate on such questions as whether the eggs of Vancouver woodpeckers, if transferred to Arizona, would hatch Arizona woodpeckers, or whether the transferred individuals would gain Arizona characters in a few generations. What the woodpeckers might or might not do depends on the amount of organic elasticity which they may happen to possess, but the experiment is unnecessary for answering the general question, since plants show a high development of these powers of prompt adjustment to diverse conditions. It is not even necessary that the eggs be hatched in Arizona. Many plants, as already noted, can adjust themselves to such changes at any stage of their existence, and are regularly accustomed to do so. They are both fish and flesh. In water they have the form, structure and functions of other strictly aquatic species; on land they are equally ready to behave as terrestrial species."

All this shows that a species should be defined by describing the range of its variations in each kind of environment in which it may occur. In other words, its form is determined by environmental causes. The species is not to be conceived as absolutely stable or as subject to accidental variations, but as determined in definite ways by conditions of life.

The general impression prevails that among the higher mammals this variability is so slight that it may be neglected, and that particularly in man lines of the same descent are stable. Still, there are a number of observations which show that bodily form is dependent upon outer conditions. Hans Przibram has investigated the influence of body temperature upon the length of the tail of rats and found, when the body temperature is made to rise by transplanting the rats from an artificial cool climate to a warm one, that the proportional length of the tail of rats living and born in the warmer climate increases.

Members of the same race live under quite different climatic and social conditions. The European is spread over the whole world. He lives in the Arctic and in the tropics, in deserts and in humid countries, in high altitudes and on low plains. In regard to mode of life we may contrast the professional, the sedentary, the laborer, the aviator and the miner. Some Europeans live in a way not so very different from that of simpler people, for the mode of life of the agricultural Indians of North America at the time of Columbus, or that of some agricultural Negro tribes, is, so far as nutrition and occupation are concerned, quite similar to theirs. Also some of the fishermen on the coast of Europe may well be compared, in their mode of life, with the fishermen of America or Asia. More direct comparisons may be made among the people of eastern Asia, where we may contrast the cultured Chinese and primitive Amur River tribes, the northern

Japanese and the Ainu, the civilized Malay and the mountain tribes of Sumatra or the Philippines. Similar comparisons are possible for the Negro race when we contrast the small educated class of Negroes in America and the African tribesmen; and for the American race when we compare the educated Indians, particularly of Spanish America, and the tribes of the prairies and of the virgin forests.

It is obvious that in all these cases we are comparing groups of the same descent, but living in distinct geographic, economic, social and other environmental conditions. If we find differences among them, they can only be due, directly or indirectly, to environment. Thus the fundamental problem presents itself, in how far are human types stable, in how far variable under the influences of environment?

It is difficult to take up this inquiry on the basis of a direct comparison between primitive and civilized types belonging to the same races, partly because material is hard to obtain, partly because the homogeneity of the race is often open to doubt; but it is at once apparent that inquiries into the variability of human types living under the effect of different types of environment will help us to gain an insight into the question at issue, so that we are led to a more general discussion of the problem of the stability or variability of the form of the human body.

The general tendency of anthropological inquiry has been to assume the permanence of the anatomical characteristics of the present races, beginning with the European races of the early neolithic times. Kollmann, the most pronounced advocate of this theory, claims that the oldest remains of man found in the neolithic deposits of Europe represent types which are still found unchanged among the modern civilized population of the continent. He has tried to identify all the varieties found in the neolithic prehistoric population with those living at the present time.

All studies of the distribution of head-forms and of other anthropometric traits have shown uniformity over considerable continuous areas and through long periods; and the natural inference has been that heredity controls anthropometric forms, and that these are therefore stable (Deniker).

Not all the features of the human body can be considered

as equally stable. Even if head-form and other proportions should be determined entirely by heredity, it is easily seen that weight depends upon the more or less favorable conditions of nutrition. More than that, the whole bulk of the body is partially determined by the conditions prevailing during the period of growth.

This has been shown by the general increase in stature in Europe which has occurred since the middle of the past century. It has been proved most clearly by a comparison of the measurements of Harvard students with those of their own fathers who had attended the college. The difference in favor of the younger generation for those who may be considered to have completed their growth is about 4 cm. (Bowles). For native-born Jews in the city of New York those measured in 1909 show throughout smaller measurements than those measured in 1937 (Boas 18). The difference is manifest in both adults and children of corresponding ages. The following table shows the average increase in per cent of the measurement of 1909:

	MALE	FEMALE
Stature	6.5	2.6
Length of Head	2.3	1.6
Width of Head	1.3	1.2
Width of Face	3.8	2.4

While the increase in total stature is greater than that of the head measurements, both the present and the Harvard series of measurements of various parts of the trunk and limbs show that there is an increase in all dimensions which does not depend solely upon the indirect influence of the increase in bulk. It is an expression of the varying reaction of the body to changes in environment.

The starvation period of Central Europe due to the blockade and its criminal extension during the period of wrangling over the spoils of the war shows the effect of insufficient nutrition upon the development of the body. Apprentices in Vienna, measured in 1919 and 1921 had the following measures (Lobzolter):

AGES	STATURE		WEIGHT KGM.	
	1919	*1921*	*1919*	*1921*
14–15	151.8	154.6	40.9	44.3
15–16	155.3	158.7	42.7	45.5
16–17	160.5	162.6	47.5	50.1
17–18	165.3	163.3	51.3	53.6

The differences between well-to-do and poor are also striking. Many observations have shown that the size of the body depends upon the economic condition of the parent. Bowditch's studies of the growth of school children in Boston and many others have proved this point. Hebrew children in New York attending private schools exceed those in an orphan asylum by from 6 to 7 cm. (Boas 16); Negro children in public schools exceed those in an orphan asylum by similar amounts (Boas 18). The findings by Gould proved that natives of every country enlisted in the West and measured during the War of the Rebellion were taller than those enlisted in the East.

The changes in the bulk of the body are necessarily related to changes in proportions. Setting aside the prenatal development, we find that at the time of birth some parts of the body are so fully developed that they are not far removed from their final size, while others are quite undeveloped. Thus the skull is, comparatively speaking, large at the time of birth, grows rapidly for a short time, but very soon approaches its full size, and then continues to grow very slowly. The limbs, on the other hand, grow rapidly for many years. Other organs do not begin their rapid development until much later in life. Thus it happens that retarding or accelerating influences acting upon the body at different periods of growth may have quite different results. After the head has nearly completed its growth, retarding influences may still influence the length of the limbs. The face, which grows rapidly for a longer period than the cranium, can be influenced later than the latter. In short, the influence of environment may be the more marked, the less developed the organ that is subject to it.

Changes in final form may also be determined by occupation. A study of the form of the hand by Buzina and Lebzelter showed that the ratio of width to length differs considerably for various occupations. The ratio was found for

Blacksmiths	46.9
Locksmiths	46.3
Bricklayers	46.4
Compositors	43.3
Postal clerks	43.8

The decrease in this ratio is largely due to a decrease in the width of the hand.

The whole trend of these studies of growth thus emphasizes the importance of the effect of rate of development upon the final form of the body. Illness in early childhood, malnutrition, lack of sunshine, fresh air and physical exercise, are so many retarding causes, which bring it about that the growing individual of a certain age is in its physiological development younger than the healthy, well-nourished one, who has plenty of fresh air, and puts his muscular system to good use. Retardation or acceleration has, however, the effect of modifying the later course of development; so that the final stage will be the more favorable, the less the retarding causes.

These facts relating to growth are of fundamental importance for a correct interpretation of the oft-discussed phenomena of early arrest of growth. Among members of the same race a prolonged period of growth due to unfavorable environment goes hand in hand with unfavorable development, while an abbreviated period of growth due to favorable environment results in larger dimensions of all physical measurements. It follows, that, in judging the physiological value of arrest of growth, the mere fact that growth ceases in one race at an earlier time than in another cannot be considered as significant in itself without observations on the conditions determining the rapidity of growth.

So far, the question still remains open, in how far there may be changes in the types of man that cannot be explained by acceleration or retardation of growth.

An attempt has been made by Rieger to explain differences in head-form as due to the effect of physiological and mechanical conditions, and Engel emphasizes the effect of pressure of the muscles upon the forms of the head. Walcher and Nyström try to explain different head-forms by the consideration of the position of the infant in the cradle. They believe that position on the back produces round heads; position on the side, long heads. It would seem, however, that the difference of head-form in large areas of Europe, in which infants are treated in the same manner, are too great to make this explanation acceptable.

A number of observations have been made which demonstrate conclusively a difference between urban and rural types. These observations were first made by Ammon who showed that the urban population in Baden differs from the rural population in head-form, stature and pigmentation. He considered this as due to selective migration, assuming a relation between the attractions of city life and head-form. His observation is in accord with observations made by Livi (p. 87) in the cities of Italy, which show also a difference when compared to the surrounding country.

An explanation, given by Livi, seems to account adequately for the difference between city and country population, without necessitating the assumption of any considerable effect of natural selection which presupposes an improbable correlation between choice of domicile, or between mortality and fertility on the one hand, and traits like head-form and pigmentation on the other. The change of type in cities, so far as it has been observed, is of such character, that the city type always shows great resemblance to the average type of the whole large district in which it is located. If the local rural population is markedly short-headed and the general type of a larger area from which the city population is drawn more long-headed, then the city population will be more long-headed, and *vice versa*.

A more careful investigation of the city population shows that this explanation is not adequate. If the movement towards the city from distant parts of the country were the cause of the changes of type we should expect to find the city dwellers much more heterogeneous than the rural population. This is not by any means the case; the difference in variability between city and country is very slight. The population of

Rome presents an excellent example of this kind. If it were assumed that the Romans who have drifted to the city for thousands of years from all parts of the Mediterranean and southern Europe had retained the bodily form of their ancestors, and if their descendants still survived we should expect a very high degree of variability. As a matter of fact, the variability is almost the same as that found in the surrounding country.

Up to quite recent times no evidence of actual changes of type was available, except the observations by Ammon and those by Livi on the physical characteristics of rural and urban populations to which I have just referred, and some others on the influence of altitude upon physical form.

A direct influence of environment upon the bodily form of man has been found in the case of American-born descendants of immigrants from Europe,[4] and in that of Japanese born in Hawaii (Shapiro). The traits of descendants of immigrants examined were head-measurements, stature, weight and hair-color. Among these, only stature and weight are closely related to the rate of growth, while head-measurements and hair-color are only slightly subjected to these influences. Differences in hair-color and head-development do not belong to the group of measurements which depend in their final values upon the physiological conditions during the period of growth. From all we know, they are primarily dependent upon heredity.

The American-born descendants differ in head-form from their parents. The differences develop in early childhood, and persist throughout life. The head index of the foreign-born is practically the same, no matter how old the individual at the time of immigration. This might be expected when the immigrants are adult or nearly mature; but even children who come here when one year or a few years old develop the head index characteristic of the foreign-born. For Hebrews this index ranges around 83, that of American-born changes suddenly. The value drops to about 82 for those born immediately after the immigration of their parents, and reaches 79 in the second generation; i.e., among the children of

[4] Boas 6, Guthe, Hirsch.

American-born children of immigrants. The effect of American environment makes itself felt immediately, and increases slowly with the increase of time elapsed between the immigration of the parents and the birth of the child. Observations made in 1909 and 1937 give the same result.

The conditions among the Sicilians and Neapolitans are quite similar to those observed among the Hebrews. The head index of the foreign-born remains throughout on almost the same level. Those born in America immediately after the arrival of their parents show slight increase of the cephalic index.

The Italian immigration is so recent, that individuals who were born many years after the arrival of their parents in America are very few in number, and no individuals of the second generation have been observed. For this reason it is hardly possible to decide whether the increase of the cephalic index continues with the length of time elapsed between the immigration of the parents and the birth of the child.

The head-forms of Puerto Ricans suggest also instability of the form as expressed by the cephalic index. Adult men who had one parent born in Spain had an index of 79.7. Native-born Puerto Ricans without or at least with very slight Negro intermixture had an index of 82.8, while those with Negro intermixture had an index of 80.8. Since American Negroes have an average index of 76.9, Mulattoes of 77.2, there must be a local cause for the increase. It is not likely that enough Indian blood survives to bring about the shortening of the head. It seems most plausible that we have here also a change due to environmental causes. Observations made in Havana are not quite in agreement with those made in Puerto Rico (Boas 2). Georges Rouma found for White children an index of 78.6, for Mulattoes 77.5, for Negroes 76.6. Perhaps a more numerous element of Spanish birth may account for the low index of the Whites.

It would be erroneous to claim that all the distinct European types become the same in America, without mixture, solely by the action of the new environment. The available data show only the conditions prevailing in a few cities. The history of the British types in America, of the Dutch in the East Indies, of the Spaniards in South America, favors the assumption of a strictly limited plasticity. Our discussion should be based on this more conservative basis unless an unexpectedly wide range of variability of types can be proved.

The effect of environment upon bodily form could best be determined if it were possible to study the bodily forms of individuals of identical genetic make-up who are living under different types of environment. This opportunity is offered by identical twins, that is twins developed from a single ovum. Unfortunately the number of cases in which we know with certainty that twins are so developed is small. Generally identity is inferred from their similarity, and their similarity is taken as a result of their identity. While it is likely that by this method the majority of identical twins may be found the logic of selection is unsatisfactory and results must be accepted as approximations.

Von Verschuer showed that during the period of adolescence identical twins are more unlike than in early childhood or as adults. This is an expression of that part of the variability in the tempo of growth which is due to external causes and which is observed in all studies of growth. A study of the head index of twins based on material collected by Dahlberg in Norway shows that the fraternal variability of head index of twins assumed to be identical is ± 1.5, while that of fraternal twins is ± 2.3.[5] The fairly large amount of variability of the identical twins must be ascribed in part to environmental causes, in part also to the probable inclusion of some non-identical pairs. How much external pathological causes may influence development is evidenced by the development of one of identical twins who is deprived of proper opportunity of developing on account of his position in the womb. There is no reason to assume that with different outer conditions the diversity of identical twins might not be considerably increased. A detailed investigation of the bodily and

[5] These variabilities are determined by the same methods as those given on p. 67. They represent the variability that would be found if these were not two identical twins but an infinite number of identical brothers or sisters in each family. The values have been derived from the coefficient of correlation for the identical twins of Dahlberg's series.

mental development of identical twins reared apart by New-man shows that the physiological and psychological functioning is markedly subject to environmental influences.

Selection is another possible cause for the change of type of a population. The extinction of tribes like the Tasmanians or of the California Indians brought about by an excessive death rate, including merciless persecution by settlers, and by a vanishing birth rate does not affect the surviving group. Within a group we must expect changes of type wherever there is a correlation between bodily form and birth rate, morbidity, mating and segregation. These correlations exist in all heterogeneous populations with social stratification. Family lines are never just the same. If the family lines are socially stratified, differences in birth rate, mortality or migration, which are socially determined, bring about shifts in the general type. Examples of such stratification are quite numerous. In countries like the United States with a strong heterogeneous immigration in which the social status and location of the immigrant are largely determined by the country of his origin, such selective changes must occur.

Even in heterogeneous populations selection can become effective only when heterogeneity of social strata is due to heredity. If it is determined by physiological causes such as differences in nutrition and occupation of the social groups, and not by hereditarily transmitted conditions, there will be no pronounced shift of type due to selection. This consideration is often neglected and for this reason many of the alleged facts are not significant.

Selection acts primarily through social stratification. It is not immediately dependent upon bodily form. The effects of selection can be determined only by an exact examination in each socially homogeneous stratum of the survivors of a given type, compared with those who died, by a study of the relation of fecundity and of the tendency to migrate to bodily form.

I know of hardly any example that proves beyond cavil the direct influence of selection in the sense that morbidity, fecundity, migration and selective mating have been proved to be solely dependent upon healthy bodily forms—setting aside cases of persecution of a social stratum that has a hereditary frequency distribution of types different from that of the general population.

It is also claimed that slightly pigmented individuals are more subject to malaria than those of darker coloring, and von Luschan (2) assumes a gradual elimination of the blond Kurds who migrate to the plains of Mesopotamia.

The strong insolation of the tropics is unfavorable to the slightly pigmented Europeans, while the darker races are better protected. Conditions of this kind will bring about a gradual change in type in population exposed to them for a long period.

There are other evidences of a relation between bodily form and the incidence of certain diseases which may have a slight influence upon the composition of a population. Modern investigations on constitution bear upon this point. It remains to be determined in how far these may have a far-reaching effect.

Chapter 6

The Morphological Position of Races

SO FAR WE HAVE discussed the composition of populations, the effect of heredity and the degree of instability of human types. We have now to turn to a consideration of the significance of fundamentally different types.

The whole problem of the relationship of races is involved in the question whether similar forms are always genetically related, or whether parallel development may have occurred here and there without genetic relationship. We have tried to demonstrate that man is a domesticated form. Bodily changes brought about by domestication have been observed in all kinds of animals. They are physiologically determined by the influence of domestication upon the organism, and all the different species react to them in similar ways. It is, therefore, necessary to assume that those traits of the human body that are determined by domestication may have developed independently in various parts of the world, and that loss of pigmentation (leucism) and increase of pigmentation (melanism), curly or frizzly hair, high or low stature, smallness of the face, when they occur in regions far apart are not necessarily proof of community of origin. This view has also been taken by Eugen Fischer (2).

The inference that may be drawn from the distribution of present domesticated forms is that the ancestors of man must have been of yellowish color, perhaps with slightly patterned hair, with moderately long heads, faces not so long and perhaps a little wider than those of the Europeans, with probably a lower nose, of smaller stature and with a large brain.

Similar reactions to environmental causes are widely spread in the organic world. In plants the peculiar habitus of desert vegetation is not confined to a single family. The Cactus family of America and the Euphoriaceae of Africa are similar in their outer appearance.

For examples of parallelism in animals I may quote Arthur

99

W. Willey, "The most striking example of the three principles of divergence, convergence and parallelism, at one and the same time, is of course that which is afforded by the parallel series presented by the Marsupial Mammals or Metatheria, on the one hand, and the ordinary Placental Mammals or Eutheria, on the other. . . . [Similar parallelisms are found when] comparing the series of Insectivora and Rodentia, the spiny armature of the hedgehogs approximating to that of the porcupines, the arboreal habit of tree-shrews (Typaiidae) to that of squirrels (Sciuridae), the terrestrial, nocturnal and semi-domesticated habit of land-shrews to that of mice and rats, while the aquatic habit and the parachute flight are also met within both orders. The musk-shrew, *Crocidura murina*, is very rat-like in general deportment, although its eyes are small and its dentition that of Insectivora.

"Parallel evolution accompanied by convergence is the expression of analogous formations in two or more animals belonging to different subdivisions, which may have acquired a similar differentiation of outward appearance or internal organization independently along different lines of descent, the points in which they resemble each other giving no indication of genetic affinity nor even of bionomical association."

Considering racial forms from a purely morphological point of view, it is noteworthy that those traits in which man is most strongly differentiated from the animals do not occur with consistency in any one race, but that each is eminently human from a different point of view. In all these features the gap between man and animal is a wide one, and the variations between the races are slight as compared with it. Thus we find, that, in comparison with the skull, the face of the Negro is larger than that of the American Indian, whose face is, in turn, larger than that of the White. The lower portion of the Negro face has larger dimensions. The alveolar arch is pushed forward, and thus gains an appearance which reminds us of the higher apes. There is no denying that this feature is a most constant character of the black races, and that it represents a type slightly nearer the animal than the European type. The same may be said of the broadness and flatness of the noses of the Negro and partly of the Mongol

If we accept the general theories of Klaatsch, Stratz and

Schoetensack, who consider the Australian as the oldest and most generalized type of man, we might also call attention to the slenderness of the vertebrae, the undeveloped curvature of the vertebral column, to which Cunningham first called attention, and the traits of the foot, which recall the needs of an animal living in trees, and whose feet had to serve the purpose of climbing from branch to branch.

In interpreting these observations, it must be strongly emphasized that the races which we are accustomed to call higher races are not by any means and in all respects farthest removed from the animal. The European and the Mongol have the largest brains; the European has a small face and a high nose—all features farther removed from the probable animal ancestor of man than the corresponding features of other races. On the other hand, the European shares lower characteristics with the Australian, both retaining in the strongest degree the hairiness of the animal ancestor, while the specifically human development of the red lip is most marked in the Negro. The proportions of the limbs of the Negro are also more distinct from the corresponding proportions in the higher apes than are those of the European.

When we interpret these data in the light of modern biological concepts, we may say that the specifically human features appear with varying intensity in various races, and that the divergence from the animal ancestor has developed in varying directions. It has been inferred from structural differences such as those here referred to that races exhibiting lower characteristics must be mentally inferior. This inference is analogous to the one that ascribes lower morphological traits to criminals and other socially maladjusted classes. In the latter case we fail to find any careful comparison with the non-criminal or socially adjusted brothers and sisters of these groups, the only means by which the claim for morphological inferiority could be substantiated.

From a strictly scientific point of view, all these inferences seem to be open to the most serious doubt. Only a few investigations have been made in relation to these problems, but their results have been entirely negative. Most important among them is the elaborate attempt made by Karl Pearson to investigate the relationship of intelligence to size and shape of the head. His conclusions are so significant that I will repeat them here: "The onus of proof that other measurements and more subtle psychological observations would lead to more definite results may now, I think, be left to those who *a priori* regard such an association as probable. Personally, the result of the present inquiry has convinced me that there is little relationship between the external physical and the psychical character in man." I think all the investigations that have been made up to the present time compel us to assume that the characteristics of the osseous, muscular, visceral or circulatory system have practically no direct relation to the mental ability of man (Manouvrier 1).

We will now turn to the important subject of the size of the brain, which seems to be the one anatomical feature which bears directly upon the question at issue. It seems plausible that the greater the central nervous system, the higher the faculty of the race, and the greater its aptitude to mental achievements. Let us review the known facts. Two methods are open for ascertaining the size of the central nervous system—the determination of the weight of the brain and that of the capacity of the cranial cavity. The first of these methods is the one which promises the most accurate results. Naturally, the number of Europeans whose brain-weights have been taken is much larger than that of individuals of other races. There are, however, sufficient data available to establish beyond a doubt the fact that the brain-weight of the Whites is larger than that of most other races, particularly larger than that of the Negroes. The investigations of cranial capacities are quite in accord with these results. According to Topinard the capacity of the skull of males of the neolithic period in Europe is about 1560 cc. (44 cases); that of modern Europeans is the same (347 cases); of the Mongolid race, 1510 cc. (68 cases); of African Negroes,[1] 1405 cc. (83 cases); and of Negroes of the Pacific

[1] The value for African Negroes is here very small. Another series quoted by Topinard (p. 622), consisting of 100 skulls of each group, gives the following averages: Parisians, 1551 cc.; Auvergnats, 1585 cc.; African Negroes, 1477 cc.; New Caledonians, 1400 cc. (a misprint in Topinard's book makes this appear as 1588 cc.).

Ocean, 1460 cc. (46 cases). Here we have, therefore, a decided difference in favor of the White race.

In interpreting these facts, we must ask, Does the increase in the size of the brain prove an increase in faculty? This would seem highly probable, and facts may be adduced which speak in favor of this assumption. First among these is the relatively large size of the brain among the higher animals, and the still larger size in man. Furthermore, Manouvrier (2) has measured the capacity of the skulls of thirty-five eminent men. He found that they averaged 1665 cc. as compared to 1560 cc. general average, which was derived from 110 individuals. On the other hand, he found that the cranial capacity of forty-five murderers was 1580 cc., also superior to the general average. The same result has been obtained through weighings of brains of eminent men. The brains of thirty-four of these showed an average increase of 93 grams over the average brain-weight of 1357 grams. Another fact which may be adduced in favor of the theory that greater brains are accompanied by higher faculty is that the heads of the best English students are larger than those of the average class of students (Galton 2). The force of the arguments furnished by these observations must, however, not be overestimated.

First of all, the brains of not all eminent men are unusually large. On the contrary, a few unusually small brains have been found in the series. Furthermore, most of the brain-weights constituting the general series are obtained in anatomical institutes; and the individuals who find their way there are poorly developed, on account of malnutrition and of life under unfavorable circumstances, while the eminent men represent a much better nourished class. As poor nourishment reduces the weight and size of the whole body, it will also reduce the size and weight of the brain. It is not certain, therefore, that the observed difference is entirely due to the higher ability of the eminent men. This may also explain the larger size of the brains of the professional classes as compared to those of unskilled laborers (Ferraira).

Notwithstanding these restrictions, the increase of the size of the brain in the higher animals, and the lack of development in microcephalic individuals, are fundamental facts which make it more than probable that increased size of the brain accompanies increased faculty, although the relation is not quite as immediate as is often assumed.

The reason for a lack of close correlation between brain-weight and mental faculties is not far to seek. The functioning of the brain depends upon the nerve cells and fibers, which do not constitute, by any means, the whole mass of the brain. A brain with many cells and complex connections between the cells may contain less connective tissue than another one of simpler nervous structure. In other words, if there is a close relation between form and ability, it must be looked for rather in the morphological traits of the brain than in its size. A correlation exists between size of brain and number of cells and fibers, but the correlation is weak (Donaldson; Pearl 2). A summary of the present state of our knowledge given by G. Levin (1937) is quite in accord with the earlier statements showing that "inferiority signs have no justification to be regarded as such." They occur in the brains of all races and both in the brains of eminent men and in those of people of ordinary intelligence. Furthermore the functioning of the same brain depends upon its blood supply. If it is inadequate the brain does not function properly.

Notwithstanding the numerous attempts that have been made to find structural differences between the brains of different races of man that could be directly interpreted in psychological terms, no conclusive results of any kind have been attained. The status of our knowledge has been well summed up by Franklin P. Mall. He holds, that, on account of the great variability of the individuals constituting each race, racial differences are exceedingly difficult to discover, and that up to the present time none have been found that will endure serious criticism.

Among the populations of the globe we find three types represented by the greatest numbers: the Mongolid, the European and the Negro. A brief consideration of recent history shows, however, that these conditions are quite modern. The great density of population of Europe has developed during the last few thousand years. Even at Caesar's time the population of northern Europe must have been very sparse. According to estimate the population of Gaul may have been 150, that of Germany 250 per square mile (Hoops), and the population of eastern Europe may have been even sparser. The great increase in population in the Mediterranean area occurred at an earlier period, but the whole process cannot have extended over more than a few thousand years. The same is true of China and India. Great density of population is everywhere a recent phenomenon. It is dependent upon the increase of food brought about by the invention of intensive agriculture under favorable climatic and cultural conditions. When these conditions become less favorable the density of population may decrease again, as in North Africa and in Persia. We shall show later on, that agriculture is a late development in human history, and that at an early time man lived by gathering food and hunting animals. Under these conditions the density of population is necessarily restricted by the size of the habitat of a people and by its productivity. On the whole in similar climates there will be the same maximum number who can live on the produce of a given area, and this number must always be small, being limited by the food supply available in unfavorable years. We may conclude, therefore, that in early times the number of individuals contained in each race was roughly proportional to the area inhabited by it, with due allowance, however, for unusual productivity or unusual sterility of the habitats.

European migrations to other continents did not begin until late. In the fifteenth century the European race had not set foot in America, Australia and South Africa. It was strictly confined to the Mediterranean area, that is, Europe, North Africa and parts of western Asia. At an earlier time it extended eastward as far as Turkestan. The great spread of the people of Mongolid features is also in part recent, at least so far as absolute numbers are concerned. The geographical extension of the race occurred particularly in the southeast where the Malay developed the art of navigation and settled on the islands of the Indian and Pacific Oceans. There is also proof of the invasion of southern Asia by Mongolid people who came from Central Asia.

On the other hand the area of the Negro race seems to have been encroached upon by late migrations. At present—setting aside the forcible transplantation of the Negro to America— we find Negroes practically all over Africa south of the

Sahara. Negroid people are, however, found also in isolated spots along the southern border of the Asiatic continent. The largest body lives in New Guinea and on the chains of islands stretching from New Guinea eastward and southeastward. Other smaller groups are found on the Philippine Islands, in the interior of the Malay Peninsula and on the Andaman Islands in the Gulf of Bengal. Since we know that recent extended migrations of West Asiatic and Central Asiatic peoples into these territories have occurred, it seems plausible, that the Negro territory in southern Asia may have been much wider in earlier times. Proof of this theory can only be given by archaeological evidence which, up to the present time, is not available.

These considerations show conclusively that the relative numbers of the races must have changed enormously in the course of time and that races which are at present quite insignificant as to numbers may have formed in earlier times a considerable part of the human species.

In a biological consideration of races the total number of individuals is irrelevant. The only question of importance is that of the degree of morphological differentiation.

Mongolids and Negroes represent the two most sharply contrasted forms of the human species: pigmentation, form of hair, form of face and nose, proportions of the body, all are characteristically distinct. The skin of the Negro is dark, that of the Mongolid light, the hair of the former frizzly and flattened in section, that of the latter straight and rounded in section; the nose of the former is flat, that of the latter much higher; the teeth of the Negro project, those of the Mongolid are vertical. Even in this case it would not be right to claim that there are not individuals who in regard to some of their characteristics differ so much from their own group that they are in all traits absolutely distinct from the other one, but in their pronounced forms the two groups form a decided, sharp contrast. It is interesting to note that the geographical distribution of these two racial types represent two well-defined areas. The Mongolid type as defined before is found in eastern Asia and in both Americas; the Negroid type occupies Africa and isolated spots on the northern and northeastern coast of the Indian Ocean. Considering eastern Asia and America as borderlands of the Pacific Ocean, Africa a borderland of the Indian Ocean, and assuming that the Negroes at one time occupied the whole of southern Asia, we may say that these two large racial groups at one time occupied the bulk of the habitable lands, and that the one may be defined as the race of the Indian Ocean, the other as that of the Pacific Ocean.

There are, however, a few principal types that are not readily brought under this single scheme. These are the Europeans, the Australians, including presumably ancient inhabitants of India, and the pygmy Negro types. In pigmentation the Europeans form an even stronger contrast to the Negroes than do the Mongolids, but in other features they take a somewhat intermediate position; the form of the hair, the proportions of the body, the form of the eye and cheeks are not so different from the Negro form as those commonly found among the Mongolids. The Australians on the other hand exhibit a number of rather primitive features that set them off sharply from other races, and make us incline to the belief that they represent a type, differentiated at an early period, that may have been crowded back by the more successful races into remote corners of the world.

The pygmy Negro types are represented in an extreme form by the South African Bushmen, a people of diminutive stature, of light yellowish skin, with extremely flat nose and face, and an exaggerated frizzliness of hair. Their general habitus is decidedly that of the Negro. They must be affiliated with this race, of which they form, however, a separate division. The present distribution of the pygmy tribes in Africa is rather irregular. They were found until recently, in a large body in South Africa. Sporadic tribes whose characteristics are, however, more Negroid, occur in many parts of Africa; in the southern bend of the Congo, in the region northwest of the Congo not far from the west coast, and in the territories that give rise to the White Nile.

Pygmy people are also found on the Andaman Islands, the Malay Peninsula, on the Philippine Islands and in New Guinea. So far as Africa is concerned, there is fairly good evidence showing that the pygmy tribes had a much wider distribution at an earlier time. There has been a very general movement southward of the Negro tribes that occupy Central

Africa at the present time, and this may have resulted in the breaking up of the more ancient population. The final answer to this question will be given by archaeological research that may disclose the remains of the easily recognized South African type in districts now occupied by tall Negroes. The question is not so clear in regard to the pygmy tribes of southeastern Asia whose relation to the tall Negro type is more obscure.

The Europeans, so far as our knowledge goes, have always been restricted to a relatively small area. Outside of northern Europe, northwestern Asia and small parts of northwestern Africa blond and blue-eyed types have never been found to constitute entire, or almost entire populations. Since nothing indicates that the type is a particularly primitive one, since it rather shows highly specialized features, its origin must be sought in or near Europe.

In order to understand the position of the type, we may turn our attention to special variations that occur in the Mongolid races. Although the typical Mongolid has black, straight hair, dark eyes, a heavy face, moderately wide and not very high nose, many variations occur. There is a marked tendency in many regions for the color of the skin to be quite light. Generally we see the natives well tanned, but there are cases in which the whiteness of the protected skin vies with that of the European. I have seen among the Haida of British Columbia women who bear no evidence of European admixture, who have on the contrary intensely developed Indian features, but who have white skin, brownish red hair and light brown eyes. It is difficult to give absolute proof of the absence of European admixture, but the high value that is placed traditionally upon a light complexion and brown hair are proof that these must have been known to the Indians for a long time. Light complexions prevail also among the Indian tribes of the upper Mississippi River. On the other hand there are cases of increased pigmentation, as among the Yuma Indians of southern California, who are so dark, that in many cases the color of the skin might be matched with that of light Negroes. Considering all the local varieties that occur we might say that the European pigmentation represents an extreme variant of the relative lack of pigment which is characteristic of Mongolid types.

Similar conditions prevail in regard to color and form of hair. While I do not know of any case of blond hair among Mongolid types, reddish brown hair is certainly common. Even in adults brownish hair is locally not very rare. Wavy hair occurs also locally. There is a decided tendency in many groups to develop large, highly elevated noses. The narrow, gracefully cut nose of the Eskimo, the heavy aquiline nose of the Indian of the Plains may be contrasted with the low snub-nose of the Indian of Puget Sound. Elevated noses are, however, also not uncommon among South Siberian tribes. In this sense the European nose is quite in line with the variants that are found in the Mongolid race. The same may be said in regard to the width of face. While in the most characteristic Mongolid type it is large, there are many cases in which the cheekbones slant backward and we obtain the impression of a narrow face. Hand in hand with this and with the increased elevation of the nose goes the attenuation of another Mongolid characteristic, the peculiar eye that may be observed in almost every young Chinaman and in most Japanese. The narrowness of the face is nowhere as great as among some modern northwest European types, and narrowness and elevation of nose is nowhere as great as among a people like the Armenians, but these types are merely exaggerated cases of a tendency that may be observed sporadically in many regions.

The tendency of the Mongolid race, to vary in the direction of types represented by the Europeans, is also expressed in the features of a number of aberrant local types. Thus the similarity between East Europeans and the Ainu of northern Japan has been pointed out, and on account of physiognomic similarity, relationship between Indonesian types and Europeans has been assumed.

It is quite suggestive that among local variants of Negroes we do not find any such approach to European forms. Pigmentation, hair, nose and face vary considerably, but it would be difficult to find a case of a pure Negro population which represents a variant that strikingly approaches European forms. Where an increased elevation of the nose is found, as in East Africa, there is also strong suspicion of West Asiatic admixture.

On account of these considerations the European seems to us most likely as a recent specialization of the Mongolid race.

It is necessary to revert here once more to some general geographic considerations. The land-mass of the world stretches continuously from the wide valley formed by the Atlantic and Arctic Oceans around the Pacific and Indian Oceans. We might say that in modern geological times the whole land-mass forms the borderland of the Pacific and Indian Oceans, so that the Old World turns its back upon the New World on the shores of the Atlantic Ocean. Any intercourse that existed must have been along the shores of the Pacific Ocean. There was no means of bridging the gap that separates the Atlantic coasts of Europe and Africa from those of America. Even if we adopt Wegener's theory of the drifting apart of the continents, there is no possibility of its occurrence at a time when man was present.

In Tertiary times these conditions were different, and if man had existed in Europe at that period, he might have migrated to America by way of the northern bridge connecting America and Europe by way of Iceland. Although no Tertiary human remains have been found in Europe, it has been claimed that certain flint objects that show split surfaces at their ends are proof of the existence at least of a forerunner of man in Tertiary times in Europe. Since the American race and the Mongolid race of Asia are fundamentally alike, and since it is extremely unlikely that man originated in America, we are compelled to assume that he reached America either by way of Asia, or in Tertiary times from Europe. It is barely conceivable that the ancestor of the Mongolid race might have lived in Europe and reached America in this way, but there is no evidence, beyond its possibility, that would support such a hypothesis. On the contrary the similarity between American and Asiatic Mongolids is so great that we must assume a very close and recent relationship between the two. It is, therefore, most probable that the area of specialization in which the Mongolid form developed was somewhere in Asia, and that the race reached

America over the land-bridge leading from Asia to America. If this is true, then the peopling of America must have occurred at a late period. We have no evidence that would support the view that races identical with the modern ones lived before the last interglacial period. Man must then have come to the American continent at a time when the present races had been established and when intercourse between the two continents was possible. During the glacial periods the northwestern part of our continent was covered with ice. Therefore the arrival of man in America will have to be assumed not later than one of the last interglacial periods.

There is another possibility, however. It is conceivable that man may have reached America at an earlier time, but then we should have to assume that the development of the Mongolid type occurred in America and that the present occupation of Asia by this race represents a backward current. From a palaeontological and geological point of view this is quite conceivable, but neither view can at present be substantiated by facts. The problem will be decided when the earliest forms of man in northern Asia and in America become better known.

As the area of specialization of the Mongolid race must be looked for somewhere around the Pacific Ocean, so the development of the Negro type must be assumed to be in the neighborhood of the Indian Ocean, since all the variants of this type are located in that region and, excepting the Grimaldi skeleton, there is no indication of Negroid characters outside of it.

If our views are correct, then the Europeans would represent a new specialized form derived from the Mongolid race, the Negro and the pygmy Negro, two types, of which the light pygmy may be more ancient than the tall Negro.

The problem of the position of the Australian race is different. If it were not for the fact that the race presents many apparently very ancient characteristics which are found in the form of the skull as well as in the vertebral column and the extremities, we might consider it to stand in a relation to the Negro type somewhat of the same kind as the relation of the European to the Mongolid, for there are many traits that both races have in common. Pigmentation, form of nose and size of brain-case show characteristics that set off both groups definitely from the Mongolid groups. The frizzliness of the Negro's hair might be considered as a variant of the curliness of the hair of the Australian. The special characteristics of the Australian are, however, of such a character that they must have belonged to a very ancient type of man, and the Australian would therefore represent the older type, the Negro the newer one. If this is the case, we should expect to find Australian forms widely distributed in southern Asia. As a matter of fact there are points of similarity between the ancient native population of India and the Australians, and our problem will be cleared up when we obtain data on the osseous remains of the prehistoric races of the whole area bordering on the Indian Ocean.

Chapter 7

Physiological and Psychological Functions of Races

IN THE PRECEDING PAGES we have described the anatomical characteristics of races. We shall next consider their physiological and psychological functions as determined by bodily form.

Function depends upon the structure and chemical constitution of the body and its organs, but not in such a way that it is rigidly determined by them. On the contrary, the same body functions differently at different times. Our pulse, breathing, the action of our digestive organs, nerves and muscles are not the same at all times. The muscles are capable of doing more work when rested than when fatigued, and even after an equal amount of rest they will not respond every time in exactly the same way. The heart beat changes according to conditions. The reaction to visual or other impressions is not always equally rapid. So it is with all organs. While the anatomical characteristics of the body are fairly stable within rather long time limits, its functions are variable.

Some anatomical elements of the body and their chemical composition share this variability, but the grosser morphological traits may be considered as stable as compared to the functions.

What is true of the physiological activity of the body is even more true of mental functions. It would seem that the more complex these are the more variable they will be. Emotional behavior, intellectual activities, energy of the will are all subject to constant fluctuations. Sometimes we can accomplish tasks that are at other times, without apparent reason, beyond our powers. Now we are subject to emotional impressions that at other times do not move us. At one time action is realized easily, at other times with difficulty.

While the variability of anatomical form in a race is due

113

solely to two sources, that of family lines and that of fraternities, we have here an added element, namely, the variability
of the individual. For this reason the variability of functions
in a racial group is greater than the variability of anatomical
form, and an analysis of the variability of a population requires a separation of three elements: of individual, fraternal
and family line variabilities.

Still, there are certain physiological phenomena that have
no individual variability because they occur only once in life.
All of these are expressions of certain events in the physiological history of the individual such as birth, eruption of
teeth, menarchy, death. For these the fraternal variability and
that of family lines can be determined.

The variability of the age at which these events occur
increases rapidly with increasing age. In early life individuals
of the same age are about on the same stage of physiological
development. As time goes on the lag of some and the acceleration of others become considerable. Using the method of
expressing variability described before, we find the range of
variability of the period of gestation to be measured by not
more than by a few days; that of the eruption of the first
teeth by two months, that of the permanent teeth by more
than a year. The time of sexual maturity varies by as much as
a year and a half, and death by old age by more than a
decade.

It would be an error to assume that the rate of development of the body proceeds as a unit. The conditions determining the eruption of the teeth, the period of adolescence,
the changes of the skeleton and of the vascular system are
not the same.

It is particularly noticeable that the eruption of the teeth
follows laws quite different from those controlling the length
of bones. In regard to the latter, girls are always physiologically more mature than boys. In regard to the teeth the boys
are, if anything, more advanced than the girls. Still, a certain
amount of correlation exists. Thus children in a socially fairly
uniform group, who erupt their permanent teeth early are
also tall,[1] while those who have a late development of per-

[1] Hellman 1, Spier, Boas 16.

manent teeth are short; children who mature early are taller and heavier than those lagging behind.

The following table gives a review of these data:

	AGE AND VARIABILITY (YEAR)		
	MALES	BOTH SEXES	FEMALES
	Years	Years	Years
Pregnancy (Boas and Wissler 14)		0.0±0.04	
First tooth		0.6±0.21	
First molar		1.6±0.31	
Three or more first molars erupted (Boas 16, p. 441)	7.0±0.9		7.7
Permanent canine, premolar 1 or 2 erupting	9.5±1.0		9.8±1.1
Second molar erupting	11.5±1.1		11.8±1.1
Three or more second molars erupted	12.7±1.4		12.9±1.3
Completion of ossification of hand (Hellman 2) ...			13.8±0.8
Appearance of pubic hair (Crampton)	13.4±1.5		
Full development of pubic hair (Boas 6, pp. 509–525)	14.6±1.7		
Full development of pubic hair (Crampton)	14.5±1.3		
Puberty (New York City) .			13.3±1.6
Menopause			44.5±5.3
Death due to arterial diseases		62.5±13.2	

The rapidity of physiological development is determined by the biological organization of the body, for children who in their early ages are advanced in their physiological development run through the whole period of development quickly. It is not yet known whether the general tempo of the physiological life cycle continues throughout life, but it seems probable, for those who show early signs of senility die on the average earlier of diseases inherent in old age, than those among whom signs of senile degenerations appear at a later age (Bernstein).

Furthermore the tempo of the life cycle is evidently determined by heredity, for brothers and sisters have a similar tempo. This has been shown by a study of brothers and sisters living in an orphan asylum under the same conditions, so that it cannot be due to the influence of a different kind of environment for each family (Boas 17). This also agrees with the observation that some families are remarkably short lived while many members of others live to a remarkably old age (Bell, Pearl 1).

In our discussion of anatomical forms (p. 67) it was found that the variability of family lines is less than the fraternal variability, at most equal to it. It would seem that in physiological traits, insofar as they occur in a uniform environment, the same is the case. For example, the variability of the time of menarchy is ± 1.2 years in New York City. The variability of sisters is ± 0.93, that of family lines ± 0.76. The variability of sisters is, therefore, 1.2 times that of family lines.

The preceding observations hold good only when we compare groups that live in identical environment. Since physiological functions are markedly influenced by outer conditions different racial groups behave in the same way when exposed to the same environment. Thus, life in high altitudes requires certain typical changes. Schneider summarizes these as follows: "Oxygen-want may cause trouble in the body which is very soon followed by compensating actions that ultimately, if residence is to be maintained, lead to acclimatization. . . . The ability to compensate for the low oxygen tensions of high altitudes varies with the individual, and the adjustments may be more rapid at one time than at another. The adjustment consists of increased respiration, chemical alteration of the blood and an increase of haemoglobin."

Observations on the maturity of girls give similar results. In New York City the average age of menarchy and its variability is practically identical for North European, Jewish and Negro girls (Boas 18) while considerable differences exist for country and city (Ploss). Girls in a well-administered orphan asylum in New York do not differ from those found in a school attended by children of well-to-do parents.

The tempo of development has become somewhat quicker during the last forty years. On the average the acceleration in

New York City for the beginning of puberty of girls in orphan asylums amounts to six months a decade (Boas 18). Bolk has observed similar acceleration in Holland.

Differences in social groups are also found in the development of teeth. The permanent incisors of poor children develop later than those of well-to-do children while their premolars develop considerably earlier (Hellman 1), presumably because early loss of milk-teeth by caries stimulates the development of the permanent teeth.

Physiological functions like heart beat, breathing, blood pressure, metabolism which show constant changes according to the condition of the subject are comparable only when greatest care is taken to make conditions stable. This is generally done by establishing a basal measure which is assumed to be constant when the subject is absolutely rested and remains at rest. The assumption that this value is stable is hardly borne out by the facts, although the variations are much smaller than they are under other partially controlled conditions (Lewis). Data that allow us to distinguish between individual, fraternal and family line variability are all but non-existent.

Psychological data excepting the simplest phenomena of physiological psychology cannot be discussed from the point of view of the individual, for in all of them the varying cultural environment plays an important role. It is not negligible in such matters as the development of the senses. When a child is kept swathed and tied to a cradle board for more than a year his sense experience is limited in many ways and it does not develop like another one who from earliest childhood on can move limbs and head freely. Infants kept in an orphan asylum with the best of medical care but so that all of the same age are in charge of a busy nurse do not hear human speech and do not learn to talk until they are thrown together with older children.

Tests of intelligence, emotions, personality are expressions of both innate characteristics and experience based on the social life of the groups to which the subject belongs. This is expressed clearly in Klineberg's tests of the intelligence of Negro children in a number of American cities. New arrivals from rural districts who were not adjusted to city life gave very poor results. Those who had lived in the city for a number of years showed that they became adjusted to the demands of city life and of the city-planned tests. The intelligence test showed a constant improvement. The longer time had elapsed since immigration into the city the better was the performance of the group. The improvement cannot be explained by a selective process which brought better material to the city in earlier years because the same phenomenon is found in analogous tests made at different times. The southern rural Negroes tested in the World War compared in the same way with city Negroes. Brigham's observations on Italians who had lived in the United States for five, ten, fifteen and more years and whose intelligence tests showed results the better the longer they had lived here are also reducible to a better adjustment. In this case the linguistic difficulties of the new arrivals and the gradual acquisition of English must have been an additional cause of the gradual improvement, much more so than among the southern Negro whose dialect and limited vocabulary must also be counted as a handicap.

Another test made by Klineberg is instructive. He tested Indian and White girls in regard to their ability to reproduce patterns such as are made in bead embroidery by Indian women. The results showed a clear dependence upon familiarity with the subject, not with its technique because the industry was obsolete in the group. The Indian girls did better than the White girls.

It follows from these and similar observations that reactions due to innate intelligence—if we admit such a term which embraces a multitude of elements—differ enormously according to the social experience of the group and show, at least in the case of city Negroes, that with a similar social experience Whites and Negroes behave in similar ways, that race is entirely subordinate to cultural setting.

Another observation made by Klineberg is relevant. Intelligence tests as well as city life drive for speed, while rural life allows a more leisurely tempo of action. His observations showed for Whites, Negroes and Indians speed and inaccuracy for citified groups, less speed and greater accuracy for rural groups.

We conclude from these observations that in all psychological observations we are confronted with influences partly organic, partly cultural. If we are to draw any inference in regard to the organic element, the cultural phase must be excluded. Variability in response may be tested for an individual by observing him under varying conditions, in repose and excitement, in joy and sadness, after a severe shock and when in mental equilibrium, in health and in sickness.

For races or populations a study of parts of the same people living under different conditions and a comparison of parents and their children brought up in new surroundings will give reliable material. For all of these observations are available.

Motor habits are one of the simpler manifestations of life that may be studied. We do not know much about the motor habits of different peoples, but enough has been observed to indicate that decided local variations exist. Rest positions are one indication of such habits. The Chinese, Melanesians and some Africans sleep resting their necks on a narrow support, a position almost insupportable to us; most primitive people sit squatting; the Eskimo and many Indians sit on their heels. The handles of tools indicate the manifold ways in which movements are performed. The Indian draws his knife toward his body, the American White whittles away from his body. A careful study of arrow release shows a variety of methods spread over continental areas (Morse, Kroeber 1).

Ida Frischeisen-Köhler has tried to show that every person has a stable rhythm that is most agreeable to his ear. While this may be true to a certain extent investigations by Dr. John Foley, Jr., show that both the most acceptable rhythm and the most natural way of tapping depend in part on outer circumstances, such as noisy or quiet environment, partly on habitual occupation. Typists have rapid rhythms, others who are attuned to slow movements have slower rhythms. He also found that the rate of walking depends upon social environment. Rural people walk slowly and deliberately; the rate of the steps is rapid in large cities. The Mexican peasant carrying loads on his back trots, the woman accustomed to carry water jars on her head walks in upright posture with a steady gait.

The posture of groups of unassimilated immigrants has a

local color. The Italian walks and stands erect with shoulders raised and thrown somewhat backward. The Jew stands slouching, knees slightly bent, shoulders drooping and head thrown slightly forward. Among the Americanized descendants of these immigrants the posture changes. Those who live among Americans adopt their erect posture.

Posture and gesture have been carefully examined by David Efrón and Stuyvesant Van Veen. The American uses emphatic, didactic and descriptive gestures much more than is usually believed. His gestures differ from those of the immigrant Italian and Jew. Both these groups are largely composed of poor people who have the habits of the European groups from which they come. The Italian has an elaborate set of symbolic gestures of definite meaning: "to eat" is indicated by the closed fingers touching the mouth; hunger by the right hand held flat horizontally striking the right side of the body. Thumb and first finger held against the teeth and moved down rapidly expresses anger. The first two fingers laid side by side mean "husband and wife" or "together"; the fingers of both hands lightly closed, both hands held in contact and then parted and joined again repeatedly "what do you want?" The first and little finger stretched out, the others closed and the hand held down means "evil eye"; shaking one's necktie "I am not a fool."

The number of these symbolic gestures is very large and many go back to antiquity. The Jew has very few symbolic gestures. The movements rather follow his lines of thought inward and outward, right and left. He accompanies the movements of the hands with others of head and shoulders. The forms of movement in the two groups are also different. The Italian moves his arms from his shoulders with a wide sweep, raising them high over his head and reaching out in all directions. The movements are even. The Jew holds the elbows close to the side of the body and gesticulates with forearm and fingers. His movements are jerky and run in much more complicated lines than those of the Italian. Henri Neuville and L. F. Clauss maintain that position and movement belong to the characteristic traits of race. Dr. Efrón's investigations disprove this view, for gesture changes with great ease. It is a common observation that Americans who have lived for some time in Mexico use Mexican gestures. Dr. Efrón observed a Scotch student who had grown up in a Jewish environment and used Jewish gestures, and an Englishman brought up in Italy, married to a Jewess and living in a circle of Jewish friends who had developed mixed Jewish and Italian gestures. The Mayor of New York, La Guardia, speaking English to Americans used American, speaking to Italians in Italian, Italian gestures.

The observations on the descendants of immigrants are convincing. The study of the groups of Italians and Jews living among native Americans shows that their gesture habits which they or their parents brought over from Europe disappear and that ultimately a complete assimilation to American habits results.

We conclude from this that motor habits of groups of people are culturally determined and not due to heredity.

This conclusion is supported by evidences of art. Every period has its own favorite posture. Thus the spread-leg position was for a while the heroic position and gave way to others.

We have followed the process of assimilation by other methods. Each country has its peculiar distribution of crime. While the crime frequency among immigrants is not the same as that of the home country it differs markedly from that of native Americans. In all European countries crimes against property are much rarer than those found in the population of New York State. Since crimes are committed with varying frequency according to age groups it was necessary to reduce all rates to a standard age distribution. A study of this subject for the New York City population conducted by Dr. Elliott Stofflet shows that in the second generation, that is among descendants of immigrants, the rates of crimes approach or exceed those of the native Americans. It has been known for a long time that the rates of crimes differ materially according to occupation, and change of occupation is undoubtedly one of the causes of rapid change. The difference between the generations has been proved for Italians, Germans and Irish.

Mental diseases also indicate that a change in social conditions influences their incidence. The subject is more difficult than others because according to American immigration laws those affected by mental diseases are not admitted to the country. Nevertheless the number of those who develop mental diseases is large. An investigation made by Dr. Bruno Klopfer embracing Italians, Germans and Irish shows that on the whole the second generation has an incidence more similar to that of native Americans than the immigrants themselves. In this case also comparability had to be attained by reducing the frequency to that of a standard population.

Language presents a somewhat complex but instructive example showing that anatomical differences between individuals are leveled out in their functioning owing to the stress of uniform cultural conditions. In any given community the anatomical forms of the articulating organs vary strongly. The mouth may be small or large, lips thin or thick, the palate high or low, the teeth may vary in position and size, the tongue in shape. Nevertheless, the articulation of the bulk of the population will depend essentially upon the traditional form of speech in the district. In a neighboring district the same varieties of anatomical form will occur, but a different mode of articulation will be found. Individuals differ in timbre of sound and in minor peculiarities which may or may not be anatomically determined, but these variations do not determine the essential character of sound production.

The very fact that language does not depend upon race and that in the literature of many nations the masters of style were not to the manor born—Dumas and Pushkin are good examples—prove the independence of cultural style and language.

It would be highly desirable to supplement these remarks with the results of investigations showing how far personality is influenced by social conditions. Unfortunately the methods of studying personality are highly unsatisfactory, partly because the features to be investigated lack in clarity. A study by Leopold Macari of immigrant Italians, all natives of one village, and their descendants in America indicates a wide breach between the personalities of the two generations which corroborates the results of our studies of crime and mental diseases. Another study made by Dr. Harriet Fjeld on the personalities of children in different types of schools also shows marked differences in the manifestations of personality. Miss Weill studied children of the same families, taking into account the intimate family situation. Her observations give the same results. The difficulty of the inquiry lies in the necessity of studying personality in its manifestations. If it could be shown that in a socially perfectly homogeneous population individuals of different types react in different ways to the same circumstances the problem might be solved. It is doubtful whether these conditions can ever be attained.

Identical twins reared apart under somewhat different environment were studied by H. H. Newman. He observed that the difference in environment had a decided influence on the mental behavior of such pairs. A. N. Mirenova subjected the one of a number of pairs of identical twins to training, the other not. This resulted in a decided difference in reactions to corresponding tests. She says: "The observations show that marked alterations took place in the whole behavior and in the general development of the trained twins. They became more active, more independent, and more disciplined. The intellectual level of the trained twins also rose in comparison with the controls. Some of the characters appeared to develop due to the direct influence of training, while others probably developed through the organization of the processes of training."

Ethnological material does not favor the view that different human types have distinct personalities, else we should not find a change like that of the warlike Indian of early times and his degraded descendant whose fate was sealed when his tribal life was broken up. Equally convincing are the differences in cultural behavior of groups that are biologically near kin, like the New Mexican sedentary Pueblo and the nomadic Navajo, or the behavior of those Mexican Indian villagers that are completely hispanized. History presents equally cogent arguments. The Scandinavians of the Bronze Age are undoubtedly the ancestors of the modern Scandinavians, still how great are the differences in their cultural behavior. Their early works of art and warlike activities contrasted with their modern intellectual achievements are indications of a changing structure of personality. The boisterous joy of life of Elizabethan England and the prudery of the Victorian age;

the transition from the rationalism of the end of the eighteenth century to the romanticism of the beginning of the nineteenth century are other striking examples of the change of the personality of a people within a short time, not to speak of the accelerated change that is going on under our very eyes.

Our consideration of both the anatomical form and the functions of the body, including mental and social activities, do not give any support to the view that the habits of life and cultural activities are to any considerable extent determined by racial descent. Families occur of pronounced characteristics, partly due to heredity, partly to cultural opportunity, but a large population, no matter how uniform in apparent type, will not reflect an innate personality. The personality— so far as it is possible to speak of the personality of a culture —will depend upon outer conditions that sway the fate of the people, upon its history, upon powerful individuals that arise from time to time, upon foreign influences.

The emotional drive to see the life of a people in its whole setting, including nature and bodily build, supported by the modern insistence of recognizing a structural unity of concomitant phenomena, has led to a complete neglect of the question of the kind and degree of their interrelation and to the unproved opinion that not only in individuals, not only in hereditary lines, but in whole populations bodily build determines cultural personality. The existence of a unity of bodily build in even the most homogeneous population known to us can be disproved and the existence of a cultural personality embracing a whole "race" is at best a poetic fiction.

During the last decade careful studies of the life histories of individuals belonging to different races and cultures have been assembled. These prove that the generalizations in which speculative students used to indulge are no longer tenable. Still, it is necessary to discuss some of the views regarding the psychology of primitive people that are widely held and according to which there are striking differences between the mental processes of culturally primitive tribes and civilized man. We might be tempted to interpret these as racially determined because at the present time no primitive tribes belong to the White race. If, on the other hand we can show that the mental processes among primitives and civilized are essentially the same, the view cannot be maintained that the present races of man stand on different stages of the evolutionary series and that civilized man has attained a higher place in mental organization than primitive man.

I will select a few only among the mental characteristics of primitive man which will illustrate our point—inhibition of impulses, power of attention, logical thinking and originality.

We will first discuss in how far primitive man is capable of inhibiting impulses.[2]

It is an impression obtained by many travellers, and also based upon experiences gained in our own country, that primitive man of all races, and the less educated of our own race, have in common a lack of control of emotions, that they give way more readily to an impulse than civilized man and the highly educated. This impression is based largely on the neglect to consider the occasions on which various forms of society demand a strong control of impulses.

Most of the proofs for this alleged peculiarity are based on the fickleness and uncertainty of the disposition of primitive man, and on the strength of his passions aroused by seemingly trifling causes. Too often the traveller or student measures fickleness by the importance he himself attributes to the actions or purposes in which they do not persevere, and he weighs the impulse for outbursts of passion by his own standard. To give an example: A traveller desirous of reaching his goal as soon as possible engages men to start on a journey at a certain time. To him time is exceedingly valuable. But what is time to primitive man who does not feel the compulsion of completing a definite work at a definite time? While the traveller is fuming and raging over the delay, his men keep up their merry chatter and laughter, and cannot be induced to exert themselves except to please their master. Would not they be right in stigmatizing many a traveller for his impulsiveness and lack of control when irritated by a

[2] Spencer, I, pp. 55 et seq.

trifling cause like loss of time? Instead of this, the traveller complains of the fickleness of the natives, who quickly lose interest in the objects which he has at heart.

The proper way to compare the fickleness of the tribesman and that of the White is to compare their behavior in undertakings which each from his own standpoint considers as important. More generally speaking, when we want to give a true estimate of the power of primitive man to control impulses, we must not compare the control required on certain occasions among ourselves with the control exerted by him on the same occasions. If, for instance, our social etiquette forbids the expression of feelings of personal discomfort and of anxiety, we must remember that personal etiquette among primitives may not require such inhibition. We must rather look for those occasions on which inhibition is required by the customs of primitive man. Such are, for instance, the numerous cases of taboo—that is, of prohibitions of the use of certain foods, or of the performance of certain kinds of work—which sometimes require a considerable amount of self-control. When an Eskimo community is on the point of starvation, and their religious beliefs forbid them to make use of the seals that are basking on the ice, the amount of self-control of the people who follow the demands of custom rather than satisfy their hunger is certainly very great. Other examples that suggest themselves are the perseverance of primitive man in the manufacture of his utensils and weapons; his readiness to undergo privations and hardships which promise to fulfill his desires—as the Indian youth's willingness to fast in the mountains, awaiting the appearance of his guardian spirit; or his bravery and endurance exhibited in order to gain admittance to the ranks of the men of his tribe; or, again, the often-described power of endurance exhibited by Indian captives who undergo torture at the hands of their enemies.

It has also been claimed that lack of control is exhibited by primitive man in his outbursts of passion occasioned by slight provocations. In this case also the difference in attitude of civilized man and of primitive man disappears if we give due weight to the social conditions under which the individual lives. We have ample proof that his passions are just as much controlled as ours, only in different directions. The numerous customs and restrictions regulating the relations of the sexes may serve as an example. The difference in impulsiveness in a given situation may be fully explained by the different weight of the motives involved. Perseverance and control of impulses are demanded of primitive man as well as of civilized man, but on different occasions. If they are not demanded as often, the cause must be looked for, not in the inherent inability to produce them, but in the social structure which does not demand them to the same extent.

Spencer mentions as a particular case of this lack of control the improvidence of primitive man. It would be more proper to say, instead of improvidence, optimism. "Why should I not be as successful tomorrow as I was today?" is the underlying feeling of primitive man. This feeling is no less powerful in civilized man. What builds up business activity but the belief in the stability of existing conditions? Why do the poor not hesitate to found families without being able to lay in store beforehand? Starvation among most primitive people is an exceptional case, the same as financial crises in civilized society; for times of need, such as occur regularly, provision is always made. The social status of most members of our society is more stable, so far as the acquiring of the barest necessities of life is concerned, so that exceptional conditions do not prevail often; but nobody would maintain that the majority of civilized men are always prepared to meet emergencies. The economic depression of 1929 and the following years has shown how ill prepared a large part of our population is to meet an emergency of such magnitude. We may recognize a difference in the degree of improvidence caused by the difference of social form, but not a specific difference between lower and higher types of man.

Related to the lack of power of inhibition is another trait which has been ascribed to primitive man of all races—his inability of concentration when any demand is made upon the more complex faculties of the intellect. An example will make clear the error committed in this assumption. In his description of the natives of the west coast of Vancouver Island, Sproat says, "The native mind, to an educated man, seems generally to be asleep. . . . On his attention being fully

aroused, he often shows much quickness in reply and ingenuity in argument. But a short conversation wearies him,
particularly if questions are asked that require efforts of
thought or memory on his part. The mind of the savage then
appears to rock to and fro out of mere weakness." Spencer,
who quotes this passage, adds a number of others corroborat-
ing this point. I happen to know through personal contact the
tribes mentioned by Sproat. The questions put by the traveller
seem mostly trifling to the Indian, and he naturally soon tires
of a conversation carried on in a foreign language, and one
in which he finds nothing to interest him. As a matter of fact,
the interest of these natives can easily be raised to a high
pitch, and I have often been the one who was wearied out
first. Neither does the management of their intricate system
of exchange prove mental inertness in matters which concern
them. Without mnemonic aids to speak of, they plan the
systematic distribution of their property in such a manner as
to increase their wealth and social position. These plans require great foresight and constant application.

Recently the question has been much discussed whether the
processes of logical thought of primitive man and of civilized
man are the same. Lévy-Bruhl has developed the thesis that
culturally primitive man thinks prelogically, that he is unable
to isolate a phenomenon as such, that there is rather a "participation" in the whole mass of subjective and objective
experience which prevents a clear distinction between logically
unrelated subjects. This conclusion is reached not from a
study of individual behavior, but from the traditional beliefs
and customs of primitive people. It is believed to explain the
identification of man and animal, the principles of magic and
the beliefs in the efficacy of ceremonies. It would seem that
if we disregard the thinking of the individual in our society
and pay attention only to current beliefs that we should reach
the conclusion that the same attitudes prevail among ourselves
that are characteristic of primitive man. The mass of material
accumulated in the collections of modern superstitions[3] proves
this point and it would be an error to suppose that these

---

[9] Von Negeloin, and *Handwörterbuch des deutschen Aberglau
bens.*

beliefs are confined to the uneducated. Material collected among American college students (Tozzer) shows that such belief may persist as an emotionally charged tradition among those enjoying the best of intellectual training. Their existence does not set off the mental processes of primitive man from those of civilized man.

Lack of originality has often been adduced as the primary reason why certain races cannot rise to higher levels of culture. It is said that the conservatism of primitive man is so strong, that the individual never deviates from the traditional customs and beliefs (Spencer). Malinowski and others have shown that conflicts between the tribal standard and individual behavior are not by any means absent. The disbeliever has his place in actual life and in folk tale.

Aside of this, originality is by no means lacking in the life of primitive people. Prophets appear among newly converted tribes as well as among pagan tribes, and introduce new dogmas. These may often be traced to the influence of the ideas of neighboring tribes, but they are modified by the individuality of the person, and grafted upon the current beliefs of the people. It is well known that myths and beliefs have been disseminated, and undergo changes in the process of dissemination (Boas 8). The increasing complexity of esoteric doctrines intrusted to the care of a priesthood suggests that this has often been accomplished by the independent thought of individuals. I believe one of the best examples of such independent thought is furnished by the history of the ghost-dance (Mooney) and peyote ceremonies (Wagner, Petrullo) in North America. The doctrines of the ghost-dance prophets were new, but based on the ideas of their own people, their neighbors and the teachings of missionaries. The notion of future life of an Indian tribe of Vancouver Island has undergone a change in this manner, insofar as the idea of the return of the dead in children of their own family has arisen. The same independent attitude may be observed in the replies of the Nicaraguan Indians to the questions regarding their religion that were put to them by Bobadilla, and which were reported by Oviedo.

The mental attitude of individuals who thus develop the beliefs of a tribe is exactly like that of the civilized philosopher. The student of the history of philosophy is well aware how strongly the mind of the greatest genius is influenced by the current thought of his time. This has been well expressed by a German writer (Lehmann), who says, "The character of a system of philosophy is, just like that of any other literary work, determined first of all by the personality of its originator. Every true philosophy reflects the life of the philosopher, as well as every true poem that of the poet. Secondly, it bears the general marks of the period to which it belongs; and the more powerful the ideas which it proclaims, the more strongly it will be permeated by the currents of thought which fluctuate in the life of the period. Thirdly, it is influenced by the particular bent of philosophical thought of the period."

If such is the case among the greatest minds of all times, why should we wonder that the thinker in primitive society is strongly influenced by the current thought of his time? Unconscious and conscious imitation are factors influencing civilized society, not less than primitive society as has been shown by G. Tarde, who has proved that primitive man, and civilized man as well, imitates not such actions only as are useful and for the imitation of which logical causes may be given, but also others for the adoption or preservation of which no logical reason can be assigned.

I think these considerations illustrate that the differences between civilized man and primitive man are in many cases more apparent than real; that the social conditions, on account of their peculiar characteristics, easily convey the impression that the mind of primitive man acts in a way quite different from ours, while in reality the fundamental traits of the mind are the same.

This does not mean that the mental reactions of different populations when observed under absolutely equal conditions might not show differences. Since individuals, according to their bodily constitution react differently, and since members of a family line are constitutionally similar, it seems likely that in individuals and family lines differences in mental reactions exist. However, every large population is composed of a great many constitutionally different family lines. Therefore any such differences would be greatly attenuated and find expression only in a different frequency distribution of qualities. Added to this is the extreme sensitiveness of mental reactions to cultural conditions, so that the greatest caution must be observed in trying to eliminate differences of social status. The failure to appreciate such differences in the colored population of Jamaica has misled Davenport and Steggerda. It also makes the observations of Porteus on Japanese, Chinese, Portuguese and Puerto Ricans as well as his comparison of Australians and Africans of doubtful value. If the same care were taken in the assessment of the bringing up of the subjects tested, in their social background, their interests and their inhibitions as in the manipulation of artificial tests we should be willing to accept the results with greater assurance. As the evidence stands today it cannot be claimed that any considerable differences in fundamental mental traits have been proven.

After we have thus found that the alleged specific differences between civilized and primitive man, so far as they are inferred from complex psychic responses, can be reduced to the same fundamental psychical forms, we have the right to decline as unprofitable a discussion of the hereditary mental traits of various branches of the White race. Much has been said of the hereditary characteristics of the Jews, of the Gypsies, of the French and Irish. Setting aside the inadequacy of such descriptions in which the diversity existing in each group is glossed over according to the subjective emphasis given to various aspects of cultural life I do not see that the external and social causes which have moulded the character of members of these people have ever been eliminated satisfactorily; and, moreover, I do not see how this can be accomplished. A number of external factors that influence body and mind may easily be named—climate, nutrition, occupation—but as soon as we enter into a consideration of social factors and mental conditions, we are unable to tell definitely what is cause and what is effect.

An apparently excellent discussion of external influences upon the character of a people has been given by A. Wernich in his description of the character of the Japanese. He finds some of their peculiarities caused by the lack of vigor of the muscular and alimentary systems, which in their turn are due to improper nutrition; while he recognizes as hereditary other physiological traits which influence the mind. And still, how weak appear his conclusions, in view of the modern economic, political and scientific development of Japan which has adopted to the fullest extent all the best and worst traits of western civilization.

Effects of malnutrition continued through many generations might be expected to affect the mental life of the Bushmen and the Lapps (Virchow); and still, after the experience just quoted, we may well hesitate before we express any definite conclusions.

One additional point of our inquiry into the organic basis of mental activity remains to be investigated; namely, the question: Has the organic basis for the faculty of man been improved by civilization, and particularly may that of primitive races be improved by this agency? We must consider both the anatomical and the psychological aspects of this question. We have seen that civilization causes anatomical changes of the same description as those accompanying the domestication of animals. It is likely that changes of mental character go hand in hand with them. The observed anatomical changes are, however, limited to this group of phenomena. We cannot prove that any progressive changes of the human organism have taken place; and no advance in the size or complexity of the structure of the central nervous system, caused by the cumulative effects of civilization, has been discovered.

The difficulty of proving a progress in mental endowment is still greater. The effect of civilization upon the mind has been much overestimated. The psychical changes which were the immediate consequence of the early domestication may have been considerable. It is doubtful whether outside of these any progressive changes, such as are transmitted by heredity, have taken place. The number of generations subjected to the influence of western civilization seems altogether too small. For large portions of Europe we cannot assume more than forty or fifty generations; and even this number is considerably too high, inasmuch as in the Middle Ages the bulk of the population lived on very low stages of civilization. Besides this, the recent tendency of human multiplication is such, that the most highly cultured families tend to disappear, while others which have been less subjected to the influences regulating the life of the most cultured class take their place. It is much less likely that advance is hereditary than that it is transmitted by means of education.

We should be clear in our minds regarding the difference between the phenomena of culture themselves and the abstract concepts of qualities of the human mind that are deduced from cultural data but that have no cultural meaning if conceived as absolute, as existing outside of a culture. The assumption that at some time the mental qualities of man existed *in vacuo* is untenable, for all our knowledge of man is derived from his behavior under given cultural conditions. We may say that the nervous condition of an individual tends to make him stable or unstable, slow to act or of rapid decision, but we can infer this only through his reaction to given cultural conditions. The way in which these characteristics manifest themselves depends upon the culture in which the individuals live.

The existence of a mind absolutely independent of conditions of life is unthinkable. Experimental psychology, in its earlier stages was sterile because it operated with the theory of the existence of an absolute mind, not subject to the environmental setting in which it lives.

The situation in morphology is analogous. The strict definition of a morphological type demands a statement of the variety of forms that an organism may take under varying conditions, for a morphological type without environmental conditions is non-existent and unthinkable. In higher animals we posit it because the variations brought about by environment are small as compared to the fundamental, stable characteristics. In contrast to this the physiological and psychological characteristics of the higher animals and particularly of man, are highly variable and can be stated only in relation to environmental, including physical and cultural conditions. The traits of personality belong to this class and have meaning only when expressed as reactions of the individual to varying types of environment, of which the existing culture is the most important.

Some of the abstractions derived from the behavior of man the world over are basic in all forms of culture. Most important are two: human intelligence—that is the ability to form conclusions from premises and the desire to seek for causal relations—and the ever present tendency to value thought and action according to the ideas of good and bad, beautiful and ugly, individual freedom or social subordination. It would be a difficult undertaking to prove an increase in intelligence, or an increase of the ability to evaluate experiences. A candid study of the inventions, observations and evaluations of man in the most diverse forms of culture gives us no basis for the claim that there has been any development of these qualities. We only find an expression of the application of these faculties to more or less highly individualized cultures.

To prove the cumulative effect of civilization through transmission, much weight is generally laid upon the relapse into primitive conditions of educated individuals belonging to primitive races. Such cases are interpreted as proofs of the inability of the child of a lower race to adapt itself to our high civilization, even if the best advantages are given to it. It is true that a number of such instances are on record. Among these are Darwin's Fuegian, who lived in England for a few years and returned to his home, where he fell back into the ways of his primitive countrymen; and the West Australian girl who was married to a White man, but suddenly fled to the bush after killing her husband, and resumed life with the natives. Not one of these cases has been described with sufficient detail. The social and mental conditions of the individual have never been subjected to a searching analysis. I should judge that even in extreme cases, notwithstanding their better education, their social position was always one of isolation, while the ties of consanguinity formed a connecting link with their uncivilized brethren. The power with which society holds us and does not give us a chance to step out of its limits cannot have acted as strongly upon them as upon us.

The station obtained by many Negroes in our civilization has just as much weight as the few cases of relapse which have been collected with much care and diligence. I should place side by side with them those White men who live alone among native tribes, and who sink almost invariably to a semi-barbarous position, and the members of well-to-do families who prefer unbounded freedom to the fetters of society, and flee to the wilderness, where many lead a life in no way superior to that of primitive man.

In the study of the behavior of members of foreign races educated in European society, we should also bear in mind the influence of habits of thought, feeling and action acquired in early childhood, and of which no recollection is retained. It is largely due to Sigmund Freud (1) that we understand the importance of these forgotten incidents which remain a living force throughout life—the more potent, the more thoroughly they are forgotten. Owing to their lasting influences many of the habits of thought and traits of personality which we are all too ready to interpret as due to heredity are acquired under the influence of the environment in which the child spends the first few years of its life. All observations on the force of habit and the intensity of resistance to changes of habit are in favor of this theory.

Our brief consideration of some of the mental activities of man in civilized and in primitive society has led us to the conclusion that the functions of the human mind are common to the whole of humanity. According to our present method of considering biological and psychological phenomena, we must assume that these have developed from previous lower conditions, and that at one time there must have been races and tribes in which the properties here described were not at all, or only slightly, developed; but it is also true that among the present races of man, no matter how primitive they may be in comparison with ourselves, these faculties are highly developed.

The average faculty of the White race is found to the same degree in a large proportion of individuals of all other races, and, although it is possible that some of these races may not produce as large a proportion of great men as our own race, there is no reason to suppose that they are unable to reach the level of civilization represented by the bulk of our own people.

It is likely that the distribution of the traits here discussed is not the same in all populations. Particularly in small, inbred groups certain traits may be rather prominent. It may be admitted that in exceptional cases where a population almost coincides with a family line innate differences may come to be important—as among the elite in the best times of Athens —but the overwhelming importance of outer, cultural conditions is, as we have seen, so great, and the quantitative racial differences between large populations are so slight in comparison that none of the claims for substantial differences between races seem to be scientifically sound.

Chapter 8

Race, Language and Culture

THE DISCUSSIONS OF the preceding chapters have shown that bodily form cannot be considered as absolutely stable and that physiological, mental and social functions are highly variable, being dependent upon external conditions, so that an intimate relation between race and culture does not seem plausible.

It remains to investigate this problem from another angle, by means of an inquiry which would show whether types, languages and cultures are so intimately connected that each human race is characterized by a certain combination of physical type, language and culture.

It is obvious, that, if this correlation should exist in a strict sense, attempts to classify mankind from any one of the three points of view would necessarily lead to the same results; in other words, each point of view could be used independently or in combination with the others to study the relations between the different groups of mankind. As a matter of fact, attempts of this kind have often been made. A number of classifications of the races of man are based wholly on anatomical characteristics, yet often combined with geographical considerations; others are based on the discussion of a combination of anatomical and cultural traits which are considered as characteristic of certain groups of mankind; while still others are based primarily on the study of the languages spoken by people representing a certain anatomical type.

The attempts that have thus been made have led to entirely different results.[1] Blumenbach, one of the first scientists who attempted to classify mankind, distinguished five races —the Caucasian, Mongolian, Ethiopian, American and Malay. It is fairly clear that this classification is based as much

[1] For a history of these attempts see Topinard, pp. 1–147.

on geographical as on anatomical considerations, although the description of each race is primarily an anatomical one. Cuvier distinguished three races—the white, yellow and black. Huxley proceeded more strictly on a biological basis. He combined part of the Mongolian and American races of Blumenbach into one, assigned part of the South Asiatic peoples to the Australian type, and subdivided the European race into a dark and a light division. The numerical preponderance of the European types evidently led him to make finer distinctions in this race, which he divided into the xanthochroic or blond, and melanochroic or dark races. It would be easy to make subdivisions of equal value in other races. Still clearer is the influence of cultural points of view in a classification like that of Klemm who distinguished the active and passive races according to the cultural achievements of the various types of man.

The most typical attempt to classify mankind from a consideration of both anatomical and linguistic points of view is that of Friedrich Müller, who takes as the basis of his primary divisions the form of hair, while all the minor divisions are based on linguistic considerations.

These and numerous other classifications that have been proposed show clearly a condition of utter confusion and contradiction; and we are led to the conclusion that type, language and type of culture are not closely and permanently connected.

Historical and ethnographical considerations prove the correctness of this view.

At the present period we may observe many cases in which a complete change of language and culture takes place without a corresponding change in physical type. This is true, for instance, among the North American Negroes, a people by descent largely African; in culture and language, however, essentially European. While it is true that certain survivals of African culture and language are found among our American Negroes the culture of the majority is essentially that of the uneducated classes of the people among whom they live, and their language is on the whole identical with that of their neighbors—English, French, Spanish and Portuguese, according to the prevalent language in various parts of the continent. It might be objected that the transportation of the African race to America was an artificial one, and that in earlier times extended migrations and transplantations of this kind did not occur.

The history of medieval Europe, however, demonstrates that extended changes in language and culture have taken place many times without corresponding changes in blood.

Recent investigations of the physical types of Europe have shown with great clearness that the distribution of types has remained the same for a long period. Without considering details, it may be said that an Alpine type can easily be distinguished from a North European type on the one hand, and a South European type on the other (Ripley, Deniker). The Alpine type appears fairly uniform over a large territory, no matter what language may be spoken and what national culture may prevail in the particular district. The Central European Frenchmen, Germans, Italians and Slavs are so nearly of the same type, that we may safely assume a considerable degree of blood-relationship, notwithstanding their linguistic differences.

Instances of similar kind, in which we find permanence of blood with far-reaching modifications of language and culture, are found in other parts of the world. As an example may be mentioned the Veddah of Ceylon, a people fundamentally different in type from the neighboring Singhalese, whose language they seem to have adopted, and from whom they have also evidently borrowed a number of cultural traits (Sarasin, Seligmann). Still other examples are the Japanese of the northern part of Japan, who are undoubtedly, to a considerable extent, Ainu in blood (Bälz, Ten Kate); and the Yukaghir of Siberia, who, while retaining to a great extent the old blood, have been assimilated in culture and language by the neighboring Tungus (Jochelson 2).

While it is therefore evident that in many cases a people, without undergoing a considerable change in type by mixture, has changed completely its language and culture, still other cases may be adduced in which it can be shown that a people has retained its language while undergoing material changes in blood and culture, or in both. As an example of this may be mentioned the Magyar of Europe, who have retained their language, but have become mixed with people speaking Indo-European languages, and who have, to all intents and purposes, adopted European culture.

Similar conditions must have prevailed among the Athapascans, one of the great linguistic families of North America. The great body of people speaking languages belonging to this group live in the northwestern part of America between Alaska and Hudson Bay, while other dialects are spoken by small tribes in California, and still others by a large body of people in Arizona and New Mexico.[2] The relationship between all these dialects is so close that they must be considered as branches of one large group, and it must be assumed that all of them have sprung from a language once spoken over a continuous area. At the present time the people speaking these languages differ fundamentally in type, the inhabitants of the Mackenzie River region being quite different from the tribes of California, and these, again, differing from the tribes of New Mexico (Boas 15, 19). The forms of culture in these different regions are also quite distinct: the culture of the California Athapascans resembles that of other Californian tribes, while the culture of the Athapascans of New Mexico and Arizona is influenced by that of other peoples of that area.[3] It seems plausible that branches of this stock migrated from one part of this large area to another, where they intermingled with the neighboring people, and thus changed their physical characteristics, while they retained their speech. Without historical evidence, this process cannot, of course, be proved.

These two phenomena—retention of type with change of language, and retention of language with change of type—apparently opposed to each other—often go hand in hand. An example is the distribution of Arabs along the north coast of Africa. On the whole, the Arab element has retained its language; but at the same time intermarriages with the native races were common, so that the descendants of the Arabs

[2] See map in *Handbook of American Indians* (Bulletin 30 of the Bureau of American Ethnology), part i (1907)

[3] Goddard, Reichard, Morice, Matthews 2.

have retained their old language and have changed their type. On the other hand, the natives have to a certain extent given up their own languages, but have continued to intermarry among themselves, and have thus preserved their type. So far as any change of this kind is connected with intermixture, both types of changes must always occur at the same time, and will be classed as a change of type or a change of language, as our attention is directed to the one people or the other, or, in some cases, as the one or the other change is more pronounced. Cases of complete assimilation without any mixture of the people involved seem to be rare, if not entirely absent.

Cases of permanence of type and language and of change of culture are much more numerous. As a matter of fact, the whole historical development of Europe, from prehistoric times on, is one endless series of examples of this process, which seems to be much easier, since assimilation of cultures occurs everywhere without actual blood-mixture, as an effect of imitation. Proof of diffusion of cultural elements may be found everywhere. Neither differences of race nor of language are effectual barriers for their spread. In North America, California offers a good example of this kind; for here many languages are spoken, and there is a certain degree of differentiation of type, but at the same time a considerable uniformity of culture prevails (Kroeber 2, 3). Another case in point is the coast of New Guinea, where, notwithstanding strong local differentiations, a fairly characteristic type of culture prevails, which goes hand in hand with a strong differentiation of languages. Among more highly civilized peoples, the whole area which is under the influence of Chinese culture might be given as an example.

The culture of Africa shows that racial differences are no hindrance to diffusion. The cattle breeding of Asia has modified the cultural life of a large part of Africa. The political and juridical forms of the Negro are to a great extent the counterpart of those of feudal Europe. It would be vain to attempt an understanding of African institutions without bearing in mind their intimate association with neighboring continents. In the extreme southern part of Africa the Bushmen and Bantu represent two people differing in type and language. Nevertheless the sounds of the language of the Southern Bantu show a similarity to the sounds of the Bushman languages that is not repeated in any other part of the continent. It consists in the occurrence of sounds which are produced by forcibly sucking in air instead of expelling it. Very weak sounds of this kind occur in other parts of the continent and may be an indication of an ancient speech habit which existed at one time over a wider area; but the particular occurrence among the Southern Bantu can be due only to a recent assimilation.

These considerations show that, at least at the present time, anatomical type, language and culture have not necessarily the same fates; that a people may remain constant in type and language, and change in culture; that it may remain constant in type, but change in language; or that it may remain constant in language, and change in type and culture. It is obvious, therefore, that attempts to classify mankind, based on the present distribution of type, language and culture, must lead to different results, according to the point of view taken; that a classification based primarily on type alone will lead to a system which represents more or less accurately the blood-relationships of the people; but these do not need to coincide with their cultural relationships. In the same way classifications based on language and culture do not need to coincide with a biological classification.

If this be true, then a problem like the Aryan problem does not exist, because it relates to the history of the Aryan languages; and the assumption that a certain definite people whose members have always been related by blood must have been the carriers of this language throughout history; and the other assumption, that a certain cultural type must have always belonged to peoples speaking Aryan languages—are purely arbitrary ones, and not in accord with the observed facts.

Nevertheless it must be granted that in a theoretical consideration of the history of the types of mankind, of languages and of cultures, we are led back to the assumption of early conditions, during which each type was much more isolated from the rest of mankind than it is at the present time. For this reason the culture and the language belonging to a single type must have been much more sharply separated from those of other types than we find them to be at the present period. Such a condition has nowhere been observed; but the knowledge of historical developments almost compels us to assume its existence at a very early period in the development of mankind. If this be true, the question would arise, whether an isolated group at an early period was necessarily characterized by a single type, a single language and a single culture, or whether in such a group different types, different languages and different cultures may have been represented.

The historical development of mankind would afford a simpler and clearer picture if we were justified in the belief that in primitive communities the three phenomena had been intimately associated. No proof, however, of such an assumption can be given. On the contrary, the present distribution of languages, as compared with the distribution of types, makes it plausible that even at the earliest times within the biological units more than one language and more than one culture were represented. I believe it may safely be said that all over the world the biological unit —disregarding minute local differences—is much larger than the linguistic one; in other words, that groups of men who are so closely related in bodily appearance that we must consider them as representatives of the same variety of mankind, embrace a much larger number of individuals than the number of men speaking languages which we know to be genetically related. Examples of this kind may be given from many parts of the world. Thus, the European race—including under this term roughly all those individuals who are without hesitation classed by us as members of the White race—would include peoples speaking Indo-European, Basque, Semitic and Ural-Altaic languages. West African Negroes would represent individuals of a certain Negro type, but speaking the most diverse languages; and the same would be true, among Asiatic types, of Siberians; among American types, of part of the Californian Indians.

So far as our historical evidence goes, there is no reason to believe that the number of languages which according to their form and content cannot now be traced back to a common mother tongue has at any time been less than it is now. All our evidence rather goes to show that the number of apparently unrelated languages was much greater in earlier times than at present. We have so far no means of determining whether a still earlier condition existed in which the languages that appear as distinct were related in some way. On the other hand, the number of types that have presumably become extinct seems to be rather small, so that there is no reason to suppose that at any time there should have been a nearer correspondence between the number of distinct linguistic and anatomical types; and we are thus led to the conclusion that presumably at an early time small isolated groups of people of similar type existed, each of which may have possessed a language and culture of its own.

Incidentally we may remark here, that, from this point of view, the great diversity of languages found in many remote mountain areas should not be explained as the result of a gradual pressing-back of remnants of tribes into inaccessible districts, but appears rather as a survival of an earlier general condition of mankind, when every continent was inhabited by small groups of people speaking distinct languages. The present conditions would have developed through the gradual extinction of many of the old stocks and their absorption or extinction by others, which thus came to occupy a more extended territory.

However this may be, the probabilities are decidedly against the theory that originally each language and culture was confined to a single type, or that each type and culture was confined to one language; in short, that there has been at any time a close correlation between these three phenomena.

If type, language and culture were by origin closely related it would follow that these three traits developed approximately at the same period and conjointly. This does not seem by any means plausible. The fundamental types of man which are represented in the Negroid and in the Mongolid race must have been differentiated long before the formation of those forms of speech that are now recognized in the linguistic families of the world. I think that even the differentiation of the more important subdivisions of the great races antedates the formation of the recognizable linguistic families. At any rate, the biological differentiation and the formation of speech were, at this early period, subject to the same causes that are acting upon them now, and our whole experience shows that these causes may bring about great changes in language much more rapidly than in the human body. In this consideration lies the principal reason for the theory of lack of correlation of type and language, even during the period of formation of types and of linguistic families.[4]

If language is independent of race this is even more true of culture. In other words, when a group of a certain racial type migrated over an extended area before their language had attained a form that we are able to recognize as a single linguistic family, and before their culture had taken forms traces of which we may still recognize among their modern descendants, it will be impossible to discover a relation between type, language and culture, even if it had existed at an early time.

It is quite possible that people of a common type expanded over a large area and that their language during this process became so thoroughly modified in each locality that the relationship of the modern forms, or rather their common descent from a common tongue, can no longer be discovered. In the same way their culture may have developed in different ways quite independently of their ancient culture, or at least in such ways that genetic relations to the primitive form, if they existed, can no longer be ascertained.

If we accept these conclusions and avoid the hypothesis of an original close association between type, language and culture it follows that every attempt to classify mankind from more than one of these points of view must lead to contradictions.

It should be borne in mind that the vague term "cul-

[4] This must not be understood to mean that every primitive language is in a constant state of rapid modification. There are many evidences of a great permanence of languages. When, however, owing to certain outer or inner causes, changes set in, they are apt to bring about a thorough modification of the form of speech.

ture" as used here is not a unit which signifies that all aspects of culture must have had the same historical fates. The points of view which we applied to language may also be applied to the various aspects of culture. There is no reason that would compel us to believe that technical inventions, social organization, art and religion develop in precisely the same way or are organically and indissolubly connected. As an example illustrating their independence we may mention the Maritime Chukchee and the Eskimo who have a similar, almost identical material culture, but differ in their religious life; or the various Indian tribes of the western Plains; or those Bantu tribes whose economic lives are alike but who differ in social structure. Lack of cohesion appears most clearly in attempts to chart cultural traits, as Ankermann, Frobenius and Wieschoff have done for Africa, and Erland Nordenskiöld (2) for South America. Notwithstanding the appearance of connected areas the discontinuities of distribution are one of the striking features of these maps. Limits of distribution do not agree, neither in reference to the distribution of types and languages, nor to that of other cultural phenomena such as social organization, religious ideas, style of art, etc. Each of these has its own area of distribution.

Not even language can be treated as a unit, for its phonetic, grammatical and lexicographic materials are not indissolubly connected, for by assimilation different languages may become alike in some features. This history of phonetics and lexicography are not necessarily tied up with the history of grammar.

The so-called "culture areas" are conveniences for the treatment of generalized traits of culture, generally based on sameness of geographic and economic conditions and on similarities of material culture. If culture areas were based on language, religion or social organization they would differ materially from those generally accepted.

Applying this consideration to the history of the peoples speaking Aryan languages we conclude that this language has not necessarily arisen among one of the types of men who nowadays speak Aryan languages; that none of them may be considered a pure, unmixed descendant of the original people that spoke the ancestral Aryan language; and that furthermore the original type may have developed other languages beside the Aryan.

It may be asked whether the cultural achievements of races may be arranged in a progressive series, some races having produced inferior values while others have created nobler ones. If a progression of culture could be established and if, at the same time, it could be shown that the simpler forms always occur in some races, higher ones in others, it might be possible to conclude that there are differences in racial ability. It is easily shown that the most varied cultural forms appear in most races. In America the high civilizations of Peru and Mexico may be compared with the primitive tribes of Tierra del Fuego or with those of northern Canada. In Asia Chinese, Japanese and the primitive Yukaghir; in Africa the Negroes of the Sudan and the hunters of the primeval forests are found side by side. Only in Australia no higher forms of culture are found, and our own modern civilization had nothing alike to it among other races until the most recent time when Japan and China participate in many of our most valued activities, as in earlier times we have taken on many of their achievements.

The errors underlying all conclusions based on the achievements of various races have been dwelt on before (p. 21). It should be emphasized again that we can never be sure whether the mental character of a primitive tribe is the cause of its low culture so that under favorable conditions it could not attain a more advanced cultural life, or whether its mental character is the effect of its low culture and would change with advancing culture. It is all but impossible to find material for answering this question, except for the peoples of eastern Asia, because nowadays no large populations of alien races are placed in a position in which they are socially and politically equal to Whites and enjoy the same opportunities for intellectual, economic and social development. The chasm between our society and theirs is the wider the greater the contrast in outer appearance. For this reason we may not expect the same kind of mental development in these groups.

The considerations which in the beginning of our discussion led us to the conclusion that in modern times primitive tribes have no opportunity to develop their innate abilities, prevents us from forming any opinion in regard to their racial hereditary faculty.

In order to answer this question we need a clearer understanding of the historical development of culture. This subject will be dealt with in the following chapters.

Chapter 9

Early Cultural Traits

CULTURE MAY BE defined as the totality of the mental and physical reactions and activities that characterize the behavior of the individuals composing a social group collectively and individually in relation to their natural environment, to other groups, to members of the group itself and of each individual to himself. It also includes the products of these activities and their role in the life of the groups. The mere enumeration of these various aspects of life, however, does not constitute culture. It is more, for its elements are not independent, they have a structure.

The activities enumerated here are not by any means the sole property of man, for the life of animals is also regulated by their relations to nature, to other animals and by the interrelation of the individuals composing the same species or social group.

It has been customary to describe culture in order as material culture, social relations, art and religion. Ethical attitudes and rational activities have generally been treated slightly, and language has seldom been included in the description of culture. Under the first of these headings the gathering, preserving and preparation of food, shelter and clothing, processes and products of manufacture, methods of locomotion are described. Rational knowledge is generally included as part of this subject. Under social relations the general economic conditions, property rights, relation to foreign tribes in war and peace, the position of the individual in the tribe, the organization of the tribe, forms of communication, sexual and other individual relations are discussed. Decorative, pictorial and plastic art, song, narrative and dance are the subject matter of art; the attitudes and activities centering around everything that is considered as sacred or outside of the sphere of ordinary human acts, that of religion. Here are generally also included customary behavior, referring to what is considered as good, bad, proper or improper and other fundamental ethical concepts.

Many phenomena of material culture and social relations are common to man and animals (Alverdes). Each species of animals has its own method of food quest. The method of hunting of the wolf is different from that of the lion; the food and food-gathering of the squirrel differs from that of the woodchuck. Some animals like the ant-lion and spider build traps to catch game. Still others prey upon other creatures and appropriate the food collected by them. Jaeger gulls rob other gulls or fishing birds of their fish. Vultures live on the offal left by animals of prey. Many rodents are accustomed to lay by stores of provisions for the winter; insects, like bees, even prepare food for the next generation.

The reactions to climate are quite different in various groups. The bear hibernates in winter, some birds migrate to warmer climes, others endure the harshness of the cold weather.

Many kinds of animals make homes for themselves for their own protection and that of their young. Antelopes make lairs and apes live in temporary nests. Even the fundamental achievement of man, the invention of artificially made objects that serve their purpose, is not entirely absent in the animal world. The nests of some birds are made with greater art than the homes of some primitive people. They are woven and plastered with great skill. Insects and spiders make elaborate structures in which they live. One species of ants even prepares suitable soil in their hills for raising fungi and keep the beds scrupulously clean. According to W. Köhler's (1) experiments the apes use tools. They will break off a suitable stick for reaching a desired object that is too far away to be taken by the hand. He even saw chimpanzees putting hollow sticks together in order to obtain a tool of appropriate length. These are, however, probably the only cases in which animals prepare tools, not instinctively, but to serve a single, specific purpose.

Parallels to the social habits of man are also found in the animal world. The herd or pack of gregarious animals forms a firmly knit unit hostile to strangers even of the same species. A pack of dogs will not allow a foreign dog in their midst. He is accepted, if at all, only after long continued fights. Penguins of the same rookery will not allow others with whom they are not acquainted, to trespass on their nesting place. Ants of one hill including foreign species that live in symbiosis, keep together but attack all foreigners that try to encroach upon their territory.

In the societies of apes and poultry there is a distinct order of rank, the strongest "personalities" being recognized as superiors by the weaker ones. Among insects the assignment of social duties is connected with bodily form, each class having its own anatomical characteristic. The various classes of workers of the leaf-cutting ants are anatomically distinct. Among higher animals, social duties belong to the leader of the herd, male or female, to scouts or watchers. Some animals live in more or less permanent monogamy, as some birds, others in herds in which the male leader has his harem, still others live in short lived temporary unions. Sometimes both male and female look after the young, in other cases the female or the male alone has to take care of them.

The feeling of ownership manifests itself particularly during the period of reproduction. The stickleback drives other fish and snails away from the region in which he has built his nest; many birds do not permit any other individuals of the same species to visit the district they inhabit. Ducks defend their particular pond against intruders. Other animals "own" permanent territories throughout the year; monkeys stay in a definite district to which others are not admitted. The same is true of eagles and hawks. Animals that lay by provisions, as some species of woodpeckers, squirrels and woodchucks, own and defend their stores.

Animals living in a social group also have their friendships and enmities, their forceful leaders and weaklings, and their social relations are of the same general kind as those found in human society.

The distribution of habits among animals shows that these must be, comparatively speaking, recent acquisitions, for many instances are known of closely allied species whose modes of life differ in important respects. We find solitary wasps and those living in elaborately organized colonies. Related species of ants differ fundamentally in their habits. Some birds are gregarious and nest in colonies, while closely related species are solitary. The migrations of birds over definite routes can be understood only as a result of a long historical process and can in no way be explained as due to their anatomical structure.

The changes in habits seem to be dependent upon the mode of life of untold generations. It is not necessary for us to discuss here the question how such habits may have come to be fixed by heredity. The facts indicate that habits may modify structure—as in the case of bees who develop a queen by proper treatment of an egg or a larva, or in those ants that have different bodily forms for individuals performing distinct social functions. The distribution of these phenomena among related forms suggests an instability of habits much greater than that of bodily form. It may also be an indication that comparatively slight changes in structure may modify the mode of life. There is, however, no indication that certain types of structure determine definite habits. Their distribution seems quite erratic.

We do not designate the activities of animals as culture, no matter whether they are purposive, or whether they are organically determined or learned. We rather speak of "mode of life" or "habits" of animals. There may be some justification in using the term culture for activities that are acquired by tradition, still it would be stretching the meaning of the term too far if we should apply it to the song of the bird or to any other acquired activity of animals. If, according to Köhler (2), chimpanzees like to adorn themselves and may even intentionally perform certain rhythmic movements, a kind of "dance," the term may seem more applicable. It is difficult to draw a sharp line between "mode of life" and "culture."

If we were to define culture by observing behavior alone there is little in the fundamental elements of human behavior that has not some kind of parallel in the animal world.

Peculiar to man is the great variability of behavior in regard to his relations to nature and to his fellow men. While among animals the behavior of the whole species is stereotyped, or as we say, instinctive, not learned, and only to a very slight extent variable and dependent on local tradition, human behavior is not stereotyped in the same sense, and cannot be called instinctive. It depends on local tradition and is learned.

Furthermore, so far as we can understand the actions of animals, there is no retrospective reasoning in regard to their actions. They are purposeful insofar as they are adapted to certain requirements, and insofar as many animals may profit by experience, but the whole problem of causality and the question why certain things happen, are foreign to the animals and common to all mankind. In other words, human culture is differentiated from animal life by the power of reasoning, and, connected with it, by the use of language. Peculiar to man is also the evaluation of actions from ethical and aesthetic viewpoints.

An examination of the oldest remains of man gives the impression of an objective parallelism with animal behavior. Setting aside the doubtful eoliths of the end of the Tertiary —since they show no definite shaping, but are merely provided with sharp edges suitable for cutting and slashing that may have been formed by use—we find definitely shaped tools in the Quaternary. These are brittle stones knocked into rough shapes by the blow of a heavier, tough stone. The strata in which these stones are found represent a period of several thousand years. No change in the form of the implements occurs from the earlier to the later part of this period. Generation after generation performed the same activities. We do not know whether their activities that left no remains may have changed during this time. We do not know whether man of this period had organized language and the concept of causal relations. Considering only the material that is actually in hand, the activities of man throughout this period might have been as permanent as those of animals. The bodily form also was still prehuman and differed from that of any of the present human races. It would be an adequate statement of the observed facts if we should claim that man of this period had developed an organic tendency to supplement the use of hands and teeth by the use of objects to which he gave somewhat serviceable form, and that the form he used was learned by imitation.

Oswald Menghin shows that in this early period the industries of mankind did not follow the same pattern everywhere, but it is impossible to determine whether such differentiation had anything to do with the distribution of races.

In later times we are able to study not only the fragmentary archaeological remains, the only indications of the cultural life of past ages, but we become acquainted also with the languages, customs and thoughts of people.

From these times on we find not only emotion, intellect and will power of man alike everywhere, but also similarities in thought and action among the most diverse peoples. These similarities are so detailed and far reaching, so utterly independent of race and language that Bastian was led to speak of the appalling monotony of the fundamental ideas of mankind all over the globe.

The art of producing fire by friction, the boiling of food, the knowledge of tools like knife, scraper and drill illustrate the universality of certain inventions.

Elementary features of grammatical structure are common to all languages. The distinctions between speaker, person addressed and person spoken of; and concepts of space, time and form are universal.

So is belief in the supernatural. Animals and the active forms of nature are seen in anthropomorphic form and endowed with superhuman powers. Other objects are seen as possessing beneficent or malevolent qualities. Magic power is ever present.

The belief in a multiplicity of worlds, one or more spanned over us, others stretching under us, the central one the home of man is generally held. The idea of a soul of man in varied forms is universal, and a home of the departed souls is commonly located in the west and may be reached after a dangerous journey.

Tylor, Spencer, Frazer, Bastian, Andree (1), Post and many others have collected instances of such similarities in vast numbers and relating to many subjects so that it is unnecessary to give further details.

Special curious analogies occur in regions far apart. Examples are the foretelling of the future from cracks in the shoulder blades of an animal (Andree 2, Speck); the occurrence of the Phaeton legend in Greece and Northwest America (Boas 12); the bleeding of animals by the use of a small bow and arrow (Høger); the use of a strap for throwing lances in ancient Rome (the pilum) and on the

Admiralty Islands; the development of an elaborate astrology in the Old World and the New; the invention of the zero in Yucatan and India; that of the blowgun in America and Malaysia; the similarity of basketry technique and design in Africa and America (Dixon 1); the balance in pre-Spanish Peru (Nordenskiöld 1, Joyce) and in the Old World, the use of the bull roarer to frighten away the profane from sacred ceremonies in Australia and South America.

Certain parallelisms in linguistic form may also be observed. Here belong the use of sounds by drawing in the breath in West Africa and in California (Dixon 2, Uldall); the use of musical pitch for differentiating the meaning of words in Africa, eastern Asia and in many parts of America; the distribution of masculine, feminine and neuter in Indo-European languages and on Columbia River in North America; the use of duplication or reduplication for expressing repetition and other concepts in some languages of America and in Polynesia; the sharp distinction of movement toward the speaker and away from the speaker.

The common cause for these similarities in the behavior of man may be explained by two theories. Similar phenomena may occur because they are historically related or they may arise independently on account of the sameness of the mental structure of man. The frequency with which analogous forms develop independently in plants and animals (see pp. 99 et seq.) indicates that there is nothing improbable in the independent origin of similar ideas among the most diverse human groups.

Historical relations may be of two kinds. They may be earlier inventions and ideas which represent early cultural achievements belonging to a period previous to the general dispersion of mankind or they may be due to later happenings.

Universal distribution of cultural achievements suggests the possibility of great antiquity. This theory should be applied only to features that occur the world over and the great antiquity of which can be proved by archaeological or other more indirect evidence. A number of ethnological traits fulfill these conditions. The use of fire, of drilling, cutting, sawing, work in stone belong to this early age, and have been the heritage of which each people built up its own individual type of culture (Weule, Ratzel 2). The occurrence of the dog as a domesticated animal in practically all parts of the world may be of equal antiquity. It seems plausible that the living-together of man and dog developed in the earliest period of human history, before the races of northern Asia and America separated from those of southeastern Asia. The introduction of the dingo (the native dog) into Australia seems to be most easily explained when we assume that it accompanied man to that remote continent.

Language is also a trait common to all mankind, and one that must have its roots in earliest times.

The activities of the higher apes favor the assumption that certain arts may have belonged to man before his dispersion. Their habit of making nests, that is, habitations, the use of sticks and stones, point in this direction.

All this makes it plausible that certain cultural achievements date back to the origin of mankind.

We have also clear evidence of the dissemination of cultural elements from tribe to tribe, from people to people and from continent to continent. These can be proved to have existed from the earliest times on. An instance of the rapidity with which cultural achievements are transmitted is presented by the modern history of some cultivated plants. Tobacco and cassava were introduced into Africa after the discovery of America, and it took little time for these plants to spread over the whole continent; so that at present they enter so deeply into the whole culture of the Negro, that nobody would suspect their foreign origin.[1] In the same way the use of the banana has pervaded almost the whole of South America (Von den Steinen). The history of Indian-corn is another example of the incredible rapidity with which a useful cultural acquisition may spread over the whole world. It is mentioned as known in Europe in 1539, and, according to Laufer (2), had reached China by way of Tibet between 1540 and 1570.[2]

[1] E. Hahn 2: pp. 464, 465; de Candolle.
[2] Regarding the introduction of tobacco into eastern Asia, J. Rein states that it was known in the most southern part of Japan during the last half of the sixteenth century and that it was known in Nagasaki in 1607.

It is easy to show that similar conditions prevailed in earlier times. Victor Hehn's investigations as well as archaeological evidence show the gradual and continuous increase of the number of domesticated animals and cultivated plants, due to their importation from Asia. The same process was going on in prehistoric times. The spread of the Asiatic horse, which was first used as a draught animal, later on for riding, that of cattle over Africa and Europe, the development of European grains many of which are derived from wild Asiatic forms, may serve as illustrations. The area over which these additions to the stock of human culture were extended is very large. We see most of them travel westward until they reach the Atlantic coast, and eastward to the shores of the Pacific Ocean. They also penetrated the African continent. It may be that the use of milk was disseminated in a similar way; for when the people of the world enter into our historic knowledge, we find milk used all over Europe, Africa and the western part of Asia.

Perhaps the best proof of transmission is contained in the folk-lore of the tribes of the world. Nothing seems to travel as readily as fanciful tales. We know of certain complex tales, which cannot possibly have been invented twice, that are told by the Berbers in Morocco, by the Italians, the Russians, in the jungles of India, in the highlands of Tibet, on the tundras of Siberia, on the prairies of North America and in Greenland; so that perhaps the only parts of the world not reached by them are South Africa, Australia, Polynesia and South America. The examples of such transmission are quite numerous, and we begin to see that the early interrelation of the races of man was almost world-wide.

It follows from this observation that the culture of any given tribe, no matter how primitive it may be, can be fully explained only when we take into consideration its inner growth as well as the effects of its relations to the cultures of its near and distant neighbors. Two enormously large areas of extended diffusion may be traced. Our brief remarks on the distribution of cultivated plants and domesticated animals prove the existence of interrelations between Europe, Asia and North Africa, from the Atlantic to the Pacific Ocean. Other cultural traits corroborate this conclusion. The gradual spread

of bronze from Central Asia westward and eastward, all over
Europe and over China; the area in which the wheel is
used; where agriculture with plough and with the help of
domesticated animals is practiced, show the same type of
distribution (Ed. Hahn 1). We may also recognize other
characteristic traits in this area. Oath and ordeal are highly
developed in Europe, Africa and Asia excepting the northeastern part of Siberia, while in America they are little
known (Laasch). Other common features of the cultural
types of the Old World appear also most clearly by contrast
with conditions in America. One of these is the importance
of formal judicial procedure and elaborate administrative
organization in the Old World, and their weak development
among those tribes of North and South America, who in their
general cultural development, might well be compared with
the African Negroes. In the domain of folk-lore the riddle,
the proverb and the moralizing fable are characteristic of an
enormous part of the Old World, while they are lacking in
northeastern Siberia and rare in America. In all these features,
Europe, a large part of Africa, and Asia except its extreme
northeastern part, and the Malay Archipelago, form a unit.

In a similar manner we may trace certain very general traits
over a large part of aboriginal America. Most convincing
among these is the use of Indian-corn as the foundation of
American agriculture. Its home was in the highlands of
Mexico, but at an early time its use spread over the continental bridge to South America as far as the Argentine and
northeastward almost to the line where climatic conditions
prevent its cultivation. A similar impression is given by the
distribution of pottery which occurs in all parts of the double
continent excepting its extreme northwestern and southern
marginal areas;[3] and by the peculiar forms of American
decorative art which flourished in South America, Central
America, Mexico and the southwest of the United States.
Notwithstanding the individuality of each region they have a
certain degree of stylistic similarity strong enough to induce
some students to look for a direct relation between the

[3] There is an intrusion of pottery in Arctic Alaska and adjoining territories.

ancient cultures of the Argentine and New Mexico. It would seem that the regions of advanced cultures in Mexico, Central America and Peru played a role not unlike that of Central Asia, insofar as on an ancient common American cultural basis new traits developed which influenced the whole continent.

The interpretation of cultural phenomena which occur sporadically in regions far apart offers serious difficulties. Some authors are inclined to consider these also as survivals of a very early period when there was still a common home of the people who have these traits in common. Or they assume that on account of historical events the customs have been lost in intervening areas. Without some more solid background than that so far given these theories must be used with utmost caution, for if we admit in our argument the loss of one feature here, another there, or a loss of whole complexes of features the door would be open to the most fanciful conclusions. When phenomena of sporadic occurrence are to be referred back to great antiquity it would be necessary first of all to prove that they do survive in various cultures unchanged through exceedingly long periods. If they are changeable the sameness cannot be explained by great antiquity. This objection may be raised to most of the arguments for an early historic connection between customs and inventions that occur sporadically in regions as far apart as South America, Australia and South Africa.

In many cases it is quite impossible to give incontrovertible arguments which would prove that these customs are not due to parallel and independent development rather than to community of origin: In some cases the decision of this question may be found through the results of prehistoric archaeology.

It is often assumed that because modern cultures are complex, those of culturally poorer groups simpler, that the chronological sequence of all cultural history has led from the simple to the complex. It is obvious that the history of industrial development is almost throughout that of increasing complexity. On the other hand, human activities that do not depend upon reasoning do not show a similar type of evolution.

It is perhaps easiest to make this clear by the example of language, which in many respects is one of the most important evidences of the history of human development. Many primitive languages are complex. Minute differences in point of view are given expression by means of grammatical forms; and the grammatical categories of Latin, and still more so those of modern English, seem crude when compared to the complexity of psychological or logical forms which primitive languages recognize, but which in our speech are disregarded. On the whole, the development of languages seems to be such, that the nicer distinctions are eliminated, and that it begins with complex and ends with simpler forms, although it must be acknowledged that opposite tendencies are not by any means absent (for examples see for instance Boas 10).

Similar observations may be made on the art of primitive man. In music as well as in decorative design we find a complex rhythmic structure which is unequaled in the popular art of our day. In music, particularly, this complexity is so great, that the art of a skilled virtuoso is taxed in the attempt to imitate it (Stumpf). On the other hand, the scope of intervals, the melodic and harmonic structure show an ever-increasing complexity.

The system of social obligations determined by the status of an individual in the group of consanguineal and affinal relatives is often exceedingly complex. The behavior of brothers and sisters, uncles and nephews, parents-in-law and children-in-law is often circumscribed by minute rules which do not exist in modern civilization. There is a general loss in the variety of obligations of individuals to society insofar as these are regulated by status.

The development of religion also is not by any means that from simple to complex forms. The lack of system in religious behavior of primitive man subjects him to a mass of disconnected, apparently arbitrary rules and regulations. Dogma as well as religious activities are manifold and often without apparent coherence. When one clear and dominating idea controls religious life the aspect of religion becomes clearer and simpler and may lead to a religion without dogma and ritual. The opposite tendency of a systematic religion taking on complex ritual forms is also common.

In a similar way the observation that in modern cultures greater logical or psychological consistency may be observed has led to the conclusion that the degree of logical or psychological cohesion has a chronological value so that the historical sequence can be reconstructed from a logical or psychological analysis of the ideas of primitive tribes. The development of the anthropomorphic view of nature and of mythology has been reconstructed on this basis by Spencer and Tylor. In reality the course of history may have been quite different. It is easily seen that the concepts involved represented by such terms as the supernatural, soul, sin existed long before a corresponding clearly defined concept developed. An analysis of their complex content could not give us a history of the development of their meaning. If we can determine that the supernatural includes the ideas of wonderful qualities of objects and the other of anthropomorphic but superhuman faculties this does not show that the one aspect is necessarily older than the other. Furthermore the sources from which these vague concepts develop are manifold and cannot be explained as a logical conclusion based on a single set of experiences. When once the idea of animism and anthropomorphism has developed, the transfer of social experiences into the anthropomorphic world must occur and it can have no other form than that of the society with which man is familiar. When a condition, like sickness or hunger is conceived as an object that may be present or absent and leads an independent existence, while others are conceived as attributes, confused lines of thought must develop in which the one group will be affected by the particular views held regarding objects, the other by those regarding attributes, but no chronological sequence is involved.

Chapter 10

The Interpretations of Culture

EVER SINCE THE TIME when the study of human cultures was recognized as a problem, attempts have been made to interpret it as a unit phenomenon even before anything like a fair amount of material had been collected. Society was considered as an organism, and its various functions were explained in the same way as the organs of the body. Under the influences of Darwinism its changing forms were viewed as the evolution of an organism, the driving force of its development being rational thought. The mental activities of primitive man have been compared to those of children and *vice versa*, so that the development of the child's mind has been looked at as a recapitulation of the development of the mind of mankind. The child's mind, it is believed, can thus explain to us the primitive mind. In recent times primitive mind is being compared with the minds of the mentally unsound, as though the mental activities of perfectly normal people of foreign cultures could be explained by the mentally affected of our own culture.

Rather recent are attempts to understand primitive culture as a phenomenon that requires painstaking analysis before a generally valid theory is accepted.

Only a few of the points of view just referred to are relevant to our problem. Suggested analogy with an organism will not help us to clear up the behavior of primitive man. The analogy with the mental life of the child is difficult to apply because the culture of child life in Europe and the life of the adult in primitive society are not comparable. We ought at least to compare the adult primitive with the child in his own culture. Children of all races undoubtedly exhibit analogies of development dependent upon the development of the body, and differences according to the demands made by their gradual initiation into the culture in which they live. The only question could be whether one culture tends to develop qualities which another one neglects.

The comparison of forms of psychoses and primitive life seems still more unfortunate. The manifestation of mental disturbances must necessarily depend upon the culture in which people live and it must be of great value to the psychiatrist to study the expression of forms of psychoses in different cultures, but an attempt to parallel forms of healthy primitive life and those of disturbances in our civilization is not based on any tangible analogy. The megalomaniac boasting and acting of the Northwest Coast Indians does not make them act like a megalomaniac insane, but their culture probably gives a particular form to that type of insanity. Particularly Freud's (2) comparison of primitive culture and the psychoanalytic interpretations of European behavior seem to lack a scientific background. They appear to me as fancies in which neither the aspect of primitive life nor that of civilized life is sustained by tangible evidence. The attempt to conceive every mental state or performance as determined by discoverable causes confuses the concepts of causality and predictability. Of course, every event has a cause, but the causes do not hang together so that they represent a single thread. Innumerable accidental causes intervene which cannot be predicted and which also cannot be reconstructed as determining the course of the past.

We must pay more detailed attention to the attempts to see cultural life developing from primitive forms to modern civilization, either as a single evolutional line or in a small number of separate lines. The question may be asked whether without regard to race, time and space, we may recognize a series of stages of culture which represent for the whole of humanity an historical sequence, so that certain ones may be identified as types belonging to an early period, others as recent.

The investigations of Tylor, Bachofen, Morgan and Spencer fixed the attention upon the data of anthropology as illustrating the gradual development and rise of civilization. The development of this side of anthropology was stimulated by the work of Darwin and his successors, and the underlying ideas can be understood only as an application to mental phenomena of the theory of biological evolution. The conception that the manifestations of ethnic life represent a time series, which from simple beginnings has progressed in a single line to the complex type of modern civilization, has been the underlying thought of this aspect of anthropological science.

The arguments in support of this theory are based on the similarities of types of culture found in distinct races the world over, and on the occurrence of peculiar customs in our own civilization, which can be understood only as survivals of older customs that had a deeper significance at an earlier time, and which are still found in full vigor among primitive people.[1]

An excellent example of the general theory of evolution of civilization is found in the theory of the development of agriculture and of the domestication of animals as outlined by Otis T. Mason, W. J. McGee and Eduard Hahn (1, 2). They point out how, in the earliest beginnings of social life, animals, plants and man lived together in a common environment and how the conditions of life brought it about that certain plants multiplied in the neighborhood of the human camp to the exclusion of others, and certain animals were suffered as camp followers. Through this condition of mutual sufferance and promotion of mutual interests, if I may use this term, a closer association between plants, animals, and man developed, which ultimately led to the beginnings of agriculture and to the actual domestication of animals.

The development of art has been reconstructed by similar methods. Since the earliest traces of art represent animals and other objects and geometric forms follow, it has been inferred that all geometrical motives have developed from representative designs.

In a similar way religion has been inferred to be the result of speculation in regard to nature.

The essential method has been to bring the observed phenomena into order according to imputed principles and to interpret this as a chronological order.

We must try to understand more clearly what the theory of a unilinear cultural development implies. It means that different groups of mankind started at a very early time from

[1] Tylor, I, p. 16.

a general condition of lack of culture; and, owing to the unity of the human mind and the consequent similar response to outer and inner stimuli, developed everywhere approximately along the same lines, making similar inventions and developing similar customs and beliefs. It also involves a correlation between industrial and social development, and therefore a definite sequence of inventions as well as of forms of organization and belief.

In the absence of historical data in regard to the earliest history of primitive man the world over, we have only three sources of historical proof for this assumption—the evidence contained in the earliest history of the civilized people of the Old World, survivals in modern civilization and archaeology. The last-named is the only method by means of which we can approach the problem in regard to people that have no history.

While it is certainly true that analogues can be found between the types of culture represented by primitive people and those conditions which prevailed among the ancestors of the present civilized peoples at the dawn of history, and that these analogues are supported by the evidence furnished by survivals, the evidence of archaeology does not support the complete generalization. The theory of parallel development, if it is to have any significance, would require that among all branches of mankind the steps of invention should have followed, at least approximately, in the same order, and that no important gaps should be found. The facts, so far as known at the present time, are entirely contrary to this view.

The example of the development of agriculture and herding will illustrate some of the objections that may be raised against the general theory. Under the simple conditions of primitive life the food supply of the family is procured by both sexes. The women collect plants and animals that are stationary or that cannot move about rapidly such as larvae and worms. This must be due to the hindrance imposed upon them by childbearing and the care of young children. The men obtain the fleet game, birds and fish. They hunt and fish. The attempt to systematize the life forms of primitive people induces us to place those who gather food and hunt at the beginning of the scale. Next will be placed others who are

farther advanced in the technical means of obtaining a liveli-
hood, or who have attained a closer connection with the vegetable world by developing property rights in regard to plants
growing near their place of abode. These relations all center
around the life of woman and her occupation with plants and
we reach, without any serious gap, the condition of earliest
agriculture. The psychological reason for accepting this arrangement as having a chronological value, lies in the conviction of the continuity of technical advance and on the other
important fact that we are dealing right along with the occupations of the same part of the population, namely, the
women. The chronological interpretation is supported by the
observation that the beginnings of agriculture are generally
supported by the gathering of wild plants; that while gathering
of plants occurs without agriculture, the opposite condition is
unknown.

The activities of men related primarily to animals. The
transition from hunting to herding cannot be shown as easily
as that from the gathering of plants to agriculture. Still it is
at least plausible that the domestication of animals—which are
almost exclusively gregarious animals—is based on the relation of the hunter to the wild herd. As soon as the hunter
began to obtain his food supply from the same herd and
prevented its being scattered by killing the animals that
pursued it, conditions developed similar to those found among
the Chukchee and Koryak in Siberia. Since in this case also
the same part of the population, namely the men, were concerned in the relation between man and animal a continued
development is possible.

These considerations are supported by archaeological evidence. If our views are correct, the cultivated plants must
have originated from the wild plants with which man was
familiar. This transition has been shown for native European
plants. According to our theory we should expect frequent
crossings between wild and domesticated forms. This has been
made plausible for early European forms. In domesticated
animals similar conditions may still be observed in the reindeer of Siberia and the dog of the Eskimo.

With this we are led to a question of fundamental importance for the theory of a unilinear evolution: What is the

chronological relation between agriculture and herding? When we approach this question from a psychological viewpoint the difficulty arises that we are no longer dealing with one single type of occupation carried on by the same group, but that we have two occupations, distinct in technique and carried on by distinct groups. The activities leading to the domestication of animals have nothing in common with those leading to the cultivation of plants. There is no bond that makes plausible a connection between the chronological development of these two occupations. It is missing because the persons involved are not the same and because the occupations are quite distinct. From a psychological point of view there is nothing that would help us to establish a time sequence for agriculture and herding.

I think this example illustrates one of the principal doubts that must be raised against a systematic, all-embracing application of a theory of evolution of culture. The steps of development must relate to an aspect of culture in which the same group of people are involved and in which the same kind of activity persists. A constant relation between loosely connected or entirely disconnected aspects of culture is improbable when the differences between the activities are great and different groups of individuals participate in the activities involved. In all these cases chronological data must be based on other sources.

Safe conclusions can be based only on archaeological evidence. Besides this, certain conditions among primitives may serve as guides. If it can be shown that certain industries occur exclusively in connection with other simpler ones and the latter alone, the former never without the simpler ones, it seems likely that the simple type of work is the earlier. If this should not occur with absolute regularity, still with sufficient frequency, we might speak of recognizable tendencies of development.

Geographical distribution may also serve as a help, for wherever there is a continuous distribution of industry it is possible, although not necessary, that the one most widely spread is the oldest. It is doubtful whether this argument can be applied outside of the domain of technique.

The more distinct the various phenomena the less they are

correlated, so that finally notwithstanding the tendency to historical development in single phases of culture no harmonious scheme for the whole of culture that would be valid everywhere is found (Thomas).

Thus it does not seem to be certain that every people in an advanced stage of civilization must have passed through all the stages of development, which we may gather by an investigation of all the types of culture which occur all over the world.

Similar objections may be raised against the general validity of the theory of the development of the family. It has been claimed that the organization of the family began with irregular and shifting relations between the sexes, that later on mother and children formed the family unit which remained attached to that of the mother's parents, brothers and sisters and that only much later developed a form in which the father was the head of the family which was attached to his parents, brothers and sisters. If the evolution of culture had proceeded in a single line the simplest forms of the family would be associated with the simplest types of culture. This is not the case, for a comparative study discloses the most irregular distribution. Some very primitive tribes, like the Eskimo and the Indian tribes of the northwest plateaus of North America, count relationship bilaterally, through father and mother; other tribes with highly developed culture recognize the maternal line alone, while still others whose economic and industrial life is of a simpler type, recognize the paternal line (Swanton). The data are contradictory and do not permit us to conclude that economic life and family organization are intimately related in regard to their inner form.

Theoretical considerations suggest that customs do not by any means necessarily develop in one way only. The relation between incest and totemism may serve as an example. Incest groups vary according to the prevalent system of relationship and associated ideas. Frequently the incest group is believed to stand in intimate relation to some animal, plant or other object, its totem. In other cases there is no such relation. In anthropological theory totemism has been described as an early stage of society from which later forms have been developed. The concept of incest is so universal that it must either have belonged to man before his dispersion or it must have developed independently in a very early period. Wherever an incest group exists a development is possible in two directions. The group while increasing in number may remain a whole, or it may break up in a number of separate groups. A conceptual unity of the group must exist, otherwise subgroups will lose consciousness of their earlier relationship when they are separated from other subgroups. The conceptualization may be brought about by naming the whole group, by common, recognizable customs or functions, or by a terminology of relationship which will differentiate members from non-members. Such a terminology may include very large numbers of individuals, because by reference to some known intermediary even distant members may be identified. It follows from this that when no conceptualization of unity exists totemism of the whole group cannot develop. The only form that is favorable to it is the one in which a group is characterized by a name or by common customs.

If, as is illustrated by this example, different customs may develop from a single source we have not the right to assume that every people that has reached a high stage of development must have passed through all the stages found among tribes of primitive culture.

A still more serious objection is based on another observation. The validity of the general sameness of the evolution of mankind is based on the assumption that the same cultural features must always have developed from the same, single causes, and that a logical or psychological sequence of steps represents also a chronological sequence.[2] We have pointed out that in special fields, when the identical social groups carry on certain occupations uninterruptedly there may be a reason for upholding this theory. Not so when these conditions are not given. Thus the inference that maternal institutions precede paternal ones, to which I referred before, is based on the generalization that because in a number of cases paternal families have developed from maternal ones, therefore all paternal families have developed in the same way. There is no proof showing that the history of family organi-

[2] See pp. 161, 164.

zation is controlled by a single set of specific conditions, that the man's or the woman's family or any other group exerted a controlling influence, nor that there is any inherent reason that one type must have preceded the other one. We may, therefore, just as well conclude that paternal families have in some cases arisen from maternal institutions, in other cases in other ways.

In the same way it is inferred that because many conceptions of the future life have evidently developed from dreams and hallucinations, all notions of this character have had the same origin. This is true only if it can be shown that no other causes could possibly lead to the same ideas.

To give another example. It has been claimed that among the Indians of Arizona, pottery developed from basketry, and it has been inferred that all pottery must therefore be later in the cultural development of mankind than basketry. Evidently this conclusion cannot be defended, for pottery may develop in other ways.

As a matter of fact, quite a number of cases can be given in which convergent evolution, beginning from distinct beginnings, has led to the same results. I have referred before to the instance of primitive art, and have mentioned the theory that geometrical form develops from realistic representations, which lead through symbolic conventionalism to purely aesthetic motives. If this were true a great diversity of objects might in this way have given rise to the same decorative motives, so that the surviving motive would not have had the same realistic origin; but more important than this, geometrical motives of the same type have developed from the tendency of the artist to play with his technique as the virtuoso plays on his instrument; that the expert basket-weaver, by varying the arrangement of her weave, was led to the development of geometrical designs of the same form as those that were developed in other places from realistic representations. We may even go a step farther and recognize that geometrical forms developed from the technique suggested animal forms, and were modified so as to assume realistic forms; so that in the case of decorative art the same forms may just as well stand at the beginning of a series of development as at the end (Boas 13).

A serious objection to the reasoning of those who try to establish lines of evolution of cultures lies in the frequent lack of comparability of the data with which we are dealing. Attention is directed essentially to the similarity of ethnic phenomena, while the individual variations are disregarded. As soon as we turn our attention to these we notice that the sameness of ethnic phenomena is more superficial than essential, more apparent than real. The unexpected similarities have attracted our attention to such an extent that we have disregarded differences. In the study of the physical traits of distinct social groups, the reverse mental attitude manifests itself. The similarity of the main features of the human form being self-evident, our attention is directed to the minute differences of structure.

Instances of such lack of comparability can easily be given. When we speak of life after death as one of the ideas which develop in human society as a psychological necessity, we are dealing with a most complex group of data. One people believes that the soul continues to exist in the form that the person had at the time of death, without any possibility of change; another one that the soul will be reborn at a later time as a child of the same family; a third one that the souls will enter the bodies of animals; and still others that the shadows continue our human pursuits, waiting to be led back to our world in a distant future. The emotional and rationalistic elements which enter into these various concepts are entirely distinct; and we perceive that the various forms of the idea of a future life have come into existence by psychological processes that are not at all comparable. In one case the similarities between children and their deceased relatives, in other cases the memory of the deceased as he lived during the last days of his life, in still other cases the longing for the beloved child or parent, and again the fear of death—may all have contributed to the development of the idea of life after death, the one here, the other there.

Another instance will corroborate this point of view. We have already referred to "totemism"—the form of a society in which certain social groups consider themselves as related in some way to a certain species of animals or to a class of objects. This is the generally accepted definition of "totemism"; but I am convinced that in this form the phenomenon is not a single problem, but embraces the most diverse psychological elements. In some cases the people believe themselves to be descendants of the animal whose protection they enjoy. In others an animal or some other object has appeared to an ancestor of the social group and promised to become his protector, and the friendship between the animal and the ancestor was then transmitted to his descendants. In still other cases a certain social group in a tribe is believed to have the power of securing by magical means and with great ease a certain kind of animal or of increasing its numbers, and a supernatural relation is established in this way. It will be recognized that here again the anthropological phenomena which are in outward appearances alike are, psychologically speaking, entirely distinct, and that consequently psychological laws covering all of them cannot be deduced from them (Goldenweiser).

Another example may not be amiss. In a general review of moral standards we observe that with increasing civilization a gradual change in the valuation of actions takes place. Among primitive man, human life has little value, and is sacrificed on the slightest provocation. The social group among whose members altruistic obligations are binding is small; and outside of the group any action that may result in personal gain is not only permitted, but approved. From this starting-point on we find an ever-increasing valuation of human life and an extension of the size of the group among whose members altruistic obligations are binding. The modern relations of nations show that this evolution has not yet reached its final stage. It might seem, therefore, that a study of the social conscience in relation to crimes like murder might be of psychological value, and lead to important results, clearing up the origin of ethical values. From an ethnological point of view murder cannot be considered as a single phenomenon. Unity is established by introducing our juridical concept of murder. As an act murder must be considered as the result of a situation in which the usual respect for human life is superseded by stronger motives. It can be considered as a unit only in regard to the reaction of society to murder which is expressed in the permission of revenge, the payment of compensation or punishment. The person who slays an enemy in revenge for wrongs done, a youth who kills his father before he gets decrepit in order to enable him to continue a vigorous life in the world to come, a father who kills his child as a sacrifice for the welfare of his people, act from such entirely different motives, that psychologically a comparison of their actions does not seem permissible. It would seem much more proper to compare the murder of an enemy in revenge with destruction of his property for the same purpose; or to compare the sacrifice of a child on behalf of the tribe with any other action performed on account of strong altruistic motives, than to base our comparison on the common concept of murder (Westermarck).

These few data may suffice to show that the same ethnic phenomenon may develop from different sources; and we may infer that the simpler the observed fact, the more likely it is that it may have developed from one source here, from another there.

When we base our study on these observations, it appears that serious objections may be made against the assumption of the occurrence of a general sequence of cultural stages among all the races of man; that rather we recognize both a tendency of diverse customs and beliefs to converge towards similar forms, and a development of customs in divergent directions. In order to interpret correctly these similarities in form, it is necessary to investigate their historical development; and only when the historical development in different areas is the same, will it be admissible to consider the phenomena in question as equivalent. From this point of view the facts of cultural contact assume a new importance (see p. 157).

Culture has also been interpreted in other ways. Geographers try to explain forms of culture as a necessary result of geographical environment.

It is not difficult to illustrate the important influence of geographical environment. The whole economic life of man is limited by the resources of the country in which he lives. The location of villages and their size depends upon the available food-supply; communication upon available trails or waterways. Environmental influences are evident in the territorial limits of tribes and peoples; seasonal changes of food-supply may condition seasonal migrations. The variety of habitations used by tribes of different areas demonstrate its influence. The snow house of the Eskimo, the bark wigwam of the Indian, the cave dwelling of the tribes of the desert, may serve as illustrations of the way in which in accordance with the available materials protection against exposure is attained. Scarcity of food may condition a nomadic life, and the necessity of carrying household goods on the back favors the use of skin receptacles and baskets as substitutes for pottery. The special forms of utensils may be modified by geographic conditions. Thus the complex bow of the Eskimo which is related to Asiatic forms takes a peculiar form owing to the lack of long, elastic material for bow staves. Even in the more complex forms of the mental life, the influence of environment may be found; as in nature myths explaining the activity of volcanoes or the presence of curious land forms, or in beliefs and customs relating to the local characterization of the seasons.

However, geographical conditions have only the power to modify culture. By themselves they are not creative. This is clearest wherever the nature of the country limits the development of culture. A tribe, living without foreign trade in a given environment is limited to the resources of its home country. The Eskimo has no vegetable food supplies to speak of; the Polynesian who lives on an atoll has no stone and no skins of large mammals; the people of the desert have no rivers furnishing fish or offering means of travel. These self-evident limitations are often of great importance.

It is another question whether external conditions are the immediate cause of new inventions. We can understand that a fertile soil will induce an agricultural people whose numbers are increasing rapidly to improve its technique of agriculture, but not, how it could be the cause of the invention of agriculture. However rich in ore a country may be, it does not create techniques of handling metals; however rich in animals that might be domesticated, it will not lead to the development of herding if the people are entirely unfamiliar with the uses of domesticated animals.

If we should claim that geographical environment is the sole determinant that acts upon the mind assumed to be the same in all races of mankind, we should be necessarily led to the conclusion that the same environment will produce the same cultural results everywhere.

This is obviously not true, for often the forms of cultures of peoples living in the same kind of environment show marked differences. I do not need to illustrate this by comparing the American settler with the North American Indian, or the successive races of people that have settled in England, and have developed from the Stone Age to the modern English. It may, however, be desirable to show that among primitive tribes, geographical environment alone does not by any means determine the type of culture. Proof of this may be found in the mode of life of the hunting and fishing Eskimo and the reindeer-breeding Chukchee (Bogoras, Boas 3); the African pastoral Hottentot and the hunting Bushmen in their older, wider distribution (Schultze); the Negrito and the Malay of southeastern Asia (Martin).

Environment always acts upon a pre-existing culture, not on an hypothetical cultureless group. Therefore it is important only insofar as it limits or favors activities. It may even be shown that ancient customs, that may have been in harmony with a certain type of environment, tend to survive under new conditions, where they are of disadvantage rather than of advantage to the people. An example of this kind, taken from our own civilization, is our failure to utilize unfamiliar kinds of food that may be found in newly settled countries. Another example is presented by the reindeer-breeding Chukchee, who carry about in their nomadic life a tent of most complicated structure, which corresponds in its type to the older permanent house of the coast dwellers, and contrasts in the most marked way with the simplicity and light weight of the Eskimo tent.[3] Even among the Eskimo, who have so marvelously well succeeded in adapting themselves to their geographical environment, customs like the taboo on the promiscuous use of caribou and seal prevent the fullest use of the opportunities offered by the country.

[3] Bogoras, pp. 177 et seq.; Boas 3: p. 551.

Thus it would seem that environment has an important effect upon the customs and beliefs of man, but only insofar as it helps to determine the special forms of customs and beliefs. These are, however, based primarily on cultural conditions, which in themselves are due to other causes.

At this point the students of anthropo-geography who attempt to explain the whole cultural development on the basis of geographical environmental conditions are wont to claim that these causes themselves are founded on earlier conditions, in which they have originated under the stress of environment. This claim is inadmissible because the investigation of every single cultural feature demonstrates that the influence of environment brings about a certain degree of adjustment between environment and social life, but that a complete explanation of the prevailing conditions, based on the action of environment alone, is never possible. We must remember, that, no matter how great an influence we may ascribe to environment, that influence can become active only by being exerted upon the mind; so that the characteristics of the mind must enter into the resultant forms of social activity. It is just as little conceivable that mental life can be explained satisfactorily by environment alone, as that environment can be explained by the influence of the people upon nature, which, as we all know, has brought about changes of watercourses, the destruction of forests and changes of fauna. In other words, it seems entirely arbitrary to disregard the part that psychical or social elements play in determining the forms of activities and beliefs which occur with great frequency all over the world.

The theory of economic determinism of culture is no more adequate than that of geographic determinism. It is more attractive because economic life is an integral part of culture and intimately connected with all its phases, while geographical conditions always remain an external element. Still, there is no reason to call all other phases of culture a superstructure on an economic basis, for economic conditions always act on a pre-existing culture and are themselves dependent upon other aspects of culture. It is no more justifiable to say that social structure is determined by economic forms than to claim the reverse, for a pre-existing social structure will influence economic conditions and *vice versa*, and no people has ever been observed that has no social structure and that is not subject to economic conditions. The claim that economic stresses preceded every other manifestation of cultural life and exerted their influences on a group without any cultural traits cannot be maintained. Cultural life is always economically conditioned and economics are always culturally conditioned.

The similarity of cultural elements regardless of race, environment and economic conditions may also be explained as a result of parallel development based on the similarity of the psychic structure of man the world over.

Bastian[4] recognizes the great importance of geographical environment in modifying the analogous ethnic phenomena, but does not ascribe to them creative power. To him the sameness of the forms of thought found in regions wide apart suggested the existence of certain definite types of thought, no matter in what surroundings man may live, and what may be his social relations. These fundamental forms of thought, "that develop with iron necessity wherever man lives," were called by him "elementary ideas." He denies that it is possible to discover the ultimate sources of inventions, ideas, customs and beliefs, which are of universal occurrence. They may have arisen from a variety of sources, they may be indigenous, they may be imported, but they are there. The human mind is so formed that it evolves them spontaneously, or accepts them whenever they are offered to it. The number of elementary ideas is limited. In primitive thought as well as in the speculations of philosophers the same ideas appear again and again in the special form given to them by the environment in which they find expression as "folk-ideas" (Völkergedanken).

The elementary ideas appear to him as metaphysical entities. No further thought can possibly unravel their origin, because we ourselves are compelled to think in the forms of these same elementary ideas.

In many cases a clear enunciation of the elementary idea

4 See Achelis, pp. 189 et seq.

gives us the psychological reason for its existence. To exemplify: The mere statement that primitive man considers the animals as gifted with all the qualities of man shows that the analogy between many of the qualities of animals and human qualities has led to the view that all the qualities of animals are human. The fact that the land of shadows is so often placed in the west suggests its localization at the place where the sun and the stars vanish. In other cases the causes are not so self-evident; for example, in the widespread customs of restrictions of marriage which have puzzled many investigators. The difficulty of this problem is proved by the multitude of hypotheses that have been invented to explain it in all its varied phases.

There is no reason why we should accept Bastian's renunciation. The dynamic forces that mould social life are the same now as those that moulded life thousands of years ago. We can follow the intellectual and emotional drives that actuate man at present and that shape his actions and thoughts. The application of these principles will clear up many of our problems.

Our previous considerations enable us also to evaluate the claim that the biological character of a race determines its culture. Let us admit for the moment that the genetic make-up of an individual determines his behavior. The actions of his glands, his basal metabolism and so on are elements that find expression in his personality. Personality in this sense means the biologically determined emotional, volitional and intellectual characteristics which determine the way in which an individual reacts to the culture in which he lives. The biological constitution does not make the culture. It influences the reactions of the individual to the culture. As little as geographical environment or economic conditions create a culture, just as little does the biological character of a race create a culture of a definite type. Experience has shown that members of most races placed in a certain culture can participate in it. In America men like Juárez, President of Mexico, or the highly educated Indians in North and South America are examples. In Asia the modern history of Japan and China; in America the successes of educated Negroes as scientists, physicians, lawyers, economists are ample proof showing that the racial position of an individual does not hinder his participation in modern civilization. Culture is rather the result of innumerable interacting factors and there is no evidence that the differences between human races, particularly not between the members of the White race have any directive influence upon the course of development of culture. Individual types, ever since the glacial period, have always found an existing culture to which they reacted.

The range of individual differences that occur within a race has never been investigated in a satisfactory manner. We have shown that the variability of bodily form of individuals composing each race is great. We cannot yet give exact data regarding the variability of fundamental physiological traits, much less of more intangible features such as physiologically determined personality, but even qualitative observation shows that the variability in each racial unit is great. The almost insurmountable difficulty lies in the fact that physiological and psychological processes and particularly personality cannot be reduced to an absolute standard that is free of environmental elements. It is, therefore, gratuitous to claim that a race has a definite personality. We have seen that on account of the variability of individuals composing a race, differences between larger groups of slightly varying human types are much smaller than the differences between the individuals composing each group, so that any considerable influence of the biologically determined distribution of personalities upon the form of culture seems very unlikely. No proof has ever been given that a sufficiently large series of normal individuals of an identical social environment but representing different European types, perhaps the one group, blond, tall, longheaded, with large nose; the other darker, shorter, roundheaded, with smaller noses will behave differently. The opposite, that people of the same type—like the Germans in Bohemia and the Czechs—behave quite differently is much more easily given. The change of personality of the proud Indian of pre-White times to his degenerate offspring is another glaring example.

Chapter 11

The Mind of Primitive Man and the Progress of Culture

WE HAVE SEEN that the attempts to reconstruct the history of culture by means of the application of the principle that the simple precedes the complex and through the logical or psychological analysis of the data of culture are misleading so far as particular cultural phenomena are concerned. Nevertheless the increasing intellectual achievements as expressed in thought, in inventions, in devices for gaining greater security of existence and in relief from the ever-pressing necessity of obtaining food and shelter, bring about differentiations in the activities of the community that give to life a more varied, richer tone. In this sense we may accept the term "advance of culture." It corresponds to common, every-day usage.

It might seem that by this definition we have also found that of primitiveness. Primitive are those people whose activities are little diversified, whose forms of life are simple and uniform, and the contents and form of whose culture are meager and intellectually inconsistent. Their inventions, social order, intellectual and emotional life should all be poorly developed. This would be acceptable if there were a close interrelation between all these aspects of ethnic life; but these relations are varied. There are people, like the Australians, whose material culture is quite poor, but who have a highly complex social organization. Others, like the Indians of California, produce excellent technical and artistic work, but show no corresponding complexity in other aspects of their lives. Furthermore this measure attains a different meaning when a large population is divided into social strata. Thus the differences between the cultural status of the poor rural population of many parts of Europe and America and even more so of the lowest strata of the proletariate on the one hand and the active minds representative of modern culture on the other, is excessive. Greater lack of cul-

tural values than that found in the inner life of some strata
of our modern population is hardly found anywhere. However these strata are not independent units like the tribes
that lack a multiplicity of inventions, for they utilize the
cultural achievements made by the people as a whole. This
apparent contrast between the cultural independence of
primitive tribes, and the dependence of social strata upon
the whole culture complex is merely the extreme form of
mutual dependence of social units.

Our discussion of the dissemination of cultural values
has shown that there is no people that is entirely untouched
by foreign influences, but that every one of them has taken
over from its neighbors and assimilated inventions and ideas.
There are also cases in which the achievements of neighbors
are not assimilated but taken over unaltered. In all these
cases an economic and social dependence of the tribe develops. Examples of this kind may be found particularly in
India. The hunting Veddah of Ceylon are certainly a tribe.
Nevertheless their occupations depend upon the steel tools
which they obtain from their skillful neighbors, and their
language and much of their religion is borrowed bodily. The
economic dependence of the Toda is still more striking. They
devote themselves entirely to the care of their herds of
buffaloes and obtain all the other necessities of life from their
neighbors in exchange for milk products. In another way this
dependence is found, at least temporarily, in warlike states
that live on robbery, subject their neighbors and appropriate
the products of their labors. In fact wherever a lively exchange of products of different countries occurs there is more
or less economic and cultural interdependence.

The assignment of the culture of a people to primitiveness
—in the sense of poverty in cultural achievements—requires
the answer to three questions: first how is poverty expressed
in various aspects of culture; second, may the people as a
whole be considered a unit in regard to its cultural pos-
sessions; third, what is the relation of the various aspects of
culture, are all liable to be equally poorly developed or may
some be advanced, others not.

These questions are most easily answered in regard to
technical skill, for every new technical invention is an ad-

dition to earlier achievements. The cases in which a new invention taken up and developed by a people suppresses an earlier valuable technique—as the metal technique supplanted the stone technique—are rather rare. They consist almost regularly of a substitution of a technique more adequate for a desired purpose for a less adequate one. Therefore it would not be difficult to classify cultures in regard to their wealth of inventions if there were any regularity in the order of their occurrences. We have seen that this is not the case. Should we rank a pastoral people as richer in inventions than an agricultural tribe? Are the poor tribes of the Okhotsk Sea less primitive than the artistic Northwest Americans because they have pottery? Is the ancient Mexican more primitive than a poor Negro tribe that happens to possess the art of smelting iron? Such a rigid, absolute valuation of cultures according to the series of inventions possessed by each does not agree with our judgment. We have seen already that these inventions do not represent a sequence in time.

Evidently the inventions alone do not determine our judgment. We value a culture the higher the less the effort required for obtaining the necessities of life and the greater the technical achievements that do not serve the indispensable daily needs. The cultural objects served by the new invention will also influence our judgments. Notwithstanding the exceptional technical skill and ingenuity of the Eskimo we do not value their culture highly, because all their skill and energy is needed in the daily pursuit of game and in procuring protection against the rigor of the climate. There is little room for the play with technique for other purposes. The conditions among Bushmen, Australians and Veddahs are similar to those of the Eskimo. We value the cultures of the Californian Indians a little more highly because they have fairly ample leisure which they employ for perfecting the technique of objects that are not absolutely indispensable. The more varied the play with techniques that furnish the amenities of life the higher we estimate a culture. Wherever spinning, weaving, basketry, carving in wood or bone, artistic stone work, architecture, pottery, metal work occur we do not doubt that an advance over the simplest primitive conditions has been made. Our judgment will not be influenced by the choice of the food, on which the people subsist, whether land animals, fish or vegetable products.

The gifts of nature are not often obtained in sufficient quantities and with such ease that opportunity is given for play. No perfection of his tools enables the hunter to gain without much labor the food-supply necessary for his own support and that of his family, and where the necessities of life, on account of the rigor of the climate or the scarcity of game require his undivided attention there is no time for the playful development of technique. Only in regions in which food is plentiful and obtained with little effort do we find a rich development of playful technique. Regions so favored are parts of the tropics with their wealth of vegetable products, and those rivers and parts of the sea that swarm with fish. In these regions the art of preserving food frees man and gives him leisure for playful activities. In other regions a plentiful supply of food is secured only when man increases the natural food supply artificially, by herding or agriculture. This is the reason why these inventions are intimately associated with a general advance in culture.

Another point should be considered. We may assume that all the earliest technical advances of man were not the result of planned inventions but that small accidental discoveries enriched his technical inventory. Only later these discoveries were recognized as new useful devices. Although planned invention played an inconspicuous part in early times, the discoveries were made by individuals. Therefore it is likely that additions to previous devices occurred the more rapidly the more individuals participated in the particular occupation. We are inclined to see in this one of the principal causes of accelerated cultural change among populous groups that share the same occupations.

Owing to the limitations set by a parsimonious nature the increase in numbers of a hunting tribe remains within well-defined bounds. Only where a plentiful supply of food is always at hand can a population increase rapidly. An abundant supply of fish may offer such opportunity; herding will increase the amount of food-supply, but a large population occupying a continuous area and basing their sustenance on the same kind of occupation is made possible solely by agriculture. For this reason agriculture is the basis of all more advanced technical culture (Carr-Saunders).

From these considerations two further consequences may be drawn.

Evidently the requirements for intellectual work are quite similar to those for technical inventions. There is no opportunity for intellectual work as long as all the time is taken up by the needs of the moment. Here also the culture will be valued the more highly the more fully the people gain time and the more energetically they apply themselves to intellectual pursuits. Intellectual activity is expressed in part in the advances of technique, but more so in the retrospective play with the inner and outer experiences of life. We can establish an objective measure of the advance of culture in this respect also, for we recognize that the continued thoughtful elaboration of the treasure of human experience according to rational forms will result in an increase of knowledge. Here also progress will be the more rapid the more time is devoted to it. The necessary intellectual work leads partly to the elimination of error and partly to a systematization of experience. Both, new approaches to truth, and a more systematic development of knowledge represent a gain. The extent and character of knowledge may be taken in this sense as a means of cultural progress.

Another element of culture is closely related to the advance of playful technique. Skill of technique is a fundamental requirement for the development of art. Decorative art does not exist when people lack the fullest control of their technique and time to play with it. We may infer from this that the same conditions that are important for the development of technique control that of art, and that with the variety of technical skills the variety of art forms will increase.

Before turning to other domains of mental activity we may summarize the results of our inquiry by the statement that in technique, intellectual pursuits and in decorative art definite, objective criteria for the evaluation of cultures exist, and that advances in these fields are closely interrelated because they are dependent upon the general advance of technical skill and insight.

The second question which we proposed to investigate relates to the extent to which the cultural achievements of a people are shared by all its members. In the poorest cultures, in which the whole energy of every individual is required for the acquisition of the barest needs of life, so much so that the obtaining of food and shelter forms the principal content of every activity, thought and emotion of every-day life; and in which no division of labor has developed, the uniformity of the habits of life will be the greater the more one-sided the methods of obtaining food. The Eskimo has to hunt sea mammals in winter, land animals in summer and the thoughts of everyone center around this occupation. This uniformity is not a necessary consequence of the geographic environment of the Eskimo, for even under these simple conditions a division of labor is possible. Thus the Chukchee who live under similar climatic conditions are divided in two economic groups that are somewhat dependent upon each other, the one devoted to reindeer breeding, the other to the hunting of sea mammals. Thus also among hunting people one person devotes himself preferably to the pursuit of one kind of animals, another to that of another one. The mode of life of hunters is not favorable to the formation of individualized groups; but *one* division exists here also as elsewhere, that of man and woman. The man is hunter or fisherman; the woman collects plants and animals that do not run away. She does the housework and takes care of the young children. The whole course of life is filled by these occupations as long as there is no time for playful technique. As soon as opportunity is given for its development differentiations of occupation according to taste and ability develop. We find wood carvers, basket makers, weavers and potters. They may not devote themselves exclusively to one or the other occupation, but they will incline more or less in one direction or another. Then we find also thinkers and poets, for the play of ideas and words exerts its attractions at an early time; probably even at a period when there is not yet opportunity for a playful technique; for although hunting and domestic occupations leave no time for handiwork, the wandering or waiting hunter, and the mother, gathering her food-supply and tending the children have opportunity and leisure for the play of imagination and for brooding thought.

Wherever a certain part of a people develops the mastery of a technique we find them to be creative artists. Where great skill is attained by man in a technique that he alone practices, he is the creative artist. Thus painting and wood carving on the Northwest coast of America are a man's art; while the beautiful pottery of the Pueblos and the basket-weaving of California are woman's arts. The technique dominates artistic life to such an extent that on the Northwest coast woman seems to be void of imagination and vigor. In her weaving and embroidery she can only imitate the art of the men. On the other hand the man among the Pueblo and Californians seems poorly endowed with artistic gifts. When both, men and women each have developed their own techniques to a high state of perfection, two separate styles of art may develop, as among the Tlingit of Alaska, among whom the women make technically perfect baskets ornamented by complex straightlined designs, while the men's art has developed highly stylized animal figures. It is sufficient to point out at this place that the progressive differentiation of activities implies an enrichment of cultural activities.

The differentiation may, however, also produce such one-sidedness in the occupations of some parts of the population that, considered alone, the separate classes are much poorer in culture than a people that has less differentiated activities. This is particularly true whenever in the course of economic development large parts of the population are reduced to the situation in which all their energy is required for the attainment of their daily needs, or when their participation in the productive life becomes impossible, as in our modern civilization. Although in such a case the cultural productivity of the whole people may be of a high order, the psychological evaluation must take into consideration the poverty of culture of large masses.

In the various aspects of culture so far considered greater or loooor achievement, and hence an objective measure of evaluation is almost self-evident; but there are others in which the question as to what is poverty of culture cannot be answered so easily. We have pointed out before that knowledge alone does not constitute richness of culture, but that the coordination of knowledge determines our judgment. However, the evaluation of intellectual coordination of experience, of ethical concepts, artistic form, religious feeling is so subjective in character that an increment of cultural values cannot readily be defined.

Any evaluation of culture means that a point has been chosen towards which changes move and this point is the standard of our modern civilization. With the increase of experience and of systematized knowledge, changes occur which we call progress, although the fundamental ideas may not have undergone any change. The human code of ethics for the closed social group to which a person belongs is everywhere the same: murder, theft, lying, rape are condemned. The difference lies rather in the extent of the social group towards which obligations are felt and the clearer discernment of human suffering; that is in an increase of knowledge.

It is still more difficult to define progress in social organization. The extreme individualist considers anarchy as his ideal, while others believe in voluntary regimentation. Control of the individual by society or subjection to leadership, individual freedom or the attainment of power by the group as a whole may be considered the ideal. Progress can be defined only in regard to the special ideal that we have in mind. There is no absolute progress. During the development of modern civilization the rigidity of the status into which an individual is born, or into which he is brought voluntarily or by compulsion, has lost much of its force, although there is a recrudescence in modern Germany where the status of the Jew is determined not by personal qualities but by birth; or in Russia, Italy and Germany where the status of a person depends upon his party affiliations. In other countries it survives in the status of the citizen and in the marital status. In an objective study of culture the concept of progress should be used with great caution (Boas 1).

In an attempt to reconstruct the forms of thought of primitive man we have to try to follow back the history of ideas as far as may be. By a comparison of the earliest forms discoverable with the forms of modern thought we may gain an understanding of the characteristics of primitive thought. We should make clear to ourselves for how long a period mental life similar to our own may have existed. There are two lines of approach to this problem: prehistory and language. In Egypt and western Asia highly developed cultures existed more than 7000 years ago. Prehistoric data prove that a long period of development must have preceded their rise. This conclusion is corroborated by finds in other parts of the world. Agriculture in Europe is very ancient and the cultural conditions accompanying it are quite analogous to those of modern tribes that have quite complex and cultural patterns. Still earlier, at the end of the glacial period, the Madeleine Culture has a highly developed industry and art which may be compared with that of modern tribes of similar achievement. It seems justifiable to assume that the cultural level of tribes so similar in their technical culture may have been alike also in other respects. We are, therefore, justified in assuming that 15,000 or 20,000 years ago the general cultural activities of man were not different from those found today.

The multiplicity of linguistic forms and the slowness of the development of radical changes in the structure of language also lead to the conclusion that the mental life of man as expressed in language must be of great antiquity.

On account of the permanence of the fundamental forms of languages which are preserved during long periods its study leads us far back into the early history of human thought. For this reason a brief description of some of the essential traits of human speech will be helpful.

In every spoken language a fairly numerous but definite number of articulations may be recognized by the grouping of which linguistic expression is formed. A limited number of articulations and groups of articulations is indispensable for rapid speech. Each articulation corresponds to a sound, and a limited number of sounds is necessary for acoustic understanding. If in a language the number of articulations were unlimited the necessary accuracy of movements needed for rapid speech and the quick recognition of sound complexes would probably never develop. The limitation of the number of movements of articulation and their constant repetition also bring it about that these accurate adjustments become automatic, and that firm association between the articulation and the corresponding sound develops.

It is a fundamental and common trait of articulate speech that the groups of sounds which are uttered serve to convey ideas, and each group of sounds has a fixed meaning. Languages differ not only in the character of their constituent phonetic elements and sound clusters, but also in the groups of ideas that find expression in fixed phonetic groups.

The total number of possible combinations of phonetic elements is unlimited, but only a limited number are in actual use. This implies that the total number of ideas that are expressed by distinct phonetic groups is limited in number. We will call these phonetic groups "word-stems."

Since the total range of personal experience which language serves to express is infinitely varied and its whole scope must be expressed by a limited number of word-stems, an extended classification of experiences must necessarily underlie all articulate speech.

This coincides with a fundamental trait of human thought. In our actual experience no two sense-impressions or emotional states are identical. We classify them, according to their similarities, in wider or narrower groups, the limits of which may be determined from a variety of points of view. Notwithstanding their individual differences, we recognize in our experiences common elements, and consider them as related or even as the same, provided they have a sufficient number of characteristic traits in common. Thus the limitation of the number of phonetic groups expressing distinct ideas is an expression of the psychological fact that many different individual experiences appear to us as representatives of the same category of thought.

This trait of human thought and speech may be compared to the limitation of the whole series of possible articulating movements by selection of a limited number of habitual movements. If the whole mass of concepts, with all their variants, were expressed in language by entirely heterogeneous and unrelated sound-complexes or word-stems, a condition would arise in which closely related ideas would not show their relationship by the corresponding relationship of their sound-symbols, and an infinitely large number of distinct word-stems would be required for expression. If this were the case, the association between an idea and its representative word-stem would not become sufficiently stable to be reproduced automatically without reflection at any given moment. In the same way as the automatic and rapid use of articulations has brought it about that a limited number of articulations only, each with limited variability, and a limited number of sound-clusters, have been selected from the infinitely large range of possible articulations and clusters of articulations, so the infinitely large number of ideas have been reduced by classification to a lesser number, which by constant use have established firm associations, and which can be used automatically.

The behavior of primitive man and of the uneducated demonstrates that such linguistic classifications never rise into consciousness, and that consequently their origin must be sought, not in rational, but in automatic mental processes.

In various cultures these classifications may be founded on fundamentally distinct principles. A knowledge of the categories under which in various cultures experience is classified will, therefore, help to an understanding of early psychological processes.

Differences of principles of classification are found in the domain of sensations. For instance: it has been observed that colors are classified in quite distinct groups according to their similarities, without any accompanying difference in the ability to distinguish shades of color. What we call green and blue is often combined under a term like "gall-color," or yellow and green are combined into one concept which may be named, "color of young leaves." In course of time we have been adding names for additional hues which in earlier times, in part also now in daily life, are not distinguished. The importance of the fact that in speech and thought the word calls forth a different picture, according to the classification of green and yellow or green and blue as one group can hardly be exaggerated.

In the domain of other senses differences of grouping occur. Thus salty and sweet, salty and bitter are sometimes conceived each as one class; or the taste of rancid oil and sugar are classed together.

Another example that illustrates the differences of principles of classification is given by the terminology of consanguinity and affinity. These are so different that it is hardly possible to translate the conceptual content of a term belonging to one system into that of another one. Thus one term may be used for the mother and all her sisters, or even for the mother and all her cousins of all grades so far as they are derived in the female line from the same female ancestor; or our term "brother" may be divided in another system into the groups of elder and younger brother. In this case also the classes cannot have been formed by intent, but they must either have arisen due to customs which combine or differentiate individuals or they may have helped to crystallize the social relation between the members of the consanguineous and affinal groups.

The groups of ideas expressed by specific word-stems show very material differences in different languages, and do not conform by any means to the same principles of classification. To take the example of "water." In Eskimo, "water" is only fresh water for drinking; sea-water is a different term and concept.

As another example of the same kind, the words for "snow" in Eskimo may be given. Here we find one word expressing "snow on the ground"; another one, "falling snow"; a third one, "drifting snow"; a fourth one, "a snowdrift."

In the same language the seal in different conditions is expressed by a variety of terms. One word is the general term for "seal"; another one signifies the "seal basking in the sun"; a third one, a "seal floating on a piece of ice"; not to mention the many names for the seals of different ages and for male and female.

As an example of the manner in which terms that we express by independent words are grouped together under one concept, the Dakota language may be selected. The terms "to kick, to tie in bundles, to bite, to be near to, to pound," are all derived from the common element meaning "to be gripped," which holds them together, while we use distinct words for expressing the various ideas.

It seems fairly evident that the selection of such simple terms must to a certain extent depend upon the chief interests of a people; and where it is necessary to distinguish a certain phenomenon in many aspects, which in the life of the people play each an entirely independent role, many independent words may develop, while in other cases modifications of a single term may suffice.

The differences in principles of classification which we have exemplified by means of a few nouns and verbs may be supported by observations that are not so closely related to linguistic phenomena. Thus certain concepts which we consider as attributes are sometimes conceived as independent objects. The best known case of this kind is that of sickness. For us sickness is a condition of the body. Most primitive people and even members of our own society consider any sickness as an object that enters the body and that may be removed. This is illustrated by the many cases in which it is removed by sucking or manipulation, and by the belief that it may be thrown into an enemy, or imprisoned in a tree, thus preventing its return. Other conditions are sometimes treated in the same way: life, exhaustion, hunger and other states of the body are considered as objects that are in the body or may act upon it from the outside. Thus also the light of the sun is considered as a something that he may put on or lay aside.

The linguistic forms alone would not be a strict proof for this conceptualization of attributes, for we also may say, that life leaves the body, or that a person has a headache. Although with us it is merely a form of speaking we know that the linguistic expression is alive among primitive people and finds expression in many ways in their beliefs and actions.

The anthropomorphic interpretation of nature prevalent among primitives may also be conceived as a type of classification of experience. It seems probable that the analogy between the ability to move of men and animals as well as of some inanimate objects, and their conflicts with the activities of men which could be interpreted as an expression of their will power led to it that all these phenomena were combined under one category. I believe that the origin of religious ideas founded on this concept is just as little founded on reasoning as that of linguistic categories. While, however, the use of language is automatic, so that before the development of a science of language the fundamental ideas never rise into consciousness, this happens frequently in the domain of religion and the subconscious beginning and its speculative development are always interwoven.

On account of the differences in principles of classification every language, from the point of view of another language, may be arbitrary in its classifications; that what appears as a single simple idea in one language may be characterized by a series of distinct word-stems in another.

We have seen before that some kind of classification of expression must be found in every language. This classification of ideas into groups, each of which is expressed by an independent word-stem, makes it necessary that concepts which are not readily rendered by a single stem should be expressed by combinations or by modifications of the elementary stems in accordance with the ultimate ideas to which the particular idea is reduced.

This classification, and the necessity of expressing certain experiences by means of other related ones—which, by limiting one another, define the special idea to be expressed—entail the presence of certain formal elements which determine the relations of the single word-stems. If each idea could be expressed by a single word-stem, languages without form would be possible. Since, however, individual ideas must be expressed by being reduced to a number of wider concepts, the devices for expressing relations become important elements in articulate speech; and it follows that all languages must contain formal elements, the number of which must be the greater, the less the number of elementary word-stems that define special ideas. In a language which commands a very large, fixed vocabulary, the number of formal elements may become quite small.

These elements are not strictly limited to those expressing the logical or psychological relations between words. In almost every language they include certain categories which *must* be expressed. Thus in European languages we cannot express any statement without defining its time relation. A man is, was or is going to be sick. A statement of this type without definition of time cannot be made in English. Only when we extend the meaning of the present over all time, as in the statement "iron is hard" do we include all aspects of time in one form. By contrast to this we have many languages in which no stress is laid upon the difference between past and present, in which this distinction is *not* obligatory. Still others substitute the locative idea for the temporal and *require* that it is stated where an action takes place, near me, near you or near him, so that it is impossible according to the grammatical structure to make a statement indefinite as to place. Again others may require a statement of the source of knowledge, whether a statement is based on own experience, on evidence or on hearsay. Such grammatical concepts as plurality, definiteness or indefiniteness (in the article) may be present or absent. To illustrate: the English sentence "the man killed a deer" contains as obligatory categories "the" definite, "man" singular, "killed" past, "a" indefinite singular. A Kwakiutl Indian would have to say "the" definite, "man," singular location given, p.e. near me visible, "killed" indefinite time, definite or indefinite object, location given, p.e. absent invisible, "deer" singular or plural location given p.e. absent invisible. He must also add the source of his information whether by own experience or by hearsay and an indication whether the man, the deer or the killing have been a previous subject of conversation or thought.

The obligatory categories of expression set off languages sharply from one another.

A few categories that are not familiar to us in European languages may be mentioned. Most Indo-European languages classify objects according to their sex and extend this principle to inanimate objects. Besides this there is a classification according to form which, however, is not expressed by grammatical devices. A house stands, water runs, an insect sits, a country lies. In other languages the classification of objects according to form as long, flat, round, erect, moving is a principle of grammatical classification; or we may find classes such as animate and inanimate, female and non-female, member of tribe and alien. Often they are missing entirely.

Similar conditions are found in the verb. Many languages designate general classes of movement and designate the direction by adverbial elements, like up, down, into, out of.

In others these devices are missing and words like "to go in," and "to go out" must be expressed by separate stems. Examples in which the instrument of action is expressed by a grammatical device have been given before. The manner of movement as in a straight line, circular, zigzag may be expressed by subordinate elements, or the modifications of the verb contained in our conjunctions may be expressed by formal modes.

Such ancient classifications continue to exist in modern languages and we have to think in their forms. The question should be asked therefore whether the form of the language may hinder clear thought. It has been claimed that the conciseness and clearness of thought of a people depend to a great extent upon their language. The ease with which in our modern European languages we express wide abstract ideas by a single term, and the facility with which wide generalizations are cast into the frame of a simple sentence, have been claimed to be one of the fundamental conditions of the clearness of our concepts, the logical force of our thought, and the precision with which we eliminate in our thoughts irrelevant details. Apparently this view has much in its favor. When we compare modern English with some of those Indian languages which are most concrete in their formative expression, the contrast is striking. When we say, "The eye is the organ of sight," the Indian may not be able to form the expression "the eye," but may have to define that the eye of a person or of an animal is meant. Neither may the Indian be able to generalize readily the abstract idea of an eye as the representative of the whole class of objects, but may have to specialize by an expression like "this eye here." Neither may he be able to express by a single term the idea of "organ," but may have to specify it by an expression like "instrument of seeing," so that the whole sentence might assume a form like "an indefinite person's eye is his means of seeing." Still it will be recognized that in this more specific form the general idea may be well expressed. It seems very questionable in how far the restriction of the use of certain grammatical forms can really be conceived as a hindrance to the formulation of generalized ideas. It seems much more likely that the lack of these forms is due to the lack of their need.

Primitive man, when conversing with his fellow man, is not in the habit of discussing abstract ideas. His interests center around the occupations of his daily life; and where philosophic problems are touched upon, they appear either in relation to definite individuals or in the more or less anthropomorphic forms of religious beliefs. Discourses on qualities without connection with the object to which the qualities belong, or of activities or states disconnected from the idea of the actor or the subject being in a certain state, will hardly occur in primitive speech. Thus the Indian will not speak of goodness as such, although he may very well speak of the goodness of a person. He will not speak of a state of bliss apart from the person who is in such a state. He will not refer to the power of seeing without designating an individual who has such power. Thus it happens that in languages in which the idea of possession is expressed by elements subordinated to nouns, all abstract terms appear always with possessive elements. It is, however, perfectly conceivable that an Indian trained in philosophic thought would proceed to free the underlying nominal forms from the possessive elements, and thus reach abstract forms strictly corresponding to the abstract forms of our modern languages. I have made this experiment in one of the languages of Vancouver Island, in which no abstract term ever occurs without its possessive elements. After some discussion, I found it perfectly easy to develop the idea of the abstract term in the mind of the Indian, who stated that the word without a possessive pronoun gives good sense, although it is not used idiomatically. I succeeded, for instance, in this manner, in isolating the terms for "love" and "pity," which ordinarily occur only in possessive forms, like "his love for him" or "my pity for you." That this view is correct, may also be observed in languages in which possessive elements appear as independent forms.

There is also evidence that other specializing elements, which are so characteristic of many Indian languages, may be dispensed with when, for one reason or another, it seems desirable to generalize a term. To use an example of a western language,[1] the idea "to be seated" is almost always expressed

---

[1] The Kwakiutl of Vancouver Island.

with an inseparable suffix expressing the place in which a person is seated, as "seated on the floor of the house, on the ground, on the beach, on a pile of things," or "on a round thing," etc. When, however, for some reason, the idea of the state of sitting is to be emphasized, a form may be used which expresses simply "being in a sitting posture."[2] In this case, also, the device for generalized expression is present; but the opportunity for its application arises seldom, or perhaps never. I think what is true in these cases is true of the structure of every single language. The fact that generalized forms of expression are not used, does not prove inability to form them, but it merely proves that the mode of life of the people is such that they are not required; that they would, however, develop just as soon as needed.

This point of view is also corroborated by a study of the numeral systems of primitive languages. As is well known, languages exist in which the numerals do not exceed three or four. It has been inferred from this that the people speaking these languages are not capable of forming the concept of higher numbers. I think this interpretation of the existing conditions is quite erroneous. People like the South American Indians (among whom these defective numeral systems are found), or like the Eskimo (whose old system of numbers probably did not exceed ten), are presumably not in need of higher numerical expressions, because there are not many objects that they have to count. On the other hand, just as soon as these same people find themselves in contact with civilization, and when they acquire standards of value that have to be counted, they adopt with perfect ease higher numerals from other languages, and develop a more or less perfect system of counting. This does not mean that every individual who in the course of his life has never made use of higher numerals would acquire more complex systems readily; but the tribe as a whole seems always to be capable of adjusting itself to the needs of counting. It must be borne in mind that counting does not become necessary until objects are considered in such generalized form that their individualities are entirely lost sight of. For this reason it is

---

[2] It has, however, the specific meaning "to sit in council."

possible that even a person who owns a herd of domesticated animals may know them by name and by their characteristics, without ever desiring to count them. Members of a war expedition may be known by name, and may not be counted. In short, there is no proof that the lack of the use of numerals is in any way connected with the inability to form the concepts of higher numbers when needed.

If we want to form a correct judgment of the influence that language exerts over thought, we ought to bear in mind that our European languages, as found at the present time, have been moulded to a great extent by the abstract thought of philosophers. Terms like "essence, substance, existence, idea, reality," many of which are now commonly used, are by origin artificial devices for expressing the results of abstract thought. In this way they would resemble the artificial, unidiomatic abstract terms that may be formed in primitive languages.

Thus it would seem that the obstacles to generalized thought inherent in the form of a language are of minor importance only, and that presumably language alone would not prevent a people from advancing to more generalized forms of thinking, if the general state of their culture should require expression of such thought; that under these conditions, the language would be moulded by the cultural state. It does not seem likely, therefore, that there is any direct relation between the culture of a tribe and the language they speak, except insofar as the form of the language will be moulded by the state of culture, but not insofar as a certain state of culture is conditioned by morphological traits of the language.

Since the foundation of human thought lies in the rise into consciousness of the categories in which our experience is classified, the principal difference between the mental processes of primitives and ourselves lies in the fact that we have succeeded by reasoning to develop from the crude, automatically developed categories a better system of the whole field of knowledge, a step which the primitives have not made.

The first impression gained from a study of the beliefs of

primitive man is, that while the perceptions of his senses are excellent, his power of logical interpretation seems to be deficient. I think it can be shown that the reason for this fact is not based on any fundamental peculiarity of the mind of primitive man, but lies, rather, in the character of the traditional ideas by means of which each new perception is interpreted; in other words, in the character of the traditional ideas with which each new perception associates itself determining the conclusions reached.

In our own community a mass of observations and thoughts is transmitted to the child. These thoughts are the result of careful observation and speculation of our present and of past generations; but they are transmitted to most individuals as traditional matter, much the same as folk-lore. The child combines his own perceptions with this whole mass of traditional material, and interprets his observations by its means. It is a mistake to assume that the interpretation made by each civilized individual is a complete logical process. We associate a phenomenon with a number of known facts, the interpretations of which are assumed as known, and we are satisfied with the reduction of a new fact to these previously known facts. For instance, if the average individual hears of the explosion of a previously unknown chemical, he is satisfied to reason that certain materials are known to have the property of exploding under proper conditions, and that consequently the unknown substance has the same quality. On the whole, he would not argue still further, and really try to give a full explanation of the causes of the explosion. In the same way the lay public is inclined to seek in every new unknown epidemic for the micro-organism that causes it, as in former times the cause was sought in miasmas and poisons.

In science also the dominating idea determines the development of theories. Thus everything that exists, animate or inanimate, had to be explained by the theory of survival of the fittest.

The difference in the mode of thought of primitive man and that of civilized man seems to consist largely in the difference of character of the traditional material with which the new perception associates itself. The instruction given to the child of primitive man is not based on centuries of experimentation, but consists of the crude experience of generations. When a new experience enters the mind of primitive man, the same process which we observe among civilized man brings about an entirely different series of associations, and therefore results in a different type of explanation. A sudden explosion will associate itself in his mind, perhaps, with tales which he has heard in regard to the mythical history of the world, and consequently will be accompanied by superstitious fear. The new, unknown epidemic may be explained by the belief in demons that persecute mankind; and the existing world may be explained as the result of transformations, or by objectivation of the thoughts of a creator.

When we recognize that neither among civilized nor among primitive men the average individual carries to completion the attempt at causal explanation of phenomena, but only so far as to amalgamate it with other previous knowledge, we recognize that the result of the whole process depends entirely upon the character of the traditional material. Herein lies the immense importance of folk-lore in determining the mode of thought. Herein lies particularly the enormous influence of current philosophic opinion upon the masses of the people, and the influence of the dominant scientific theory upon the character of scientific work.

It would be vain to try to understand the development of modern science without an intelligent understanding of modern philosophy; it would be vain to try to understand the history of medieval science without a knowledge of medieval theology; and so it is vain to try to understand primitive science without an intelligent knowledge of primitive mythology. "Mythology," "theology" and "philosophy" are different terms for the same influences which shape the current of human thought, and which determine the character of the attempts of man to explain the phenomena of nature. To primitive man—who has been taught to consider the heavenly orbs as animate beings; who sees in every animal a being more powerful than man; to whom the mountains, trees and stones are endowed with life or with special virtues—explanations of phenomena will suggest themselves entirely different from those to which we are accustomed, since we still base our conclusions upon the existence of matter and force as bringing about the observed results. The confusion of the popular mind by the modern theories of relativity, of matter, of causality shows how profoundly we are influenced by ill understood theories.

In scientific inquiries we should always be clear in our own minds of the fact that we always embody a number of hypotheses and theories in our explanations, and that we do not carry the analysis of any given phenomenon to completion. If we were to do so, progress would hardly be possible, because every phenomenon would require an endless amount of time for thorough treatment. We are only too apt, however, to forget entirely the general, and for most of us purely traditional, theoretical basis which is the foundation of our reasoning, and to assume that the result of our reasoning is absolute truth. In this we commit the same error that is being committed, and has always been committed, by all the less educated, including members of primitive tribes. They are more easily satisfied than we are at the present time; but they also assume as true the traditional element which enters into their explanations, and therefore accept as absolute truth the conclusions based on it. It is evident that the fewer the number of traditional elements that enter into our reasoning, and the clearer we endeavor to be in regard to the hypothetical part of our reasoning, the more logical will be our conclusions. There is an undoubted tendency in the advance of civilization to eliminate traditional elements, and to gain a clearer and clearer insight into the hypothetical basis of our reasoning. It is therefore not surprising, that, in the history of civilization, reasoning becomes more and more logical, not because each individual carries out his thought in a more logical manner, but because the traditional material which is handed down to each individual has been thought out and worked out more thoroughly and more carefully. While in primitive civilization the traditional material is doubted and examined by only a very few individuals, the number of thinkers who try to free themselves from the fetters of tradition increases as civilization advances.

An example illustrating this progress and at the same time the slowness of this progress is found in the relations between individuals belonging to different tribes. There are a number of primitive hordes to whom every stranger not a member of the horde is an enemy, and where it is right to damage the enemy to the best of one's power and ability, and if possible to kill him. Such behavior is founded largely on the solidarity of the horde, on the feeling that it is the duty of every member of the horde to destroy all possible enemies. Therefore every person not a member of the horde must be considered as belonging to a class entirely distinct from the members of the horde, and is treated accordingly. We can trace the gradual broadening of the feeling of fellowship during the advance of civilization. The feeling of fellowship in the horde expands to the feeling of unity of the tribe, to a recognition of bonds established by a neighborhood of habitat, and further on to the feeling of fellowship among members of nations. This seems to be the limit of the ethical concept of fellowship of man which we have reached at the present time. When we analyze the strong feeling of nationality which is so potent at the present time and which has superseded the local interests of lesser units, we recognize that it consists largely in the idea of the preeminence of that community whose member we happen to be—in the preeminent value of its bodily build, its language, of its customs and traditions, and in the belief that all external influences that threaten these traits are hostile and must be combated, not only for the justifiable purpose of preserving its peculiarities but even with the wish to impose them upon the rest of the world. The feeling of nationality as here expressed, and the feeling of solidarity of the horde, are of the same order, although modified by the gradual expansion of the idea of fellowship; but the ethical point of view which makes it justifiable at the present time to increase the well-being of one nation at the cost of another, the tendency to value our own form of civilization as higher—not as dearer to our hearts—than that of the whole rest of mankind, are the same as those which prompt the actions of primitive man, who considers every stranger as an enemy, and who is not satisfied until the enemy is killed. It is somewhat difficult for us to recognize that the value which we attribute to our own civilization is due to the fact that we participate in this civilization, and that it has been controlling all our actions since the time of our birth; but it is certainly conceivable that there may be other civilizations, based perhaps on different traditions and on a different equilibrium of emotion and reason which are of no less value than ours, although it may be impossible for us to appreciate their values without having grown up under their influence. The general theory of valuation of human activities, as developed by anthropological research, teaches us a higher tolerance than the one we now profess.

Chapter 12

The Emotional Associations of Primitives

AFTER WE HAVE thus seen that a large number of traditional elements enter into the reasoning of both primitive man and civilized man, we are better prepared to understand some of the more special typical differences in their ways of thinking.

A trait of primitive life that early attracted the attention of investigators is the occurrence of close associations between mental activities that appear to us as entirely disparate. In primitive life, religion and science; music, poetry and dance; myth and history; fashion and ethics—appear inextricably interwoven. We may express this general observation also by saying that primitive man views every action not only as adapted to its main object, every thought related to its main end, as we should perceive them, but that he associates them with other ideas, often of a religious or at least of a symbolic nature. Thus he gives them a higher significance than they seem to us to deserve. Every taboo is an example of such associations of apparently trifling actions with ideas that are so sacred that a deviation from the customary mode of performance creates the strongest emotions of abhorrence. The interpretation of ornaments as charms, the symbolism of decorative art, are other examples of association of aspects of behavior that, on the whole, are foreign to our mode of thought.

In order to make clear the point of view from which these phenomena seem to fall into an orderly array, we will investigate whether all vestiges of similar forms of thought have disappeared from our civilization.

In our intense life, which is devoted to activities requiring the full application of our reasoning powers and a repression of emotional life, we have become accustomed to a cold, matter-of-fact view of our actions, of the incentives that lead to them, and of their consequences. It is not necessary, however, to go far afield to find minds open to different moods. If those among us who move in the midst of the current of our quickly pulsing life do not look beyond their rational motives and aims, others who stand by in quiet contemplation recognize in it the reflection of an ideal world that they have built up in their own consciousness. To the artist the outer world is a symbol of the beauty he feels; to the fervent religious mind it is a symbol of the transcendental truth which gives form to his thought. Instrumental music that the one enjoys as a work of purely musical art calls forth in the mind of another a group of definite concepts that are connected with the musical themes and their treatment only by the similarity of the emotional states they evoke. In fact, the manner in which different individuals react to the same stimulus, the variety of associations elicited in their minds, are so self-evident that they hardly call for special remarks.

Most important for the purpose of our investigation is the observation that all of us who live in the same society react to certain stimuli in the same way without being able to express the reasons for our actions. A good example of what I refer to are breaches of social etiquette. A mode of behavior that does not conform to the customary manners, but differs from them in a striking way, creates, on the whole, unpleasant emotions; and it requires a determined effort on our part to make it clear to ourselves that such behavior does not conflict with moral standards. Among those who are not trained in courageous and rigid thought, the confusion between traditional etiquette—so-called good manners—and moral conduct is habitual. In certain lines of conduct the association between traditional etiquette and ethical feeling is so close, that even a vigorous thinker can hardly emancipate himself from it. This was true until very recent times, of acts that were considered breaches of modesty. The most cursory review of the history of costume shows that what was considered modest at one time has been immodest at other times. The custom of habitually covering parts of the body has at all times led to the strong feeling that exposure of such parts is immodest. This feeling of propriety is so erratic, that a costume that is appropriate on one occasion may be considered opprobrious on other occasions; as, for instance, a low-cut evening dress in a street-car during business hours, or a modern bathing suit in a formal assembly. What kind of exposure is felt as immodest depends always upon fashion. It is quite evident that fashion is not dictated by modesty, but that the historical development of costume is determined by a variety of causes. Nevertheless fashions are typically associated with the feeling of modesty, so that an unwonted exposure excites the unpleasant feelings of impropriety. There is no conscious reasoning why the one form is proper, the other improper; but the feeling is aroused directly by the contrast with the customary. Many of us will feel instinctively the strong resistance that we should have to overcome, even in a different society, if required to perform an action that we are accustomed to consider as immodest, and the feelings that would be excited in our minds if we were thrown into a society in which the standards of modesty differed from our own.

Even setting aside modesty, we find a variety of reasons which make certain styles of dress appear improper. To appear in the fashion of our forefathers of two centuries ago would expose us to ridicule. To see a man wear a hat in company indoors nettles us: it is considered rude. To wear a hat in church or at a funeral would cause more vigorous resentment, on account of the greater emotional value of the feelings concerned. A certain tilt of the hat, although it may be very comfortable to the wearer, would stamp him at once as an uneducated brute. Novelties in costume opposed to current fashion may hurt our aesthetic feelings, no matter how bad the taste of the prevailing fashion may be.

Another example will make clear what I mean. It will readily be recognized that most of our table manners are purely traditional, and cannot be given any adequate explanation. To smack one's lips is considered bad style, and may excite feelings of disgust; while among some Indian tribes it would be considered bad taste not to smack one's lips when invited to dinner, because it would suggest that the guest does not enjoy his meal. Both for the Indian and for ourselves the constant performance of these actions which constitute good table manners make it practically impossible to act otherwise.

An attempt to act differently would not only be difficult on account of the lack of adjustment of muscular motions, but also on account of the strong emotional resistance that we should have to overcome. The emotional displeasure is also released when we see others act contrary to custom. To eat with people having table manners different from our own excites feelings of displeasure which may rise to such an intensity as to cause qualmishness. Here, also, explanations are often given which are probably based solely on attempts to explain the existing manners, but which do not represent their historical development. We often hear that it is improper to eat with a knife because it might cut the mouth; but I doubt very much if this consideration has anything to do with the development of the custom, for the use of the fork is recent and the older type of sharp steel forks might as easily hurt the mouth as the blade of the knife.

It may be well to exemplify the characteristics of our opposition to unwonted actions by a few additional examples, which will help to clear up the mental processes that lead us to formulate the reasons for our conservatism.

One of the cases in which the development of such alleged reasons for behavior is best traced is that of the taboo. Although we ourselves have hardly any definite taboos, our failure to use certain animals for food might easily appear as such to an outsider. Supposing an individual accustomed to eating dogs should inquire among us for the reason why we do not eat dogs, we could only reply that it is not customary; and he would be justified in saying that dogs are tabooed among us, just as much as we are justified in speaking of taboos among primitive people. If we were hard pressed for reasons, we should probably base our aversion to eating dogs or horses on the seeming impropriety of eating animals that live with us as our friends. On the other hand, we are not accustomed to eat larvae and we should probably decline to eat them from feelings of disgust. Cannibalism is so much abhorred that we find it difficult to convince ourselves that it belongs to the same class of aversions as those mentioned before. The fundamental concept of the sacredness of human life, and the fact that many animals will not eat others of the same species, set off cannibalism as a custom by itself, considered as one of the most horrible aberrations of human nature. In these three groups of aversions, disgust is probably the first feeling present in our minds, by which we react against the suggestion of partaking of these kinds of food. We account for our disgust by a variety of reasons, according to the groups of ideas with which the suggested act is associated in our minds. In one case there is no special association, and we are satisfied with the simple statement of disgust. In another the most important reason seems to be an emotional one, although we may feel inclined, when questioned regarding the reasons of our dislike, to bring forward also habits of the animals in question that seem to justify our aversion. In the third case the immorality of cannibalism would stand forth as the one sufficient reason.

Other examples are the numerous customs that had originally a religious or semi-religious aspect, and which are continued and explained by more or less certain utilitarian theories. Such are the customs relating to marriages in the incest group. While the extent of the incest group has undergone material changes, the abhorrence of marriages inside the existing group is the same as ever; but instead of religious laws, a utilitarian concept, the fear of unhealthy offspring owing to intermarriage of close relatives, is brought forward as the reason for our feelings. People affected with loathsome diseases were once shunned because they were believed to be stricken by God, while at present the same avoidance is due to the fear of contagion. The disuse into which profanity has fallen in English was first due to religious reaction, but has come to be simply a question of good manners.

This emotional reaction is equally intense when points of view are involved that run counter to the opinions of the time. They are opposed most violently when the affective value of the current ideas is great, when these are part and parcel of ourselves, and when the new ideas conflict with the fundamental attitudes that have been instilled in us since our earliest youth, or that have become identified with those aims to which we devote our lives. The violence of opposition to heresy as well as to new social and economic doctrines can be understood on this basis alone. The reasons given for opposition are in most cases rationalizations for an emotional resistance.

It is important to note that in all the cases mentioned the rationalistic explanation of the opposition to a change is based on that group of concepts with which the excited emotions are intimately connected. In the case of costume, reasons are adduced why the new style is improper; in the case of heresy, proof is given that the new doctrine is an attack against eternal truth; and so with all the others.

A close introspective analysis shows these reasons to be only attempts to interpret our feelings of displeasure; that our opposition is not by any means dictated by conscious reasoning, but primarily by the emotional effect of the new idea which creates a dissonance with the habitual.

In all these cases the custom is obeyed so often and so regularly that the habitual act becomes automatic; that is to say, its performance is ordinarily not combined with any degree of consciousness. Consequently the emotional value of these actions is very slight. It is noteworthy, however, that the more automatic an action, the more difficult it is to perform the opposite action, that it requires a strong effort to do so, and that ordinarily the opposite action is accompanied by marked feelings of displeasure. It may also be observed that to see the unusual action performed by another person excites intense attention, and causes feelings of displeasure. Thus it happens that when an infraction of the customary occurs, all the groups of ideas with which the action is associated are brought into consciousness. A dish of dog's meat would bring up all the ideas of companionship; a cannibal feast, all the social principles that have become our second nature. The more automatic any series of activities or a certain form of thought has become, the greater is the conscious effort required for breaking away from the old habit of acting and thinking, and the greater also the displeasure, or at least the surprise, produced by an innovation. The antagonism against it is a reflex action accompanied by emotions not due to conscious speculation. When we become conscious of this emotional reaction, we endeavor to interpret it by a process of reasoning. This reason must be based necessarily on the ideas which rise into consciousness as soon as a break in the established custom occurs; in other words, our rationalistic explanation will depend upon the character of the associated ideas.

These tendencies are also the basis of the success of fanatics and of skillfully directed propaganda. The fanatic who plays on the emotions of the masses and supports his teachings by fictitious reasons, and the unscrupulous demagogue who arouses slumbering hatreds and designedly invents reasons that give to the gullible mass a plausible excuse to yield to the excited passions make use of the desire of man to give a rational excuse for actions that are fundamentally based on unreasoning emotion. Pope Urban II succeeded in his appeal to religious devotion by the pretext that the sacred land was in the hands of the infidel, although the driving forces were largely political and economic. Peter the Hermit took up this issue as a fanatic and carried it all over Europe. In the World War propaganda based on alleged cruelties was used to inflame the people. Hitler and his entourage use race prejudice for the purpose of furthering their own purposes. He as well as Houston Stewart Chamberlain admit cynically that a distortion of truth, if it serves to bolster up their aims, is permissible.

All these examples illustrate that even in our civilization popular thought is primarily directed by emotion, not by reason; and that the reasoning injected into emotionally determined behavior depends upon a variety of conditions and is, therefore, in course of time, variable.

We will now turn to a consideration of analogous phenomena in primitive life. Here the dislike of anything deviating from the custom of the land is even more strongly marked than in our civilization. If it is not the custom to sleep in a house with feet turned towards the fire, a violation of this custom is dreaded and avoided. If in a certain society members of the same clan do not intermarry, the most deepseated abhorrence against such unions will arise. It is not necessary to multiply examples, for it is a well-known fact that the more primitive a people, in the more varied ways it is bound by customs regulating the conduct of daily life in all its details. This does not imply that every individual adheres equally rigidly to every usage; characteristic is the multiplicity of habitual customs that control life. We are justified in concluding from our own experience, that as among ourselves, so among primitive tribes, the resistance to a deviation from firmly established customs is due to an emotional reaction, not to conscious reasoning. This does not preclude the possibility that the first special act, which became in course of time customary, may have been due to a conscious mental process; but it seems likely that many customs came into being without any conscious activity. Their development must have been of the same kind as that of the categories which are reflected in the morphology of languages, and which can never have been known to the speakers of these languages. For instance, Cunow's theory of the origin of Australian social systems is well conceivable, although not the only possible one. Some tribes are divided into four exogamic groups. The laws of exogamy demand that a member of the first group must marry a member of the second group, and a member of the third group one of the fourth group. Cunow explains these customs by showing that when custom provides that a man in a tribe that is divided into two exogamic units, and in which only members of the same generation are allowed to intermarry, conditions like those found in Australia will naturally develop, if each group has a name, and one set of names is used for the odd, and another set of names for the even generations. If we designate the two tribal divisions by the letters A and B, the generations by "odd" and "even," the names of the four divisions would be A odd, A even, B odd, B even, and in marriages in which is placed first the sex that determines the group to which the offspring belongs we find that—

A odd must marry B odd, and his children are A even
B odd   "   "   A odd, "   "   "   " B even
A even "   "   B even, "   "   "   " A odd
B even "   "   A even, "   "   "   " B odd

We may suppose that originally each generation kept to themselves, and therefore marriages between members of two succeeding generations were impossible, because only marriageable men and women of one generation came into contact. Later on, when the succeeding generations were not so diverse in age, and their social separation ceased, the custom had been established, and did not lapse with the changed conditions.

There are a number of cases in which it is at least conceivable that the older customs of a people under a new surrounding, develop into taboos. I think, for instance, that it is not unlikely that the Eskimo taboo forbidding the use of caribou and of seal on the same day may be due to the alternating inland and coast life of the people. When they hunt inland, they have no seals, and consequently can eat only caribou. When they hunt on the coast, they have no caribou, and consequently can eat only seal. The simple fact that in one season only caribou can be eaten, and that in another season only seal can be eaten, may have led to a resistance to a change of this custom; so that from the fact that for a long period the two kinds of meat could not be eaten at the same time, the law developed that the two kinds of meat must not be eaten at the same time. I think it is also likely that the fish taboo of some of our southwestern tribes may be due to the fact that the tribes lived for a long time in a region where no fish was available, and that the impossibility of obtaining fish developed into the custom of not eating fish. These hypothetical cases make it clear that the unconscious origin of customs is quite conceivable, although of course not necessary. However, it seems certain that even when there has been a conscious reasoning that led to the establishment of a custom, it soon ceased to be so and instead we find a direct emotional resistance to an infraction of the custom.

Other actions which are considered proper or improper are continued solely through the force of habit; and no reasons are assigned for their occurrence, although the reaction against an infringement of the custom may be strong. If among the Indians of Vancouver Island it is bad form for a young woman of nobility to open her mouth wide and to eat fast, a deviation from this custom would also be deeply felt, in this case as an impropriety which would seriously damage the social standing of the culprit. The same group of feelings are concerned when a member of the nobility, as in

Europe, marries below his or her station. In other, more trifling cases, the overstepping of the boundaries of custom merely exposes the offender to ridicule, on account of the impropriety of the act. All these cases belong psychologically to the same group of emotional reactions against breaks with established automatic habits.

It might seem that in primitive society opportunity could hardly be given to bring into consciousness the strong emotional resistance against infractions of customs, because they are on the whole rigidly adhered to. There is one feature of social life, however, that tends to keep the conservative attachment to customary actions before the minds of the people. This is the education of the young. The child in whom the habitual behavior of his surroundings has not yet developed will acquire much of it by unconscious imitation. In many cases, however, it will act in a way different from the customary manner, and will be corrected by its elders. Any one familiar with primitive life will know that the children are constantly exhorted to follow the example of their elders, and every collection of carefully recorded traditions contains numerous references to advice given by parents to children, impressing them with the duty to observe the customs of the tribe. The greater the emotional value of a custom, the stronger will be the desire to inculcate it in the minds of the young. Thus ample opportunity is given to bring the resistance against infractions into consciousness.

These conditions exert a strong influence upon the development and conservation of customs; for, as soon as the breach of custom is raised into consciousness, occasions must arise when people, either led by children's questions or following their own bent to speculation, find themselves confronted with the fact that certain ideas exist for which they cannot give any explanation except that they are there. The desire to understand one's own feelings and actions, and to get a clear insight into the secrets of the world, manifests itself at a very early time, and it is therefore not surprising that man in all stages of culture begins to speculate on the motives of his own actions.

We have seen before, that there need not be a conscious motive for many of these, and for this reason the tendency develops to discover the motives that may determine our customary behavior. This is the reason why, in all stages of culture, customary actions are made the subject of secondary explanations that have nothing to do with their historical origin, but which are inferences based upon the general knowledge possessed by the people. The existence of such secondary interpretations of customary actions is one of the most important anthropological phenomena, hardly less common in our own than in more primitive society. It is a common observation that we desire or act first, and then try to justify our desires and our actions. When, on account of our early bringing-up, we act with a certain political party, most of us are not prompted by a clear conviction of the justice of the principles of our party, but we do so because we have been taught to respect it as the right party to which to belong. Then only do we justify our standpoint by trying to convince ourselves that these principles are the correct ones. Without reasoning of this kind, the stability and geographical distribution of political parties as well as of church denominations would be entirely unintelligible. This view is corroborated by the mental agonies that accompany the freeing of the mind from traditional opinions that have a sentimental value. A candid examination of our own minds convinces us that the average man, in by far the majority of cases, does not determine his actions by reasoning, but that he first acts, and then justifies or explains his acts by such secondary considerations as are current among us.

We have discussed here that class of actions in which a break with the customary brings into consciousness their emotional value and releases a strong resistance to change, secondarily explained by reasons that forbid a change. We have also seen that the traditional material with which man operates determines the particular type of explanatory idea that associates itself with the emotional state of mind. Primitive man generally bases these explanations of his customs on concepts that are intimately related to his general views of the constitution of the world. Some mythological idea may be considered the basis of a custom or of the avoidance of certain actions, or the custom may be given a symbolic significance, or it may merely be connected with the fear of ill luck. Evidently this last class of explanations is identical with those of many superstitions that linger among us.

The essential result of this inquiry is the conclusion that the origin of customs of primitive man must not be looked for in rational processes. Most investigators who have tried to clear up the history of customs and taboos express the view that their origin lies in speculations on the relations between man and nature; that to primitive man the world is filled with objects of superhuman power and with agencies which may harm man at the slightest provocation; that the careful treatment of such objects and attempts to avoid conflict with these powers dictate the innumerable superstitious regulations. The impression is given that the habits and opinions of primitive man have been formed by conscious reasoning. It seems evident, however, that this whole line of thought would remain consistent if it were assumed that the processes arise without conscious reasoning from the classification of sense experience. Even if so considered the important function played in their formation by emotional drives would fail to receive its proper weight.

The theory needs extension, because it would seem that many customs and beliefs may have arisen without any kind of active participation of the mind, such as became established by the general conditions of life, and came into consciousness as soon as these conditions changed. I do not doubt at all that there are cases in which customs originated by more or less conscious reasoning; but I am just as certain that others originated without it, and that our theories should cover both points.

The study of primitive life exhibits a large number of associations of a different type, which are not so easily explained. Certain patterns of associated ideas may be recognized in all types of culture.

Somber colors and depressed feelings are closely connected in our minds, although not in those of peoples of foreign culture. Noise seems inappropriate in a place of sadness, although among primitive people the loud wail of the mourner is the natural expression of grief. Decorative art serves to please the eye, yet a design like the cross has retained its symbolic significance.

On the whole, such associations between groups of ideas apparently unrelated are rare in civilized life. That they once existed is shown by historical evidence as well as by survivals in which the old ideas have perished, although the outer forms remain. In primitive culture these associations occur in great numbers. In discussing them we may begin with examples that have their analogues in our own civilization, and which therefore are readily intelligible to us.

The most extended domain of such customs is that of ritual. Accompanying important actions numerous stated ritual forms occur which have no relation to the action itself but are formally applied in many situations. For our present consideration their early meaning is irrelevant. Many are so old that their origin must be looked for in antiquity or even in prehistoric times. In our day the domain of ritual is restricted, but in primitive culture it pervades the whole life. Not a single action of any importance can be performed that is not accompanied by prescribed rites of more or less elaborate form. It has been proved in many cases that rites are more stable than their explanations; that they symbolize different ideas among different people and at different times. The diversity of rites is so great, and their occurrence so universal, that here the greatest possible variety of associations is found.

This point of view may be applied to many of the most fundamental traits of primitive life, the rise and history of which become more readily intelligible when considered as due to associations between heterogeneous thoughts and activities.

In our modern society, except among the adherents of the still flourishing astrology, the consideration of cosmic phenomena is constantly associated with the efforts to give adequate explanations for them, based on the principle of causality. In primitive society the consideration of the same phenomena leads to a number of typical associations different from our own, but occurring with remarkable regularity among tribes of the most remote parts of the world. An excellent instance of this kind is the regular association of observations relating to cosmic phenomena with purely human happenings; in other words, the occurrence of nature myths. The characteristic trait of nature myths is the association between the observed cosmic events and what might be called a novelistic plot based on the form of social life with which people are familiar. The plot as such might as well develop as a tale of human adventure. Its association with the heavenly bodies, the thunderstorm or the wind make it a nature myth. The distinction between folk-tale and nature myth lies in the association of the latter with cosmic phenomena. This association does not naturally develop in modern society. If it is still found every now and then, it is based on the survival of the traditional nature myth. In primitive society, on the other hand, it is found constantly. The investigation of the reason for this association is an attractive problem, the solution of which can only in part be surmised.

A number of other examples will demonstrate that the kind of association here referred to is quite common in primitive life. An excellent instance is furnished by certain characteristics of primitive decorative art. With us almost the sole object of decorative art is aesthetic. We wish to beautify the objects that are decorated. We recognize a certain appropriateness of decorative motives in accordance with their emotional effect and the uses to which the decorated objects are to be put. In primitive life the conditions are quite different. Extended investigations on decorative art in all continents have proved that very commonly the decorative design is readily given a symbolic significance. Among many primitive tribes some sort of explanation for the designs in use can be given. In some cases the symbolic significance may be exceedingly weak, perhaps merely a name, sometimes it is highly developed. The triangular and quadrangular designs of our Plains Indians, for instance, often convey symbolic meanings. They may be records of warlike deeds, they may be prayers, or they may in some way convey other ideas relating to the supernatural. It would almost seem that among many primitive tribes decorative art for its own sake does not exist. The only analogues in modern decorative art are such as the use of the flag, of the cross or of emblems of secret societies for decorative purposes; but their frequency is insignificant as compared to the general symbolic tendencies of primitive art. We have here another type of association characteristic of primitive society and quite different from that found among ourselves. Among primitive people the aesthetic motive is combined with the symbolic, while in modern life the aesthetic motive is either quite independent or associated with utilitarian ideas. Modern symbolic art seems ineffectual because in our culture we have no generally recognized style of symbolism, and an individual symbolism remains unintelligible for everyone except its creator.

On the North Pacific coast of America the animal design, which is found in many other parts of the world, has associated itself firmly with the totemic idea, and has led to an unparalleled application of animal motives. This may also have helped to preserve the realistic character of this art (Boas 13). Among the Sioux the high valuation of military prowess, and the habit of exploiting deeds of war before the tribe, have been the causes that led the men to associate the decoration on their garments with events of war; so that among them a military symbolism has developed, while the women of the same tribe explain the same design in an entirely different manner (Wissler). In this last case we have no particular difficulty in following the line of thought that leads to the association between forms of decoration and military ideas, although in general our mind requires a much more conscious effort than that of primitive man. The very fact of the widespread occurrence of decorative symbolism shows that this association must establish itself automatically and without conscious reasoning.

The objection might be raised that what we have called associations are in reality survivals of much older units; that every nature myth was in its origin a tale attached to natural phenomena; that decorative art served the expression of definite ideas; or that the imagination of primitive man saw natural phenomena in the form of human actions and human fate, and that the ancient representative forms became symbolic in course of time. Since, according to our previous arguments we conclude that the mental activities of all primitives are essentially alike, it would follow that these tendencies can still be observed.

Experience shows that such an original unity underlying mythical tales or decorative art does not exist. There is no firm relation between the contents of a tale and the natural phenomenon which it represents. Neither is there such a relation between decorative form and its symbolism.

This is brought out clearly by the study of the migration of tales and of art styles. The symbolic character of decorative art does not hinder the spread of designs or of a whole style from one people to another. This has been the case, for instance, among the tribes of our Northwestern Plains, who have borrowed much of their art from their more southern neighbors; but they have not adopted at the same time its symbolical interpretations. They invented interpretations of their own.

An example of this kind is the isosceles triangle from the base of which a number of short vertical lines descend. In the arid southwest this is interpreted as a cloud from which the desired rain descends; among the mobile tribes of the Plains it is a tent with its pegs holding down the tent cover; among others a mountain at the foot of which there are a number of springs; on the coast of Alaska it represents the foot of a bear with its claws. Similar examples may be given from other regions, such as the spirals of Siberia which are reinterpreted as birds' heads by the Gilyak (Laufer 1), and as hoofs of horses by the Yakut (Jochelson 1). The engraved Y ornament of the Eskimo has been changed into a whale's tail by broadening its base and arms, or into a flower by adding small circles at the points of the arms.

I presume the explanation of borrowed patterns was the result of a process which began when the patterns were found pleasing and were imitated. According to the prevailing culture interests an interpretation was expected and found in accord with the type of thought of the tribe. In all these cases the pattern must be older than its interpretation.

Primitive mythology offers a similar example. The same kind of tales are current over enormous areas, but the mythological use to which they are put is locally quite different. Thus an ordinary adventure relating to the exploits of some animal may sometimes be made use of to explain some of its particular characteristics, at other times it is made to account for the origin of certain customs, or of constellations in the sky. T. T. Waterman has collected many data of this kind. The story of the woman who became the mother of a litter of dogs is a typical example. Among the Eskimo it explains the origin of the Europeans; in southern Alaska that of the Milky Way, the rainbow and of thunderstorms; on Vancouver Island that of a number of reefs, and among still others the origin of the tribe. In the interior of British Columbia it accounts for the origin of a taboo; farther north for the origin of Orion and for the characteristics of several kinds of animals; among the Blackfoot the origin of the dog society, and among the Arapaho why the dog is the friend of man. Examples of this kind may be found in great numbers. There is not the slightest doubt in my mind that the tale as such is older than its mythological significance. The characteristic feature of the development of the nature myth is, first, that the tale has associated itself with attempts to explain cosmic conditions (this has been referred to before); and, secondly, that when primitive man became conscious of the cosmic problem, he ransacked the entire field of his knowledge until he happened to find something that could be fitted to the problem in question, giving an explanation satisfactory to his mind. While the classification of concepts, the types of association and the resistance to change of automatic acts developed unconsciously, the secondary explanations are due to conscious reasoning.

I will give still another example of a form of association characteristic of primitive society. In modern society, social organization, including the grouping of families, is essentially based on blood-relationship and on the social functions performed by each individual. Except insofar as the Church concerns itself with birth, marriage and death, there is no connection between social organization and religious belief. These conditions are quite different in primitive society, where we find an inextricable association of ideas and customs relating to society and to religion. As in art form tends to associate itself with ideas entirely foreign to it, so the social unit tends to associate itself with various impressions of nature, particularly with the divisions of the animal world. This form of association seems to me the fundamental trait of totemism as found among many American tribes, as well as in Australia, Melanesia and in Africa. I have mentioned before its characteristic trait, which consists in a peculiar connection that is believed to exist between a certain class of objects, generally animals, and a certain social group, a relation valid for one group, but replaced in others by another one, different in content, but identical in form. Frequently the social group related to the same totem consists of real or supposed blood-relatives. On account of this marriage regulations are frequently involved in the customs and beliefs relating to totemism. Furthermore the relation of man to the related class of objects or animals is often given a religious significance, so that to each group are ascribed certain supernatural powers or disabilities connected with their totem. That such feelings are not by any means improbable, or even rare, is sufficiently shown by a psychological analysis of the attitudes of the European high nobility, or by the national emotions in their pronounced form. It is not at all difficult to understand how an overbearing enthusiasm of self-appreciation of a community may become a powerful emotion or a passion, which, on account of the lack of rational explanation of the world, will tend to associate the members of the community with all that is good and powerful. Psychologically, therefore, we may compare totemism with those familiar forms of society in which certain social classes claim privileges by the grace of God, or where the patron saint of a community favors its members with his protection. Notwithstanding these analogous forms it is difficult for us to understand the wealth of forms of associations occurring in primitive society, for this type of thought has lost much of its force in our civilization.

The way in which such associations arise is indicated, in part at least, by developments of modern art. The programmatic music of modern times is in sharp contrast to the music of the eighteenth century. The latter was a music of formal beauty. It existed essentially for the sake of music alone or of music and dance. The former associates the musical elements with elements taken from experiences entirely foreign to the domain of music.

All these considerations indicate that the separation of these complex phenomena is not due to a disintegration of ancient units, that for instance art and symbolism, narrative and myth were by origin indissolubly united, that rather the various groups of ideas and activities always existed interconnected, but that their associations were in a constant state of flux.

However these associations may have been brought about, there is no doubt that they do exist, and that, psychologically considered, they are of the same character as those previously discussed, and that the rationalizing mind of man soon lost the historic thread, and reinterpreted the established customs in conformity with the general trend of thought of his culture. We are therefore justified in concluding that these customs must also be studied by the historical method, because their present associations are not likely to be original, but rather secondary.

It is perhaps venturesome to discuss at the present moment the origin of these types of association; yet it may be admissible to dwell on a few of the most generalized facts which seem to characterize primitive culture as compared to civilization. From our point of view, the striking features of primitive culture are the great number of associations of entirely heterogeneous groups of phenomena, such as natural phenomena and emotional states, social groupings and religious concepts, decorative art and symbolic interpretation. These tend to disappear with the approach to our present civilization, although a careful analysis reveals the persistence of many, and the tendency of each automatic action to establish its own associations according to the mental situations in which it regularly occurs. One of the great changes that has taken place may perhaps best be expressed by saying that in primitive culture the impressions of the outer world are associated intimately with subjective impressions, which they call forth regularly, but which are determined largely by the social surroundings of the individual. Gradually it is recognized that these connections are more uncertain than others that remain the same for all mankind, and in all forms of social surroundings; and thus sets in the gradual elimination of one subjective association after another, which culminates in the scientific method of the present day. We may express this also by saying that when we have our attention directed to a certain concept which has a whole fringe of incident concepts related to it, *we* at once associate it with that group which is represented by the category of causality. When the same concept appears in the mind of primitive man, it associates itself with those concepts related to it by emotional states.

If this is true, then the associations of the primitive mind are heterogeneous, and ours homogeneous and consistent only from our own point of view. To the mind of primitive man, only his own associations can be rational. Ours must appear to him just as heterogeneous as his own to us, because the bond between the phenomena of the world, as it appears after the emotional associations have been eliminated by increasing knowledge, does not exist for *him*, while we can no longer feel the subjective associations that govern his mind.

This peculiarity of association is also another expression of the conservatism of primitive culture and the changeability of many features of our civilization. We tried to show that the resistance to change is largely due to emotional sources, and that in primitive culture emotional associations are the prevailing type: hence resistance against the new. In our civilization, on the other hand, many actions are performed merely as means to a rational end. They do not enter sufficiently deeply into our minds to establish connections which would give them emotional values: hence our readiness to change. We recognize, however, that we cannot remodel, without serious emotional resistance, any of the fundamental lines of thought and action which are determined by our early education, and which form the subconscious basis of all our activities. This is evinced by the attitude of civilized communities towards religion, politics, art and the fundamental concepts of science.

In the average individual among primitive tribes, reasoning cannot overcome this emotional resistance, and it therefore requires a destruction of the existing emotional associations by more powerful means to bring about a change. This may be effected by some event which stirs up the mind of the people to its depths, or by economic and political changes against which resistance is impossible. In civilization there is a constant readiness to modify those activities that have no emotional value. This is true not only of activities designed to meet practical ends, but also of others that have lost their associations, and that have become subject to fashion. There remain however, others which are retained with great tenacity, and which hold their own against reasoning, because their strength lies in their emotional values. The history of the progress of science yields example after example of the power of resistance belonging to old ideas, even after increasing knowledge of the world has undermined the ground on which they were erected. Their overthrow is not brought about until a new generation has arisen, to whom the old is no longer dear and near.

Besides this, there are a thousand activities and modes of thought that constitute our daily life—of which we are not conscious at all until we come into contact with other types of life, or until we are prevented from acting according to our custom—that cannot in any way be claimed to be more reasonable than others, and to which, nevertheless, we cling. These, it would seem, are hardly less numerous in civilized than in primitive culture, because they constitute the whole series of well-established habits according to which the necessary actions of ordinary every-day life are performed, and which are learned less by instruction than by imitation.

We may also express these conclusions in another form. While in logical processes we find a decided tendency with the development of civilization to eliminate traditional elements, no such marked decrease in the force of traditional elements can be found in our activities. These are controlled by custom almost as much among ourselves as they are among primitive man. We have seen why this must be the case. The mental processes which enter into the development of judgments are based largely upon associations with previous judgments. This process of association is the same among primitive as among civilized man, and the difference consists largely in the modification of the traditional material with which our new perceptions amalgamate. In the case of activities, the conditions are somewhat different. Here tradition manifests itself in an action performed by the individual. The more frequently this action is repeated, the more firmly it will become established, and the less will be the conscious equivalent accompanying the action; so that customary actions which are of very frequent repetition become entirely subconscious. Hand in hand with this decrease of consciousness goes an increase in the emotional value of the omission of such activities, and still more of the performance of actions contrary to custom. A greater will power is required to inhibit an action which has become well established; and combined with this effort of the will power are feelings of intense displeasure.

Thus an important change from primitive culture to civilization seems to consist in the gradual elimination of what might be called the emotional, socially determined associations of sense-impressions and of activities, for which intellectual associations are gradually substituted. This process is accompanied by a loss of conservatism which, however, does not extend over the field of habitual activities that do not come into consciousness, and only to a slight extent over those generalizations which are the foundation of all knowledge imparted in the course of education.

Chapter 13

The Race Problem in Modern Society

UNTIL THE FIRST decade of our century the opinion that race determines culture had been, in Europe at least, rather a subject of speculation of amateur historians and sociologists than a foundation of public policy. Since that time it has spread among the masses. Slogans like "blood is thicker than water," are expressions of its new emotional appeal. The earlier concept of nationality has been given a new meaning by identifying nationality with racial unity and by assuming that national characteristics are due to racial descent. It is particularly interesting to note that in the anti-Semitic movement in Germany of the time of 1880 it was not the Jew as a member of an alien race who was subject to attack, but the Jew who was not assimilated to German national life. The present policy of Germany is based on an entirely different foundation, for every person is supposed to have a definite, unalterable character according to his racial descent and this determines his political and social status. The conditions are quite analogous to the status assigned to the Negro at an earlier period, when licentiousness, shiftless laziness, lack of initiative were considered as racially determined, unescapable qualities of every Negro. It is a curious spectacle to see that serious scientists, wherever free to express themselves, have on the whole been drifting away from the opinion that race determines mental status, excepting however those biologists who have no appreciation of social factors because they are captivated by the apparent hereditary determinism of morphological forms, while among the uninformed public to which unfortunately a number of powerful European politicians belong, race prejudice has been making and is still making unchecked progress. I believe it would be an error to assume that we are free of this tendency: if nothing else the restrictions imposed upon members of certain "races," abridging their right to own real estate, to tenancy in apartment houses, membership of clubs, to their right to visit hotels and summer resorts, to admission to schools and colleges shows at least that there is no abatement of old prejudices directed against Negroes, Jews, Russians, Armenians or whatever they may be. The excuse that these exclusions are compelled by economic considerations, or by the fear of driving away from schools or colleges other social groups is merely an acknowledgment of a widespread attitude.

I may perhaps restate in briefest form the errors which underlie the theory that racial descent determines mental and social behavior. The term race, as applied to human types, is vague. It can have a biological significance only when a race represents a uniform, closely inbred group, in which all family lines are alike—as in pure breeds of domesticated animals. These conditions are never realized in human types and impossible in large populations. Investigations of morphological traits show that the extreme genetic lines represented in a so-called pure population are so different, that if found in different localities they would be counted as separate races, while the middle forms are common to races inhabiting adjoining territories, excepting the occurrence of small groups that may have been inbred for centuries. If the defenders of race theories prove that a certain kind of behavior is hereditary and wish to explain in this way that it belongs to a racial type they would have to prove that the particular kind of behavior is characteristic of all the genetic lines composing the race, that considerable variations in the behavior of different genetic lines composing the race do not occur. This proof has never been given and all the known facts contradict the possibility of uniform behavior of all the individuals and genetic lines composing the race.

Added to this is the failure to see that the many different constitutional types composing a race cannot be considered as absolutely permanent, but that the physiological and psychological reactions of the body are in a constant state of flux according to the outer and inner circumstances in which the organism finds itself.

Furthermore the varying reactions of the organism do not *create* a culture but *react* to a culture. On account of the difficulties involved in defining personality and separating the endogene and exogene elements that make up a personality it is difficult to measure the range of variation of biologically determined personalities within a race. The endogene elements can only be those determined by the structure and chemism of the body and these show a wide range of variation within each race. The claim that a race is in any way identical with a personality cannot be given.

It is not difficult to show that a very general primitive attitude of mind is involved in the identification of the characteristics of an individual with the supposed typical characteristics of the group to which he belongs. It has always found expression in the prohibition of marriage between the members of different groups and the substitution of an imputed biological difference in place of a sociological one. Examples are particularly the laws forbidding marriages between members of different religious denominations.

The diversity of local types found in Europe is a result of the intermingling of the various earlier types that lived on the continent. Since we do not know the laws of intermixture it is impossible to reconstruct the early constituent purer types, if such ever existed (see p. 75). We may not assume on the basis of a low variability that a type is pure, for we know that some mixed types are remarkably uniform. This has been shown for American Mulattoes, Dakota Indians, and made probable for the city population of Italy.[1] It is also not certain in how far exogene elements may be partly determinants of local types or how social selection may have acted upon a heterogeneous population. In short we have no way of identifying a pure type. It must be remembered that although by inbreeding in a small local group the family lines may become alike, this is no proof of purity of type, because the ancestral forms themselves may be mixed.

Setting aside these theoretical considerations we may ask what kind of evidence is available for the claim that there is any pure race in Europe or, for that matter, in any part of the world. European national types are certainly not pure stocks. It is only necessary to look at a map illustrating the racial types of any European country—like Italy, for instance

[1] Herskovits, Sullivan, Boas 9, 11.

—to see that local divergence is the characteristic feature, uniformity of type the exception. Thus Dr. Ridolfo Livi, in his fundamental investigations on the anthropology of Italy, has shown that the types of the extreme north and those of the extreme south are quite distinct—the former tall, short-headed, with a considerable sprinkling of blond and blue-eyed individuals; the latter short, long-headed and remarkably dark. The transition from one type to the other is, on the whole, quite gradual; but, like isolated islands, distinct types occur here and there. The region of Lucca in Tuscany, and the district of Naples, are examples of this kind, which may be explained as due to the survival of an older stock, to the intrusion of new types, or to a peculiar influence of environment.

Historical evidence is quite in accord with the results derived from the investigation of the distribution of modern types. In the earliest times we find on the peninsula of Italy groups of heterogeneous people, the linguistic relationships of many of which have remained obscure up to the present time. From the earliest prehistoric times on, we see wave after wave of people invading Italy from the north. Very early Greeks settled in the greater part of southern Italy, and Phoenician influence was well established on the west coast of the peninsula. A lively intercourse existed between Italy and northern Africa. Slaves of Berber blood were imported, and have left their traces. Slave trade continued to bring new blood into the country until quite recent times, and Livi believes that he can trace the type of Crimean slaves who were introduced late in the Middle Ages in the region of Venice. In the course of the centuries, the migrations of Celtic and Teutonic tribes, the conquests of the Normans, the contact with Africa, have added their share to the mixture of people on the Italian peninsula.

The fates of other parts of Europe were no less diversified. The Pyrenaean Peninsula, which during the last few centuries has been one of the most isolated parts of Europe, has had a most checkered history. The earliest inhabitants of whom we know were presumably related to the Basques of the Pyrenees. These were subjected to Oriental influences in the pre-Mycenaean period, to Punic conquest, to Celtic invasions, Roman colonization, Teutonic invasions, the Moorish conquest, and later on to the peculiar selective process that accompanied the driving-out of the Moors and the Jews.

England was not exempt from the vicissitudes of this kind. It seems plausible that at a very early period the type which is now found principally in Wales and in some parts of Ireland occupied the greater portion of the islands. It was swamped by successive waves of Celtic, Roman, Anglo-Saxon and Scandinavian migration. Thus we find change everywhere.

The history of the migrations of the Goths, the invasions of the Huns, who in the short interval of one century moved their habitations from the borders of China into the very center of Europe, are proofs of the enormous changes in population that have taken place in early times.

Slow colonization has also brought about fundamental changes in blood as well as in diffusion of languages and cultures. Perhaps the most striking recent example of this change is presented by the gradual Germanization of the region east of the Elbe River, where after the Teutonic migrations, people speaking Slavic languages had settled. The gradual absorption of Celtic communities and of the Basque, in ancient times the great Roman colonization, and later the Arab conquest of North Africa, are examples of similar processes.

Intermixture in early times was not by any means confined to peoples which, although diverse in language and culture, were of fairly uniform type. On the contrary, the most diverse types of southern, northern, eastern and western Europe, not to mention the elements which poured into Europe from Asia and Africa, have been participants in this long-continued intermixture. The Jews also have been proved by physical examination as well as by blood tests to be of highly mixed origin (Brutzkus).

In Europe the belief in hereditary mental qualities of human types finds expression principally in the mutual evaluation of the cultural achievement of nations. In present-day Germany the hatred of the Government against the Jew is a relapse into cruder forms of these beliefs.

Since we have not been able to establish organically determined differences in the mental faculties of different races, such as could claim any importance as compared with the differences found in the genetic lines composing each race; since furthermore, we have seen that the alleged specific differences between the cultures of different peoples must be reduced to mental qualities common to all mankind, we may conclude that there is no need of entering into a discussion of alleged hereditary differences in mental characteristics of various branches of the White race. Much has been said and written on the hereditary character of the Italian, German, Frenchman, Irish, Jew and Gypsy, but it seems to me that not the slightest successful attempt has been made to establish causes for the behavior of a people other than historical and social conditions; and I consider it unlikely that this can ever be done. An unbiased review of the facts shows that the belief in hereditary racial characteristics and the jealous care for purity of race is based on the assumption of non-existing conditions. Since a remote period there have been no pure races in Europe and it has never been proved that continued intermixture has brought about deterioration. It would be just as easy to claim and to prove by equally valid—or rather invalid—evidence that peoples which have had no admixture of foreign blood lacked the stimulus for cultural progress and became decadent. The history of Spain, or, outside of Europe, that of the remote villages of Kentucky and Tennessee might be given as striking examples.

The actual effects of racial mixture cannot be answered by general historical considerations. The adherents of the belief—for it is nothing else—that long-headed groups lose their bodily and mental preeminence by mixture with round heads, will never be satisfied with a proof of the improbability and impossibility of proving their cherished beliefs, for the opposite view also cannot be proved by rigid methods. The real course of race mixture in Europe will never be known accurately. We do not know anything in regard to the relative number and composition of mixed and "pure" lines; nothing in regard to the history of the mixed families. Evidently the question cannot be solved on the basis of historical data but requires the study of strictly controlled material showing the movements of population. With all this nothing in the known historical facts suggests that preservation of racial purity assures a high cultural development; else we should expect to find the highest state of culture in every small, secluded village community.

In modern times extended mixtures between different nationalities, involving migration of large masses from one country to another are rare in Europe. They occur when the rapid rise of industry in a particular locality attracts labor. This was the origin of a large Polish community in the industrial district of Westphalia. The present political terrorism directed against political opponents in Russia, Italy, Germany and other countries, and the throttling of the Jews in Germany have also led to migrations, but these are minor phenomena when compared with the oversea migration from Europe to America, South Africa and Australia. The development of the American nation through the amalgamation of diverse European nationalities, the presence of the Negro, Indian, Japanese and Chinese, and the whole ever-increasing heterogeneity of the component elements of our people, involve a number of problems to the solution of which our inquiries contribute important data.

Our previous considerations make clear the hypothetical character of many of the generally accepted assumptions, and indicate that not all of the questions involved can be answered at the present time with scientific accuracy. It is disappointing that we have to take this critical attitude, because the political question of dealing with all these groups of people is of great and immediate importance. However, it should be solved on the basis of scientific knowledge, not according to emotional clamor. Under present conditions, we seem to be called upon to formulate definite answers to questions that require the most painstaking and unbiased investigation; and the more urgent the demand for final conclusions, the more needed is a critical examination of the phenomena and of the available methods of solution.

Let us first recall to our minds the facts relating to the origins of our nation. When British immigrants first flocked to the Atlantic coast of North America, they found a continent inhabited by Indians. The population of the country was thin, and vanished rapidly before the influx of the more numerous Europeans. The settlement of the Dutch on the

Hudson, of the Germans in Pennsylvania, not to speak of other nationalities, is familiar to all of us. We know that the foundations of our modern state were laid by Spaniards in the Southwest, by French in the Mississippi Basin and in the region of the Great Lakes, but that the British immigration far outnumbered that of other nationalities. In the composition of our people, the indigenous element has never played an important role, except for short periods. In regions where the settlement progressed for a long time entirely by the immigration of unmarried males of the White race, families of mixed blood have been of some importance during the period of gradual development, but they have never become sufficiently numerous in any populous part of the United States to be considered an important element in our population. Without any doubt, Indian blood flows in the veins of quite a number of our people, but the proportion is so insignificant that it may well be disregarded.

Much more important has been the introduction of the Negro, whose numbers have increased many fold, so that they form now about one-tenth of our whole nation.

More recent is the problem of the immigration of people representing all the nationalities of Europe, western Asia and northern Africa. While until late in the second half of the nineteenth century the immigrants consisted almost entirely of people of northwestern Europe, natives of Great Britain, Scandinavia, Germany, Switzerland, Holland, Belgium and France, the composition of the immigrant masses has changed completely since that time. Italians, the various Slavic peoples of Austria, Russia and the Balkan Peninsula, Hungarians, Roumanians, East European Hebrews, not to mention the numerous other nationalities, have arrived in ever-increasing numbers. For a certain length of time the immigration of Asiatic nations seemed likely to become of importance in the development of our country. There is no doubt that these people of eastern and southern Europe represent physical types distinct from the physical type of northwestern Europe; and it is clear, even to the most casual observer, that their present social standards differ fundamentally from our own.

It is often claimed that the phenomenon of mixture pre-

234 / The Mind of Primitive Man

sented in the United States is unique; that a similar intermixture has never occurred before in the world's history; and
that our nation is destined to become what some writers
choose to term a "mongrel" nation in a sense that has never
been equaled anywhere.

The period of immigration may now be considered closed,
for the present economic and political conditions have brought
it about that, as compared to the total population, immigration is insignificant.

The history of European migrations as outlined before
shows that the modern transatlantic migration merely repeats
in modern form the events of antiquity. The earlier migrations
occurred at a period when the density of population was,
comparatively speaking, small. The number of individuals
concerned in the formation of the modern types of Great
Britain were comparatively few as compared with the millions
who have come together to form a new nation in the United
States; and it is obvious that the process of amalgamation
which takes place in communities that must be counted by
millions differs in character from the process of amalgamation that takes place in communities that may be counted by
thousands. Setting aside social barriers, which in early times
as well as now undoubtedly tended to keep intermingling
peoples separate, it would seem that in the more populous
communities of modern times a greater permanence of the
single combining elements might occur, owing to their larger
numbers, which make the opportunities for segregation more
favorable.

Among the early, smaller communities the process of
amalgamation must have been an exceedingly rapid one.
After the social distinctions had once been obliterated,
pure descendants of one of the component types must have
decreased greatly in number, and the fourth generation of a
people consisting originally of distinct elements must have
been almost homogeneous.

We may dismiss the assumption of a process of mon-
grelization in America different from anything that has taken
place for thousands of years in Europe. Neither are we right
in assuming that the phenomenon is one of a more rapid
intermixture than the one prevailing in olden times. The

difference is based essentially in the masses of individuals concerned in the process.

If we confine our consideration for the present to the intermixture of European types in America, it will be clear, from what has been said before, that the concern that is felt by many in regard to the continuance of racial purity of our nation is to a great extent imaginary.

Two questions stand out prominently in the study of the physical characteristics of the immigrant population. The first is the question of the selection of immigrants and the influence of environment upon them. The second is the question of the effect of intermixture.

We have been able to throw some light upon both of these.

We found that both in regard to bodily form and mental behavior the immigrants are subject to the influence of their new environment. While the causes of bodily changes and their direction are still obscure, it has been shown that the mental and social behavior of the descendants of immigrants shows in all those features that have been investigated an assimilation to American standards.

A number of data have also been obtained for a better understanding of race-mixture. Let us recall that one of the most powerful agents modifying human types is the breaking-up of the continuance of strains in small communities by a process of rapid migration, which occurs both in Europe and in America, but with much greater rapidity in our country, because the heterogeneity of descent of the people is much greater than in modern Europe.

What effect these processes may have upon the ultimate type and variability of the American people cannot be determined at the present time; but no evidence is available that would allow us to expect a lower status of the developing new types of America. Much remains to be done in the study of this subject; and considering our lack of knowledge of the most elementary facts that determine the outcome of this process, I feel that it behooves us to be most cautious in our reasoning, and particularly to refrain from all sensational formulations of the problem that are liable to add to the prevalent lack of calmness in its consideration; the more so,

236 / The Mind of Primitive Man

since the answer to these questions concerns the welfare of millions of people.

The problem is one in regard to which speculation is as easy as accurate studies are difficult. Basing our arguments on ill-fitting analogies with the animal and plant world, we may speculate on the effects of intermixture upon the development of new types—as though the mixture that is taking place in America were in any sense, except a sociological one, different from the mixtures that have taken place in Europe for thousands of years; looking for a general degradation, for reversion to remote ancestral types, or towards the evolution of a new ideal type—as fancy or personal inclination may impel us. We may enlarge on the danger of the impending submergence of the northwest European type, or glory in the prospect of its dominance over all others. Would it not be a safer course to investigate the truth or fallacy of each theory rather than excite the public mind by indulgence in the fancies of our speculations? That these are an important help in the attainment of truth, I do not deny; but they must not be promulgated before they have been subjected to a searching analysis, lest the credulous public mistake fancy for truth.

If I am not in a position to predict what the effect of mixture of distinct types may be, I feel confident that this important problem may be solved if it is taken up with sufficient energy and on a sufficiently large scale. An investigation of the anthropological data of people of distinct types—taking into consideration the similarities and dissimilarities of parents and children, the rapidity and final result of the physical and mental development of children, their vitality, the fertility of marriages of different types and in different social strata—such an investigation is bound to give us information which will allow us to answer these important questions definitely and conclusively.

The final result of race-mixture will necessarily depend upon the fertility of the present native population and of the newer immigrants. It is natural that in large cities, where nationalities separate in various quarters, a great amount of cohesion should continue for some time; but it seems likely that intermarriages between descendants of foreign nationalities will increase rapidly in later generations. Our experience with Americans born in New York whose grandparents immigrated into this country is, on the whole, that most social traces of their descent have disappeared, and that many do not even know to what nationalities their grandparents belonged. It might be expected—particularly in Western communities where frequent changes of location are common—that this would result in a rapid mixture of the descendants of various nationalities. This inquiry, which it is quite feasible to carry out in detail, seems indispensable for a clear understanding of the situation.

During the last decade studies of the population problem have made rapid strides. We refer merely to the careful analysis of population problems by Frank Lorimer and Frederick Osborn. As a result of the accumulating work it may be said that as long as the problems involved are conceived as racial problems in the usually accepted meaning of the term little progress will be made. The biological well-being of a nation is rather dependent upon the distribution of hereditary constitutional types in social classes. These are not indissolubly connected with racial types. No such relation has ever been discovered that is not adequately accounted for by historical or sociological conditions, and all the traits of personality that have ever been investigated point invariably to a high degree of pliability of the representatives of a racial group, to a greater uniformity in a mixed group subjected to similar social stresses.

At present the European nations and their descendants on other continents are deeply impressed by the fear of a threatening degeneration. Certainly, it is important to combat strictly hereditary pathological tendencies and to improve the health of the people by eugenic means as far as this is possible; but the complex conditions of modern life should receive proper consideration. Statistics show an increase of the socially weak, who become the wards of almshouses, institutions for the care of the insane, the imbecile, those afflicted by chronic diseases; and who fill our prisons and penitentiaries. We live in a period of a rapid increase in the differentiation of our population, that is of increasing variability. This would bring about an increase of the number of the weakest as well as of the strongest, without necessarily implying a lowering of the average. In many respects this seems to correspond to the actual conditions. The weak can be counted, because they are cared for by the State. The strong cannot be counted. Their presence is expressed in the greater intensity of our lives.

The aim of eugenics, namely, the improvement of constitutional health, is highly commendable, but we are still far from seeing how it can be attained. Certainly not by the panacea of many eugenists, sterilization. The decrease in the frequency of hereditary diseases by the elimination of those actually affected is so slow that an effect will not be felt for many generations; and more important than this: we do not know how often the same conditions may arise as hereditary mutations and whether the unfavorable conditions under which large classes live do not result in such mutations. The theory that recessive hereditary diseases have sprung up once only is untenable on account of its implications. It would lead us to the conclusion that we are the offspring of a number of diseased populations almost without a healthy ancestor. It is the most important and at the same time the most difficult task of our studies to find the conditions under which hereditary pathological conditions arise.

The Negro problem as it presents itself in the United States is from a biological viewpoint not essentially different from those just discussed. We have found that no proof of an inferiority of the Negro type could be given, except that it seemed barely possible that perhaps the race would not produce quite so many men of highest genius as other races, while there was nothing at all that could be interpreted as suggesting any material difference in the mental capacity of the bulk of the Negro population as compared with the bulk of the White population. There will undoubtedly be endless numbers of men and women who will be able to outrun their White competitors, and who will do better than the defectives whom we permit to drag down and retard the healthy children of our public schools.

Ethnological observation does not countenance the view that the traits observed among our poorest Negro population are in any sense racially determined. A survey of African tribes exhibits to our view cultural achievements of no mean order. To those unfamiliar with the products of native African art and industry, a walk through one of the large museums of Europe would be a revelation. Few of our American museums have made collections that exhibit this subject in any way worthily. The blacksmith, the wood carver, the weaver, the potter—these all produce ware original in form, executed with great care, and exhibiting that love of labor, and interest in the results of work, which are apparently so often lacking among the Negroes in our American surroundings. No less instructive are the records of travelers, reporting the thrift of the native villages, of the extended trade of the country, and of its markets. The power of organization as illustrated in the government of native states is of no mean order, and when wielded by men of great personality has led to the foundation of extended empires. All the different kinds of activities that we consider valuable in the citizens of our country may be found in aboriginal Africa. Neither is the wisdom of the philosopher absent. A perusal of any of the collections of African proverbs that have been published will demonstrate the homely practical philosophy of the Negro, which is often proof of sound feeling and judgment.

It would be out of place to enlarge on this subject, because the essential point that anthropology can contribute to the practical discussion of the adaptability of the Negro is a decision of the question how far the undesirable traits that are at present undoubtedly found in our Negro population are due to racial traits, and how far they are due to social surroundings for which we are responsible. To this question anthropology can give the decided answer that the traits of African culture as observed in the aboriginal home of the Negro are those of a healthy primitive people, with a considerable degree of personal initiative, with a talent for organization, with imaginative power, with technical skill and thrift. Neither is a warlike spirit absent in the race, as is proved by the mighty conquerors who overthrew states and founded new empires, and by the courage of the armies that follow the bidding of their leaders.

It may be well to state here once more with some emphasis that it would be erroneous to claim as proved that there are

240 / The Mind of Primitive Man

no differences in the mental make-up of the Negro race taken as a whole and of any other race taken as a whole, and that their activities should run in exactly the same lines. This would be a result of the varying frequency of personalities of various types. It may be that the bodily build of the Negro race taken as a whole tends to give a direction to its activities somewhat different from those of other races. An answer to this question cannot be given. There is, however, no evidence whatever that would stigmatize the Negro as of weaker build, or as subject to inclinations and powers that are opposed to our social organization. An unbiased estimate of the anthropological evidence so far brought forward does not permit us to countenance the belief in a racial inferiority which would unfit an individual of the Negro race to take his part in modern civilization. We do not know of any demand made on the human body or mind in modern life that anatomical or ethnological evidence would prove to be beyond his powers.

The traits of the American Negro are adequately explained on the basis of his history and social status. The tearing-away from the African soil and the consequent complete loss of the old standards of life, which were replaced by the dependency of slavery and by all it entailed, followed by a period of disorganization and by a severe economic struggle against heavy odds, are sufficient to explain the inferiority of the status of the race, without falling back upon the theory of hereditary inferiority.

In short, there is every reason to believe that the Negro when given facility and opportunity, will be perfectly able to fulfill the duties of citizenship as well as his White neighbor.

The anthropological discussion of the Negro problem requires also a word on the "race instinct" of the Whites, which plays a most important part in the practical aspect of the problem. Ultimately this phenomenon is a repetition of the old instinct and fear of the connubium of patricians and plebeians, of the European nobility and the common people or of the castes of India. The emotions and reasonings concerned are the same in every respect. In our case they relate particularly to the necessity of maintaining a distinct social status in order to avoid race-mixture. As in the other cases mentioned, the so-called instinct is not a physiological dislike. This is proved by the existence of our large Mulatto population, as well as by the more ready amalgamation of the Negro with Latin peoples. It is rather an expression of social conditions that are so deeply ingrained in us that they assume a strong emotional value; and this, I presume is meant when we call such feelings instinctive. The feeling certainly has nothing to do with the question of the vitality and ability of the Mulatto.

Still the questions of race mixture and of the Negro's adaptability to our environment represent a number of important problems.

I think we have reason to be ashamed to confess that the scientific study of these questions has never received the support either of our government or of any of our great scientific institutions; and it is hard to understand why we are so indifferent toward a question which is of paramount importance to the welfare of our nation. The investigations by Melville J. Herskovits on the American Negro are a valuable beginning; but we should know much more. Notwithstanding the oft-repeated assertions regarding the hereditary inferiority of the Mulatto, we know hardly anything on this subject. If his vitality is lower than that of the full-blooded Negro, this may be as much due to social as to hereditary causes. Herskovits has pointed out that contrary to conditions during the time of slavery the tendency among Mulattoes is for a lighter man to marry a darker woman and that in consequence of this the colored population tends to become darker —an undesirable condition, if we believe that a decrease of strong contrasts in racial types is desirable because it helps to weaken class-consciousness.

Our tendency to evaluate an individual according to the picture that we form of the class to which we assign him, although he may not feel any inner connection with that class, is a survival of primitive forms of thought. The characteristics of the members of the class are highly variable and the type that we construct from the most frequent characteristics supposed to belong to the class is never more than an abstraction hardly ever realized in a single individual, often not even a result of observation, but an often heard tradition that determines our judgment.

Freedom of judgment can be attained only when we learn to estimate an individual according to his own ability and character. Then we shall find, if we were to select the best of mankind, that all races and all nationalities would be represented. Then we shall treasure and cultivate the variety of forms that human thought and activity has taken, and abhor, as leading to complete stagnation, all attempts to impress one pattern of thought upon whole nations or even upon the whole world.

Bibliography

Achelis, Th., *Moderne Völkerkunde*, Stuttgart, 1896.

Allen, J. A. "Report on the Mammals Collected in Northeast Siberia by the Jesup North Pacific Expedition," *Bulletin, American Museum of Natural History*, 19 (1903), p. 126.

Alverdes, F., *Tiersoziologie*, Leipzig, 1925; English Edition, *Psychology of Animals*, New York, 1932.

Ammon, Otto, *Die natürliche Auslese beim Menschen*, Jena, 1893; *Zur Anthropologie der Badener*, Jena, 1899, p. 641.

Andree, Richard,
  1. *Ethnographische Parallelen und Vergleiche*, Stuttgart, 1878; *Neue Folge*, Leipzig, 1889.
  2. "Scapulimantia," *Boas Anniversary Volume*, New York, 1906, pp. 143 et seq.

Ankermann, B., "Kulturkreise und Kulturschichten in Afrika," *Zeitschrift für Ethnologie*, 37 (1905), pp. 54 et seq.

Bachofen, J. J., *Das Mutterrecht*, Basel, 1861 (1897).

Bälz, E., "Menschenrassen Ost-Asiens mit specieller Rücksicht auf Japan," *Verhandlungen der Berliner Anthropologischen Gesellschaft*, 33 (1901), pp. 166–189.

Barth, Henry, *Travels and Discoveries in North and Central Africa*, 2nd Edition, London, 1857–58, ii, pp. 253 et seq.; iii, pp. 425 et seq., 528 et seq.; iv, pp. 406 et seq., 579 et seq.

Bastian, A., An exposition of Bastian's point of view may be found in Th. Achelis, *Moderne Völkerkunde*, Stuttgart, 1896.

Baur, E., Fischer, E., and Lenz, F., *Menschliche Erblehre*, Munich, 1936, p. 712. English Edition, *Human Heredity*, New York, 1931.

Beckmann, L., *Geschichte und Beschreibung der Rassen der Hunde*, Brunswick, 1894–95.

Beddoe, John, *The Races of Britain*, London, 1885, pp. 249, 251.

Bell, Alexander G., *The Duration of Life and Conditions Associated with Longevity*, Washington, 1918.

Bernstein, Felix, "Zukunftsaufgaben der Versicherungmathematik," *Zeitschrift für die gesamte Versicherungs-Wissenschaft*, 31 (1931), p. 141.

Boas, Franz,
  1. *Anthropology and Modern Life*, 2nd Edition, New York, 1932, pp. 216–231.
  2. "Anthropometry of Porto Rico," *American Journal of Physical Anthropology*, 3 (1920), p. 247.
  3. "The Central Eskimo," *Sixth Annual Report of the Bureau of Ethnology*, Washington, 1888.
  4. "The Cephalic Index," *American Anthropologist*, N. S., 1 (1899), p. 453.

5. "The Cephalic Index in Holland and Its Heredity," *Human Biology*, 5, No. 4 (1933), p. 594.

6. *Changes in Bodily Form of Descendants of Immigrants* (Final Report), Washington, Government Printing Office, 1911 (61st Congress, 2nd Session, Senate Document 208). Also issued by Columbia University Press, 1912.

7. "Eruption of Deciduous Teeth among Hebrew Infants," *Journal of Dental Research*, 7, No. 3 (1927), pp. 245 et seq.

8. "The Growth of Indian Mythologies," *Journal of American Folk-Lore*, 9 (1896), pp. 1–11.

9. "The Half-Blood Indian," *Popular Science Monthly*, 45 (1894), pp. 761 et seq.

10. *Handbook of American Indian Languages*, Bulletin 40, Bureau of American Ethnology, Washington, 1911.

11. "The Head-Forms of Italians as Influenced by Heredity and Environment." With Helene M. Boas, *American Anthropologist*, N. S., 15 (1913), pp. 163–188.

12. *Indianische Sagen von der Nord-Pacifischen Küste Amerikas*, Berlin, 1895, pp. 338–339.

13. *Primitive Art*, Oslo and Cambridge, 1927.

14. Boas and Clark Wissler, "Statistics of Growth," *Report of the United States Commissioner of Education for 1904*, Washington, 1905, pp. 25–132.

15. "A. J. Stone's Measurements of Natives of the Northwest Territories," *Bulletin, American Museum of Natural History*, 14 (1901), pp. 53–68.

16. "Studies in Growth I," *Human Biology*, 4, No. 3 (1932); II, *Human Biology*, 5, No. 3 (1933).

17. "The Tempo of Growth of Fraternities," *Proceedings of the National Academy of Sciences*, 21, No. 7 (July, 1935).

18. Unpublished material.

19. "Zur Anthropologie der Nordamerikanischen Indianer," *Verhandlungen der Berliner Gesellschaft für Anthropologie, Ethnologie und Urgeschichte*, 27 (1895), pp. 367 et seq.

Bogoras, W., *The Chukchee*, Publications of the Jesup North Pacific Expedition, 7, Leiden, 1904–09.

Bolk, L., "Untersuchungen über die Menarche bei der niederländischen Bevölkerung," *Zeitschrift für Geburtshülfe und Gynäkologie*, 89 (1925–26), pp. 364–380.

Boulainvilliers, Comte de, *Histoire de l'ancien Gouvernement de la France*, Paris, 1727.

Boule, Marcellin, *Fossil Men*, Edinburgh, 1923, pp. 238 et seq.

Bowditch, H. P., "The Growth of Children," *Eighth Annual Report of the State Board of Health of Massachusetts*, Boston, 1877.

Bowles, G. T., *New Types of Old Americans at Harvard*, Cambridge, Mass., 1932, p. 18.

Brigham, C. C., "Intelligence Tests of Immigrant Groups," *Psychological Review*, 37 (1930), pp. 158–65.

Brutzkus, J., Paper read before the Congrès de la Population, Paris, 1937.

Buschan, G., *Illustrierte Völkerkunde*, Stuttgart, 1922–26.

Buzina, E., and Lebzelter, V., "Über die Dimensionen der Hand bei verschiedenen Berufen," *Archiv für Hygiene*, 92 (1923), pp. 53 et seq.

Candolle, A. de, *Origin of Cultivated Plants*, New York, 1886, pp. 59 et seq., 139 et seq.

Carr-Saunders, A. M., *The Population Problem*, Oxford, 1922.

Carus, C. G., *System der Physiologie*, 1838; 2nd Edition, Leipzig, 1847.

Chamberlain, H. S.,
1. *Briefwechsel zwischen Cosima Wagner und Houston Stewart Chamberlain*, Leipzig, 1934, pp. 565 et seq.
2. *Die Grundlagen des neunzehnten Jahrhunderts*, 3rd Edition, Munich, 1901, p. 274; English Edition, *Foundations of the Nineteenth Century*, London, New York, 1911, p. 271.

Clauss, L. F., *Rasse und Seele*, Munich, 1926.

Cook, O. F., "Aspects of Kinetic Evolution," *Proceedings of the Washington Academy of Sciences*, 8 (1906), pp. 209–10.

Crampton, C., "Physiological Age," *American Physical Education Review*, 13 (1908), Nos. 3–6.

Cunningham, D. J., *The Lumbar Curve in Man and Apes*, Cunningham Memoirs, Dublin, 1886.

Cunow, H., *Die Verwandtschafts-Organisationen der Australneger*, Stuttgart, 1894.

Dahlberg, G., *Twin Births and Twins from an Hereditary Point of View*, Stockholm, 1926.

Darwin, Charles, *Journal of Researches into the Natural History and Geology of the Countries Visited during the Voyage of H.M.S. Beagle round the World*, New York, 1895, pp. 228–29.

Davenport, B., and Steggerda, M., *Race Crossing in Jamaica*, Washington, 1929.

Deniker, J., *The Races of Man*, London, 1900.

Dixon, Roland B.,
1. "Basketry Designs of the Indians of Northern California," *Bulletin, American Museum of Natural History*, 17 (1902), p. 28.
2. "The Maidu," in Franz Boas, *Handbook of American Indian Languages*, Bulletin 40, Bureau of American Ethnology, Washington, 1911.
3. *The Racial History of Man*, New York, 1923.

Donaldson, H. H., *The Growth of the Brain*, London, 1895.

Durkheim, E., *Les formes élémentaires de la vie religieuse*, Paris, 1912; English Edition, *The Elementary Forms of the Religious Life*, London, 1915.

Efron, David, and Van Veen, S., unpublished material; Efron and Foley, John P., Jr., "Gestural Behavior and Social Setting," *Zeitschrift für Sozialforschung*, 6 (1937), Heft 1, pp. 152–161.

Eickstedt, E. von, *Grundlagen der Rassenpsychologie*, Stuttgart, 1936, p. 35.

Engel, Joseph, *Untersuchungen über Schädelformen*, Prag, 1851.

Ferraira, A. de Costa, "La capacité du crâne chez les Portugais," *Bulletins et Mémoires de la Société d'Anthropologie de Paris*, Série V, 4 (1903), pp. 417 et seq.

Fischer, Eugen,
1. "Das Problem der Rassenkreuzung," *Die Naturwissenschaften*, 1, Berlin (1913), p. 1007.
2. "Die Rassenmerkmale des Menschen als Domestikationserscheinungen," *Zeitschrift für Morphologie und Anthropologie*, 18 (1914).
3. *Die Rehobother Bastards*, Jena, 1913.

Fjeld, Harriet, unpublished material.

Foley, John P., Jr., "Factors Conditioning Motor Speed and Tempo," *Psychological Bulletin*, 34, No. 6 (1937). See also Efron.

Frazer, J. G., *The Golden Bough*, London, New York, 1911–19; *Totemism and Exogamy*, London, 1910.

Freud, S.,
1. A brief résumé of Freud's theory will be found in *The American Journal of Psychology*, 27 (1910).
2. *Totem and Taboo*, New York, 1918.

Friedenthal, H., *Beiträge zur Naturgeschichte des Menschen*, Jena, 1908.

Frischeisen-Köhler, I., *Das persönliche Tempo. Eine erbbiologische Untersuchung*, Leipzig, 1933.

Fritsch, Gustav, *Die Eingeborenen Süd-Afrikas*, Breslau, 1872, pp. 30 et seq.

Frobenius, L., *Atlas Africanus*, Munich, 1921; *Die Atlantische Götterlehre*, Jena, 1926.

Galton, Francis,
1. "Head Growth in Students at Cambridge," *Journal of the Anthropological Institute of Great Britain and Ireland*, 18 (1889), p. 156.
2. *Hereditary Genius*, London, 1869.
3. *Natural Inheritance*, London, 1889.

Gerland, Georg, *Das Aussterben der Naturvölker*, Leipzig, 1868.

Gobineau, A. de, *Essai sur l'inégalité des races humaines*, Paris, 1853–55; English translation, *The Inequality of Human Races*, New York, 1915.

Goddard, Pliny E., *Life and Culture of the Hupa*, University of

California Publications in American Archaeology and Ethnology, 1 (1903–04).

Goldenweiser, A. A., "Totemism, an Analytical Study," *Journal of American Folk-Lore*, 23 (1910), pp. 179 et seq.

Gould, B. A., *Investigations in the Military and Anthropological Statistics of American Soldiers*, New York, 1869, pp. 126–128.

Grant, Madison, *The Passing of the Great Race*, New York, 1916.

Guthe, G. E., "Notes on the Cephalic Index of Russian Jews in Boston," *American Journal of Physical Anthropology*, 1 (1918), pp. 213 et seq.

Haberlandt, G., *Physiologie und Ökologie*, I. Botanischer Teil (H. von Guttenberg), Leipzig, 1917.

Hahn, Eduard,
1. *Die Entstehung der Pflugkultur*, Heidelberg, 1909.
2. *Die Haustiere und ihre Beziehungen zur Wirtschaft des Menschen*, Leipzig, 1896.
3. In *Zeitschrift für Ethnologie*, 47 (1915), pp. 253, 254, note, where references to the original observations are given.

Hahn, Ida, "Dauernahrung und Frauenarbeit," *Zeitschrift für Ethnologie*, 51 (1919), p. 247.

Handwörterbuch des deutschen Aberglaubens, Berlin, 1927, et seq.

Hauschild, M. W., "Untersuchungen über die Pigmentation im Auge verschiedener Menschenrassen," *Zeitschrift für Morphologie und Anthropologie*, 12 (1909).

Heger, Franz, "Aderlassgeräthe bei den Indianern und Papuas," *Mittheilungen der Anthropologischen Gesellschaft in Wien*, 23 (1893), *Sitzungsberichte*, pp. 83–87.

Hehn, Victor, *Kulturpflanzen und Haustiere*, 2nd Edition, Berlin, 1874.

Hellman, Milo,
1. "Nutrition, Growth and Dentition," *Dental Cosmos* (Jan. 1932).
2. "Ossification of Cartilages of Hand," *American Journal of Physical Anthropology*, 11 (1928), pp. 223 et seq.

Herder, J. G., *Ideen zur Philosophie der Geschichte der Menschheit*, Riga, 1784–91.

Herskovits, M., *The American Negro*, New York, 1928; *Anthropometry of the American Negro*, Columbia University Contributions to Anthropology, 11, 1930.

Hirsch, N. D. M., "Cephalic Index of American-born Children of Three Foreign Groups," *Journal of Physical Anthropology*, 10 (1927), pp. 79 et seq.

Hoops, J., *Waldbäume und Kulturpflanzen*, Strassburg, 1915.

Huxley, H., "On the Geographical Distribution of the Chief Modifications of Mankind," *Journal of the Ethnological Society*, N. S. 2 (1870), pp. 404–412.

Jankowsky, W., *Die Blutsverwandschaft im Volk und in der Familie*, Stuttgart, 1934, pp. 119 et seq.

Jenks, A. E., *Indian-White Amalgamation*, Studies in Social Science, University of Minnesota, No. 6, 1916.

Jochelson, W.,
1. "Kumiss Festivals of the Yakut and the Decoration of Kumiss Vessels," *Boas Anniversary Volume*, New York, 1906, p. 257.
2. *The Yukaghir and the Yukaghirized Tungus*, Publications of the Jesup North Pacific Expedition, 9, Leiden, 1910, p. 59.

Johannsen, W., *Elemente der exakten Erblichkeitslehre*, Jena, 1909.

Joyce, Thomas A., *South American Archaeology*, New York, 1912, p. 15.

Keller, Conrad, "Die Haustiere als menschlicher Kulturerwerb" in *Der Mensch und die Erde*, Berlin, 1906, 1, pp. 165–304; *Naturgeschichte der Haustiere*, Berlin, 1905.

King, H. D., "Studies in Inbreeding," *Journal of Experimental Zoology*, 29 (1919), No. 1.

Klaatsch, H., "The Skull of the Australian Aboriginal," *Reports from the Pathological Laboratory of the Lunacy Department, New South Wales Government*, i, part iii, Sydney, 1908, pp. 3–167; "Der Primitive Mensch der Vergangenheit und Gegenwart," *Verhandlungen der Gesellschaft deutscher Naturforscher und Aerzte, 80te Versammlung zu Cöln* (1908), part i, p. 95.

Klatt, B., "Studien zum Domestikationsproblem," *Bibliotheca Genetica*, II, Leipzig, 1921, pp. 160 et seq.: "Mendelismus, Domestikation und Kraniologie," *Archiv für Anthropologie*, 18 (1921), pp. 225 et seq.; "Ueber die Veränderung der Schädelkapazität in der Domestikation," *Sitzungsberichte der Gesellschaft Naturf. Freunde*, Berlin, 1912.

Klemm, G., *Allgemeine Cultur-Geschichte der Menschheit*, Leipzig, 1843.

Klineberg, Otto, *Race Differences*, New York, 1935.

Klopfer, Bruno, unpublished material.

Köhler, W.,
1. "Intelligenzprüfungen an Anthropoiden," *Abhandlungen der Königlich Preussischen Akademie der Wissenschaften (Physikalisch-Mathematische Klasse)*, Berlin, 1917, pp. 78 et seq.
2. "Zur Psychologie der Schimpansen," *Psychologische Forschungen*, 1 (1921), p. 33.

Kollmann, J., "Beiträge zur einer Kraniologie der Europäischen Völker," *Archiv für Anthropologie*, 13 (1881), pp. 79, 179; 14 (1883), p. 1; "Die Rassenanatomie der Hand und die Persistenz der Rassenmerkmale," *ibid.*, 28 (1903), pp. 91 et seq.

Kretschmer, E., *Körperbau und Charakter*, Berlin, 1921 (10th Edition).

Kroeber, A. L.,
1. *Arrow Release Distributions*, University of California Publications in American Archaeology and Ethnology, 23 (1927), pp. 283 et seq.
2. *Handbook of the Indians of California*, Bulletin 78, Bureau of American Ethnology, Washington, 1925.
3. *Types of Indian Culture in California*, University of California Publications in American Archaeology and Ethnology, 2 (1904–07), pp. 81–103.

Laasch, R., *Der Eid*, Stuttgart, 1908.

Laufer, B.,
1. *The Decorative Art of the Amur Tribes*, Publications of the Jesup North Pacific Expedition, 4, Leiden, 1902.
2. "The Introduction of Maize to Eastern Asia," *Congrès International des Américanistes, xvᵉ Session, Quebec*, 1907, 1, pp. 223 et seq., particularly pp. 250–52.

Lebzelter, V., "Grösse und Gewicht der Wiener Arbeiterjugend in den Jahren 1919 und 1921," *Mitteilungen des Volksgesundheitsamtes im Bundesministerium für soziale Verwaltung.*

Lehmann, R., *Schopenhauer*, Berlin, 1894.

Lenz, F., see under Baur.

Levin, G., "Racial and 'Inferiority' Characters in the Human Brain," *American Journal of Physical Anthropology*, 22 (1937), p. 376.

Lévy-Bruhl, L., *La mentalité primitive*, Paris, 1922; English Edition, *Primitive Mentality*, New York, 1923.

Lewis, Carolyn A., "Relation between Basal Metabolism and Adolescent Growth," *American Journal of Diseases of Children*, 51 (May, 1936), pp. 1014–38.

Lissauer, in *Zeitschrift für Ethnologie*, 24 (1892), p. (429).

Livi, R., *Antropometria Militare*, Rome, 1896.

Lorenz, Ottokar, *Lehrbuch der gesammten wissenschaftlichen Genealogie*, Berlin, 1898, pp. 289 et seq., 308, 310, 311.

Lorimer, F., and Osborn, F., *Dynamics of Population*, New York, 1934; with full bibliography.

Lotry, J. A., *Evolution by Means of Hybridization*, The Hague, 1916, pp. 22 et seq.

Luschan, F. von,
1. "Die Tachtadschy und andere Ueberreste der alten Bevölkerung Lykiens," *Archiv für Anthropologie*, 19, pp. 31–53.
2. *Völker, Rassen, Sprachen*, Berlin, 1922, p. 92.

Macari, Leopold, unpublished material.

MacCurdy, G. G., *Human Origins*, New York, 1924.

Malinowski, B., *Crime and Custom in Savage Society*, London, New York, 1926.

Mall, Fr. P., "On Several Anatomical Characters of the Human

Brain, Said to Vary According to Race and Sex, etc.," *American Journal of Anatomy*, 9 (1909), pp. 1–32.

Manouvrier, L.,
1. "Les aptitudes et les actes dans leur rapport avec la constitution anatomique et avec le milieu extérieur," *Bulletins de la Société d'Anthropologie de Paris*, 4 series, 1 (1890), pp. 918 et seq.
2. "Sur l'interprétation de la quantité dans l'encéphale," *Mémoirs de la Société d'Anthropologie de Paris*, 2nd series, 3 (1866–77), pp. 284, 277, 281.

Martin, R., *Die Inlandstämme der Malayischen Halbinsel*, Jena, 1905.

Mason, Otis T., *The Origins of Invention*, London, 1895, pp. 315 et seq.

Matthews, W.,
1. "Human Bones of the Hemenway Collection in the U.S. Army Medical Museum," *Memoirs of the National Academy of Sciences*, 6 (1893), pp. 139 et seq.
2. *Navaho Legends*, Memoir of the American Folk-Lore Society, 5 (1897).

McGee, W. J., "The Beginning of Zoöculture," *American Anthropologist*, 10 (1897), pp. 215 et seq.

Menghin, Oswald, *Weltgeschichte der Steinzeit*, Vienna, 1931.

Mirenova, A. N., "Psychomotor Education and the General Development of Preschool Children," *Proceedings of the Maxim Gorky Medico-biological Research Institute*, 3 (1934), pp. 102–03.

Mooney, J., "The Ghost-Dance Religion," *14th Annual Report of the Bureau of American Ethnology*, Washington, 1896, pp. 641 et seq.

Morgan, L. H., *Ancient Society*, New York, 1878.

Morice, P. A. G., "The Great Déné Race," *Anthropos*, 1, 2, 4 (1906, 1907, 1909).

Morse, Edward S., "Ancient and Modern Methods of Arrow-Release," *Bulletin, Essex Institute, Salem, Massachusetts* (1885), pp. 145 et seq.

Morton, Samuel G., *Crania Americana*, Philadelphia, 1839.

Müller, Friedrich, *Allgemeine Ethnographie*, Vienna, 1879.

Nachtigal, G., *Saharâ und Sûdân*, Berlin, 1879–81.
1. ii, pp. 391 et seq.; iii, pp. 270 et seq.
2. ii, pp. 424 et seq.

Negelein, J. von, *Weltgeschichte des Aberglaubens*, Berlin, i (1931); ii (1935).

Neuville, Henri, "L'Espèce, la race et le métissage en Anthropologie," *Archive de l'Institut de Paléontologie Humaine*, Paris, 1933.

Newman, H. H., Freeman, F. N., and Holzinger, K. J., *Twins, a Study of Heredity and Environment*, Chicago, 1937.

Nordenskiöld, E.,
1. "Emploi de la balance romaine en Amérique du sud," *Journal de la Société des Américanistes de Paris,* N. S. 13 (1921), p. 169.
2. *Vergleichende Ethnographische Forschungen,* 1, 3, Göteborg (1918, 1924).

Nott, J. C., and Gliddon, G. R., *Types of Mankind,* Philadelphia, 1854; *Indigenous Races of the Earth,* Philadelphia, 1857.

Nyström, A., "Ueber die Formenveränderungen des menschlichen Schädels und deren Ursachen," *Archiv für Anthropologie,* 27 (1902), pp. 211 et seq., 317 et seq.

Oviedo y Valdés, *Historia General y Natural de las Indias* 1535-57, Madrid, 1851-55, Bk. xlii, Chapters 2, 3 (quoted from Spencer, *Descriptive Sociology,* No. ii, pp. 42-43).

Ovington, Mary White, *Half a Man, the Status of the Negro in New York,* New York, 1911.

Pearl, Raymond,
1. "A Note on the Inheritance of Duration of Life in Man," *American Journal of Hygiene,* 2 (1922), p. 229; see also *Scientific Monthly,* 1921, p. 46.
2. "Variation and Correlation in Brain-Weight," *Biometrika,* 4 (June, 1905), pp. 13 et seq.
3. "On the Relation of Race Crossing to Sex Ratio." With M. D. Pearl, *Biological Bulletin,* 15 (1908), pp. 194 et seq.

Pearson, Karl, "On the Relationship of Intelligence to Size and Shape of Head, and to Other Physical and Mental Characters," *Biometrika,* 5 (1906), pp. 136 et seq.

Penck, A., "Das Alter des Menschengeschlechts," *Zeitschrift für Ethnologie,* 40 (1908), pp. 390 et seq.; Penck and Brückner, *Die Alpen im Eiszeitalter,* Leipzig, 1909.

Petrullo, V., *The Diabolic Root,* Philadelphia, 1934.

Ploetz, Alfred, "Sozialanthropologie," in *Anthropologie,* edited by G. Schwalbe and E. Fischer, Part 3, Section 5, Kultur der Gegenwart, Leipzig and Berlin, 1923, pp. 591 et seq.

Ploss, H., *Das Weib in der Natur- und Völkerkunde,* edited by Ferdinand von Reitzenstein, 11th Edition, Berlin, 1927, i, p. 672.

Porteus, S. D., *Primitive Intelligence and Environment,* New York, 1937.

Post, Albert H., *Grundriss der Ethnologischen Jurisprudenz,* Oldenburg and Leipzig, 1894.

Przibram, H., "Entwicklungs-Mechanik der Tiere," in *Junk's Tabulae Biologicae,* 4 (1927), p. 284.

Ranke, Johannes, *Der Mensch,* Leipzig, 1894, ii, p. 177.

Ratzel, F., *Anthropogeographie,* Stuttgart, 1891.
1. II, pp. 330 et seq.
2. II, p. 693.

Reichard, G. A., *Social Life of the Navajo Indians*, Columbia University Contributions to Anthropology, 7, 1928.

Rein, J., "Zur Geschichte der Verbreitung des Tabaks und Mais in Ost-Asien," *Petermann's Mittheilungen*, 24 (1878), pp. 215 et seq.

Rieger, C., *Über die Beziehungen der Schädellehre zur Physiologie, Psychiatrie und Ethnologie*, Würzberg, 1882.

Ripley, W. Z., *The Races of Europe*, New York, 1899.

Risley, H. H., and Gait, E. A., *Census of India, 1901*, Calcutta, 1903, i, pp. 489 et seq.

Ritter, Karl, *Die Erdkunde im Verhältniss zur Natur und zur Geschichte des Menschen*, Berlin, 1817.

Rouma, Georges, *El Desarrolo Fisico del Escolar Cubano Sus Curvas Normales del Crecimiento*, Havana, 1920.

Sarasin, F., *Ergebnisse naturwissenschaftlicher Forschungen auf Ceylon*, Wiesbaden, 1892–93, iii, pp. 569 et seq.

Schneider, Edward C., "Physiological Changes Due to Altitude," *Physiological Review*, 1 (1921), p. 656.

Schoetensack, O., "Die Bedeutung Australiens für die Heranbildung des Menschen aus einer niederen Form," *Zeitschrift für Ethnologie*, 33 (1901), pp. 127 et seq.

Schultz, A. H., "Fetal Growth in Man," *American Journal of Physical Anthropology*, 6 (1923), pp. 389–399.

Schultze, Leonhard, *Aus Namaland und Kalahari*, Jena, 1907.

Seligmann, C. G. and B. Z., *The Veddas*, Cambridge, 1911, p. 380.

Shapiro, H. L., "Quality in Human Populations," *Scientific Monthly*, 1937, pp. 109 et seq.

Speck, F. G., *Naskapi*, Norman, Oklahoma, 1935, pp. 127 et seq.

Spencer, Herbert, *Principles of Sociology*, New York, 1893.

Spier, Leslie, "The Growth of Boys, Dentition and Stature," *American Anthropologist*, N. S. 20 (1918), pp. 37 et seq.

Sproat, G. M., *Scenes and Studies of Savage Life*, London, 1868, p. 120.

Steinen, Karl von den, *Durch Centralbrasilien*, Leipzig, 1886, pp. 310 et seq.; *Unter den Naturvölkern Zentral-Brasiliens*, Berlin, 1894, pp. 210–12.

Stoddard, Lothrop, *The Rising Tide of Color*, New York, 1920

Stofflet, Elliott, unpublished material.

Stratz den Haag, C. H., "Das Problem der Rasseneinteilung der Menschheit," *Archiv für Anthropologie*, N. S. 1 (1904), pp 189 et seq.

Studer, Th., *Die prähistorischen Hunde in ihrer Beziehung zu den gegenwärtig lebenden Rassen*, Zürich, 1901.

Stumpf, Carl, *Die Anfänge der Musik*, Leipzig, 1911.

Sullivan, L. R., "Anthropometry of the Siouan Tribes," *Anthropological Papers, American Museum of Natural History*, 2? (1920), pp. 81 et seq.

Sumner, W. G., and Keller, A. G., *The Science of Society*, New Haven, 1927; Sumner, W. G., *Folkways*, Boston, 1906.

Swanton, John R., "Social Organization of American Tribes," *American Anthropologist*, N. S. 7 (1905), p. 670.

Tarde, G., *Les Lois de l'Imitation*, Paris, 1900; English Edition, *The Laws of Imitation*, New York, 1903.

Ten Kate, H., "Anthropologisches und Verwandtes aus Japan," *Internationales Centralblatt für Anthropologie*, 7 (1902), p. 659.

Thomas, William I., *Source Book for Social Origins*, Chicago, 1909, p. 25.

Topinard, P., *Éléments d'Anthropologie générale*, Paris, 1885.

Tozzer, A. M., *Social Origins and Social Continuities*, New York, 1925, p. 239.

Tylor, E. B., *Primitive Culture, Researches into the Development of Mythology, Philosophy, Religion, Language, Art and Custom*, New York, 1874.

Uldall, H. J., Manuscript.

Verschuer, I. von, "Ergebnisse der Zwillingsforschung," *Verhandlungen der Gesellschaft für physische Anthropologie*, 6 (1931–32), p. 52.

Virchow, Rudolf, "Die physischen Eigenschaften der Lappen," *Verhandlungen der Berliner Gesellschaft für Anthropologie, Ethnologie und Urgeschichte*, 7 (1875), pp. 34 et seq.; also 22 (1890), p. 411.

Wagner, G., "Entwicklung und Verbreitung der Peyote-Kultur," *Baessler-Archiv*, 15 (1932), pp. 59 et seq.

Waitz, Theodor, *Introduction to Anthropology*, Anthropology of Primitive Peoples, Publications of the Anthropological Society of London, London, 1863, 1, p. 324.

Walcher, G., "Über die Entstehung von Brachy- und Dolichokephalie," *Zentralblatt für Gynäkologie*, 29 (1904), No. 7.

Waterman, T. T., "Explanatory Element in the Folk-Tales of the North American Indians," *Journal of American Folk-Lore*, 27 (1914), pp. 1–54.

Wegener, Alfred, *The Origin of Continents and Oceans*, New York, 1926.

Weill, Blanche C., *The Behavior of Young Children of the Same Family*, Cambridge, 1928.

Wernich, A., *Geographisch-medicinische Studien nach den Erlebnissen einer Reise um die Erde*, Berlin, 1878, pp. 81 et seq.

Westermarck, E., *The Origin and Development of the Moral Ideas*, London, 1906.

Weule, K., *Die Kultur der Kulturlosen*, Stuttgart, 1910.

Wiedersheim, R., *The Structure of Man an Index to His Past History*, London, New York, 1895.

Wieschoff, Heinz, *Die afrikanischen Trommeln*, Stuttgart, 1933.

Willey, Arthur W., *Convergence in Evolution,* London, 1911, pp 79 et seq.

Wissler, Clark, "Decorative Art of the Sioux Indians," *Bulletin American Museum of Natural History,* 18 (1904), pp. 231–78

Wundt, W., *Völkerpsychologie,* Leipzig, 1900–20; *Elemente der Völkerpsychologie,* Leipzig, 1912; Engiish Edition, *Elements o Folk Psychology,* New York, 1916.

Wuttke, A., *Geschichte des Heidentums,* Breslau, 1852–53, i, p. 36